Gringo

A Coming-of-Age in Latin America

Chesa Boudin

Scribner

New York   London   Toronto   Sydney

SCRIBNER
A Division of Simon & Schuster, Inc.
1230 Avenue of the Americas
New York, NY 10020

First Scribner hardcover edition April 2009

SCRIBNER and design are registered trademarks of The Gale Group, Inc.,
used under license by Simon & Schuster, Inc., the publisher of this work.

For information about special discounts for bulk purchases,
please contact Simon & Schuster Special Sales at 1-866-506-1949
or business@simonandschuster.com.

The Simon & Schuster Speakers Bureau can bring authors to your
live event. For more information or to book an event, contact the
Simon & Schuster Speakers Bureau at 866-248-3049 or visit our
website at www.simonspeakers.com.

Map © 2008 by Jason Snyder

Text set in Sabon

Manufactured in the United States of America

10 9 8 7 6 5 4 3 2 1

Library of Congress Control Number: 2008045839

ISBN-13: 978-1-4165-5911-5
ISBN-10: 1-4165-5911-6

For all the people from the Rio Grande down to the Strait of Magellan whose trust, generosity, and friendship made this book possible.

Overland travel is a great deal more trouble and very slow, but it is uncomfortable in a way that is completely human and often reassuring. . . . A book like this, or any book I have written, is not a problem to study and annotate. It is something I wrote to give pleasure; it is something to enjoy. You should be able to see these people and places, to hear them and smell them. Of course, some of it is painful, but travel—its very motion—ought to suggest hope. Despair is the armchair; it is indifference and glazed, incurious eyes. I think travelers are essentially optimists, or else they would never go anywhere; and a travel book ought to reflect that same general optimism.

—Paul Theroux, *The Old Patagonian Express*

Contents

Gringo

Note to the Reader

I've been called gringo dozens of times. My first day in Latin America I stepped out of the airport in Guatemala City and baggage handlers, taxi drivers, money changers, and beggars greeted me with a cacophony of "*oye gringo, mira gringo, vamos gringo, compra dolares gringo, ayúdame gringo, yo te llevo gringo, buen precio para mi amigo gringo.*" I was scared, overwhelmed, and I didn't speak enough Spanish to understand much more than "Listen up, gringo." I also wasn't sure how to interpret my new nickname: was it offensive, racist, disrespectful? Over the years gringo became a second name but rarely employed with malice or ill will. There was the occasional *gringo de mierda, pinche gringo,* or *gringo culiado,* but much more common was the neutral *oye gringo,* or the warm *gringito,* or the sweet *mi amigo gringo.* Since the word was generally used as a friendly nickname when people didn't know, or couldn't pronounce, my name—and I can't really blame them for that—I decided that it didn't bother me. Usage was key.

I heard plenty of theories about the word gringo: Mexicans yelled at Yankee troops in green uniforms during the battle of the Alamo to go home, "green-go"; during the Mexican-American War beginning in 1846, the troops invading Mexico sang a song called "green grow the lilacs" and the Mexicans who heard them started calling them the "green grows"; a United States citizen with the last name Green was in charge of administering a huge banana plantation in Central America and during a labor protest the workers started chanting "Green

1

go home!" But none of those seems likely given how geographically limited they were—the word gringo is used most everywhere Spanish is spoken—and the fact that the United States Army didn't start wearing green uniforms until decades after the Alamo and the Mexican-American War.

The word gringo first appeared in Spanish dictionaries in the late 1700s and was defined as a word used to describe foreigners who had difficulty speaking the language. This version suggests that the word is a bastardization of the Spanish word for Greek, *griego,* as in "it's all Greek to me." It might be that the Mexican-American War coincided with a shift in usage of the word to mean English-speaking foreigners in particular and perhaps a negative connotation as well.

Semantics aside, I have been a gringo, for better or worse, going on ten years. Between 1999 and 2008, I was itinerant. I visited seven continents and more than eighty countries and slept on hundreds of couches and sandy beaches. But I concentrated most of my travel time in Latin America, where the languages, landscapes, and politics (not to mention the fried sweet plantains that I devoured every chance I got) captivated me from day one. Over the years, I traveled in search of adventure, to learn a bit about the planet, and to find myself.

Being on the road, traveling the earth, testing myself against a constantly changing backdrop became addictive. Settling down in one place for more than a week seemed undesirable, impossible even. I built a network of friends and responsibilities that spanned the continents and kept me on the move. I resisted certain commitments—less in terms of relationships or work or responsibility and more in terms of anything that would require me to be in one place for an extended period of time—in a way that made it hard to build a stable life. Months in advance, I accepted short-term obligations in random, far-flung parts of the globe that prevented me from staying put. As my Spanish and Portuguese slowly improved I found travel in Latin America more rewarding. In Rwanda or China I had limited communication and, as a result, my ability to understand and access the people, politics, and places was more restricted: language was either a great wall separating me from people and places or a skeleton key opening every door. Drawn back to Latin America again and again, I ended up exploring virtually every country in the region. Of course, I concentrated my time in some countries, and in those places built more intimate relationships with people, politics, and geography than I was able to in others.

My personal journey was set against a constantly changing political backdrop. As I grew and changed, so did the region. I was born into a North American family with anti-imperialist politics at the dinner table and in their blood, but many of my conscious formative personal experiences took place in Latin America. During the decade that I explored myself and the region, Latin America was in the process of making a significant political shift. This book then has two narrative threads: my personal journey, and the places I was passing through. Weaving them together on the page was more challenging than it was in real life. The written word has a unique sort of permanence. In life I can do something one way today and another tomorrow. I can recognize my current perspective and understanding as inherently limited, flawed, and subject to change. Conveying that sense of change, that possibility for evolution in a project that is necessarily finite, sometimes eluded me. The risks of dogma, ideology, and partisanship become all the more perilous on the printed page.

In the chapters that follow, I write about the countries that resonated most with me personally; they are also representative of the region's shifting politics. Cuba, Mexico, and Nicaragua are notably absent from this book. I've visited all three but those stories will have to wait for another time.

The places I focus on are those that offered meaningful lessons, often from personal, on-the-ground experiences. Many of the people I met and profile here are smarter, more open-minded, and richer in life experiences than I am. I was glad to be an observer of—and sometimes participant in—their lives, struggles, and conversations. I hope my accounts of them, even through what are inevitably partial sketches, provide a window into this dynamic, fascinating region.

I have changed names throughout, to protect privacy. Not all events have been recounted in exact chronological order, and the conversations and descriptions are approximations re-created on the page from memory, notes, and daily journal entries rather than formal reportage or tape-recorded interviews. Memory is a slippery beast, and getting a firm grip on it is, at times, an unattainable goal; I tried my best.

Border Crossings

The rugged handmade wooden canoe fitted with a powerful outboard motor pushed up against the dirt shore of Lake Petén Itzá where the town's first houses nestled the beach. There was no "Welcome to San Andrés" sign. A handful of chickens clucked around, a few pigs rooted in the dirt, and the sweet smell of burning plastic garbage filled the air. San Andrés, with its rapidly growing population of five thousand, covered the steep hill leading up from the lake and back toward a lush tropical jungle where an ancient civilization had reached its peak some six hundred years ago. Mayan stone cities and temples, long abandoned, were the region's primary attraction for foreigners.

On the journey across the lake from the triple city of Flores–San Benito–Santa Elena, with its few tens of thousands of people, I had sat in the rear of the boat near the loud motor and intense fumes: being the gringo and a first-time visitor, I had no way of knowing better. Riding in the back, I had the additional disadvantage of waiting while the rest of the passengers—all Guatemalans—disembarked. A group of young men with neatly pressed school uniforms and meticulously gelled straight black hair got out first. Next, an old woman with an impossibly large bag was helped ashore; then a younger woman with an infant at her breast and two smaller ones following behind with sacks balanced on their heads. A couple of men carried machetes and wore muddy knee-high rubber boots—workers in the fields or the jungle.

As the people in front of me climbed onto the dirt embankment,

5

I looked down the beach and saw small groups of young women and girls washing clothes by hand and carrying water in plastic tubs. On the other side of the beach, heading away from town toward more trees and unsettled jungle between the villages dotting the lakefront, partially clothed families bathed and splashed in the shallows of the cool water. *"Oye gringo!"* Hey gringo, time to go. The boatman, no more than twenty with a thin mustache and sneakers well cared for but far past their prime, wanted me off his boat. Sporting new, sturdy boots and a big hiking bag that was strapped, unnecessarily secure, to my back, I jumped out onto the wet ground and started walking up the hill. I passed one-story cinder-block and wood houses on narrow, partially paved streets and footpaths. The sun burned down, scorching everything it touched, and the people I passed stayed in the shadows while children played and ran freely. A few blocks up, climbing steeply, I stumbled on Eco-Escuela. It was a one-room language school built on stilts out over the hill. The back wall was cut away to provide a panoramic view of the lake.

This was to be my new school but I didn't stop there. Instead I continued farther up the hill to the small wooden house of Doña Eugenia, which was where I had arranged to stay for my two-month-long visit. I was to share my new home with Doña Eugenia's only daughter, Delia, and, when he got back from working in the jungle, her quiet, amiable husband, Jesús. Doña Eugenia had short hair and was one of the only married women in town with just one child—an oddity in a community where contraception was rarely used. Her daughter was sixteen, with a squat frame and feet more used to flip-flops than shoes. The women were both tiny, coming up no higher than my chest. It would be a week or more before I met Jesús. He had a warm smile, and like most men in town who worked in the fields or the jungle, carried a machete wherever he went. I wasn't the first gringo they had hosted, so my Birkenstocks, headlamp, and wide array of sunscreens came as no surprise.

Dinner on my first night at their house was handmade corn tortillas fried into tostadas and covered with cabbage and grated cheese. While I ate hungrily, I tried out the various getting-to-know-you one-liners I remembered from Spanish class in high school. *Soy de Chicago; tengo dieciocho años; me llamo Chesa: C-H-E-S-A. ¿Cómo estás?* We struggled to get to know one another, but my Spanish was a severe limitation, often slowing conversation to a total halt. While on my third or fourth tostada Doña Eugenia asked me *¿Qué hacen sus padres?* Small talk about what her exchange students' parents did was probably a safe ice-breaking question for most of the gringos Doña Eugenia had hosted in the past. But her question left me with a dilemma.

I've been open and matter-of-fact about my family situation since before I can remember—as a kid I just took it for granted that it was as normal as saying my parents were doctors or teachers; eventually, I even preferred my whole class to know at the beginning of the year rather than lying or worrying about who knew what—and I didn't see why I should hide it now. But what were the words for jail or adoption in Spanish anyway? *"Tengo cuatro padres."* That part was easy, but I saw the puzzled look on Doña Eugenia's and Delia's faces.

"¿Cómo así? ¿Son divorciados?" came the inevitable reply. No, they were not divorced. They were . . . I had to rely on my pocket dictionary for this one . . . *encarcelados.* If I thought having parents in prison was going to give me street credibility in San Andrés, the distraught look that passed between my hosts dispelled that misconception immediately. They were worried. I started talking fast, making up the words I didn't know. *Bebé, padres, crimen, tres muertos, político, negros, imperialismo, Nueva York.*

How could I, with only the most basic Spanish, articulate to my now concerned hosts that in October 1981, when I was just fourteen months old, my biological parents, Kathy Boudin and David Gilbert, had left their Manhattan apartment and dropped me off at my Dominican babysitter's house, only to head off into a tragedy? How could I explain that, while I played and fussed as an infant, my parents made a terrible mistake, the worst of their lives? They had waited in a U-Haul in Nyack, New York, as a couple of miles away, members of a radical armed group of black nationalists robbed a Brinks truck of $1.6 million. Tragically bungled, the Brinks robbery left three men dead and an entire community traumatized. By the time my mother and father received a twenty-years-to-life sentence and a seventy-five-years-to-life sentence, respectively, friends of theirs, Bill Ayers and Bernardine Dohrn, had taken me into their family and become my other parents. How could I explain to Delia what the political turmoil of the 1960s and 1970s had been about, or how my parents, white Jews, got involved in antiracist and antiwar activism and ultimately armed robbery?

For more than a decade before I was born, all four of my parents had lived on the run from the FBI as members of the militant political group called the Weather Underground; they had a common history. In 1980, after the Underground had fallen apart, Bill and Bernardine surfaced, and voluntarily turned themselves in to the authorities—the most serious charges against both of them had been dismissed because of illegal activities, including wiretaps, break-ins, and mail interceptions, initiated by the attorney general and an FBI assistant director. Bernardine was given three years probation for charges stemming from a protest. When I landed in my new household, Bill and Bernardine already had two sons: Zayd and Malik became my older brothers. With the support of my new family, through visits, letters, and phone calls, before I can even remember, I began to build relationships with my other parents from the distance incarceration creates. Somewhere in the gray area between collective family memory and where my own recollections start, I grew accustomed to going through a metal detector and steel gates every time I wanted to give my biological parents a hug.

As I grew up, my four parents' group efforts made feasible the transitions between the mostly white, middle-class, private school day-to-day and the mostly poor, black, and Latino prison system that was a constant thread in my life. I lived in parallel worlds. My family taught me radical politics from the beginning, but I also learned to prove myself in elite institutions. Brought up with the privileges and opportunities the United States offers some people, and a political line that condemned the very existence of an elite, I lived a contradiction. Life's incongruities were not merely between theory and practice. Much of the left-wing politics took root, despite the exclusive networks and institutions, because prisons can be a great equalizer. The line for the metal detector at Attica Correctional Facility didn't move any faster for me because I attended the same private school where Nobel Prize winners and billionaires sent their kids.

With one hand cuffed to a barely visible abyss of poverty and incarceration, and the other grasped in the confident handshakes of those accustomed to privilege and comfort, I learned to move freely between different universes. Almost miraculously these existences came to complement each other. Each served as a lens through which life could be viewed and understood, a bridge to reach out and connect with people around the planet in the most unlikely places. Metal detectors, languages, planes, and buses have come to serve as portals between my different worlds.

There was no way I could articulate all this with the little Spanish I knew at the time of arrival in San Andrés, and my fifth tostada was getting cold while I fumbled with my dictionary. Even looking up every word I could barely explain to Doña Eugenia and Delia that my parents were kind, generous, well-meaning people, *buenas personas,* that we loved one another with the complexity of any strong family, *mucho amor,* that their crime had been politically motivated, *crimen político,* that despite their incarceration I had grown up in a stable, middle-class family, *familia estable.* Their tight faces suggested confusion, concern, maybe even fear. I didn't want them to be scared to have me in their home, but the more I tried to explain in broken Spanish and infinitive verbs plucked straight out of the dictionary, the more confused I seemed to make them. I wanted them to see me as a friend, to articulate a self-portrait of a good gringo, an ally, but I wasn't so sure who I was myself.

While I was in Doña Eugenia's kitchen, in January 1999, my classmates were beginning the last semester of senior year of high school. I had finished my credits early and decided I would see how well Mr. Fuentes's intensive Spanish class could serve me during an immersion experience in rural Guatemala. It was my first trip to Latin America and my first-ever journey outside the United States without my family.

In Venezuela, a few hours flying south from San Andrés, Hugo Chávez was being sworn in as president and would soon begin shaking up the region. Later that year, at the Battle in Seattle, a burgeoning global protest movement would target institutions like the World Trade Organization, the International Monetary Fund, and the World Bank that propagated neoliberal policies—classical liberal economic policies with the goal of transferring control of the economy from the public to the private sector. By the 1990s, neoliberal economic and social policies had become the norm throughout Latin America, though politicians advocating them openly were rarely elected democratically.

On the flight south I had read Stephen Schlesinger's and Stephen Kinzer's *Bitter Fruit: The Untold Story of the American Coup in Guatemala,* which described the role of the United States government in overthrowing Guatemala's democracy back in 1954. It was one of a number of books my parents had suggested to help me understand the role North American companies and the CIA played in Guatemala's tragic history of poverty and civil war. Che Guevara happened to be living in Guatemala City at the time of the coup; the events the young Argentine witnessed would forever change his life and with it pan-American history.

The CIA-sponsored 1954 Guatemalan coup, justified in the name of fighting communism, was followed closely by brutal military dictatorships and a thirty-six-year-long bloody civil war that ravaged the country. Dictators and death squads left an estimated 200,000 dead, mostly unarmed indigenous civilians, and the country deep within the United States policy fold. But when I flew into Guatemala for the first time I only had the vaguest idea of what a neoliberal policy was, let alone what it would look like on the ground.

From Chicago I had signed up to study at a language school in the sparsely populated northern region of Guatemala called the Petén, and it was through the school that I was assigned to live with Doña

Eugenia. My school tuition of $150 a week included four hours of one-on-one classes per day, and a home stay with all my meals included. The school had an inviting, progressive-sounding name, Eco-Escuela. A family friend who had studied there recommended it.

After collecting my new backpack from the baggage claim in Guatemala City's international airport, I wandered over to the airport information desk. A woman in a light green dress suit who was working there spoke more English than I did Spanish. She said that I had two basic choices for getting to the Petén: I could board a one-hour flight for $65 or I could take a twelve-hour bus ride for about $9. In a decision that would foreshadow much of my travel over the next decade I decided that a plane ride was too expensive and straightforward. Nervous though I was, I wanted to get into the mix and travel like a Guatemalan: the bus it was.

A taxi driver charged me $4.30 for a ride to the private coach terminal of a passenger bus company called Fuente del Norte, Fountain of the North. It wasn't until I stepped out of the taxi into the sun and smog of downtown Guatemala City that I realized what I had thought to be perfect low-key travel gear—Timberland boots, khaki cargo pants, and oversized photojournalist vest with twenty-three pockets (I counted them, though I could never figure out what the little mesh pouch on top of the left breast pocket was for), along with my stuffed backpack that had more straps and hooks and snaps than could possibly be useful—was conspicuous against the dirty gray central city. There were several rows of seats in the open-air waiting area just off the busy street where the cab left me. In one corner a few men in short-sleeve button-down shirts and thick jeans ate fried chicken and drank Gallo beers. One row of seats was occupied by a family of six with bags, parcels, bundles, and boxes of all sizes spread out around them. Several other travelers sat on duffel bags up against the back wall and kids played on the floor. A steady stream of travelers walked in and out of the terminal from the narrow sidewalks. I realized I was stepping, uninvited, into a new world that I understood practically nothing about and I wasn't at all sure that I was welcome. In my mind's eye I regarded myself as a comrade in arms with the downtrodden *guatemaltecos* I had read about. But how were the dozens of people in the bus station to know that? I had the uncomfortable feeling, standing there in my new gear, that I looked like another rich white tourist dropping into a foreign reality for exotic thrills and narcissistic self-exploration.

I made my way to the ticket office, a dirty Plexiglas cubicle in one corner of the room, and bought a $9 ticket that was handwritten on a recycled paper template. The bus would leave in an hour. I didn't want to wander around the center city, known for street crime, with a bag that could easily be confused for Santa's sack by any of the handful of street kids I saw sitting on the sidewalks. So I found a seat in one of the rows of empty blue chairs and took in my surroundings.

People all over were selling junk food, magazines, pens, watches, hairclips, and sunglasses. A young Mayan girl, a toddler, tried to sell me a newspaper. I started talking to a chubby-cheeked young woman but we didn't get far because my Spanish wasn't up to it. I managed to figure out that she was seventeen and married, which seemed to me, at eighteen, an unfortunate state of affairs. Her husband, a powerful-looking man with black eyes and strong jaw, showed up carrying a large machete. I relaxed after he shared a smile. They were as helpful as my Spanish permitted them to be.

Eventually, with the assistance of the young couple, I figured out that my bus was starting to board. The attendant who took my ticket made me check my big backpack. I worried about it disappearing and resolved to look out the window every time we stopped to make sure it wasn't being offloaded along with someone else's belongings. After boarding, I squeezed down the aisle, maneuvering around large sacks of potatoes and live chickens tied together in a bunch by their legs. Many of the seats were broken and the bus was filthy. There was no bathroom and I regretted not having visited the one in the bus station.

The attendant led me past people standing in the aisle to the one seat that was still empty. I was drenched in sweat and overwhelmed by my surroundings. Only later did it occur to me that I owed my seat to my white skin and my helplessness. The attendant had reserved it for me because I was a gringo. In Latin America, at least, a United States passport and a little confidence open doors to an elite world of perks and preferential treatment. Later I was to feel much more uncomfortable about drawing on this kind of white-skinned privilege, what I came to know as the gringo wild card, but on this occasion I was just glad to sit down.

As we rolled out of Guatemala City, we passed by what seemed an endless landscape of industrial parks and free trade zones. The sprawling boxlike factories were surrounded by fences and barbed wire. I later learned that the number of maquiladoras, industrial sweatshops that import raw materials and equipment on a duty-free basis for assembly and then export to mass consumer markets like the United States, had more than quadrupled from 1994 to 1999. Most of them made textiles and apparel products, but the word *maquila* came from the portion of grain the miller traditionally charged as a service fee. The millers still took their share in rural corn-growing areas but Guatemala's economy, like that of the region, was in flux. Throughout the previous decades the government had privatized the mail, electricity supply, and telephone companies. The Guatemalan state had long since abandoned its role as an agent of social development, cutting social spending across the spectrum and leaving the country's poor without a safety net. It also opened the economy to foreign, mainly North American, imports while simultaneously implementing policies aimed at consolidating agricultural holdings to maximize cash crop exports that could be used to pay off the foreign debt. Peasant farmers who lost their land converged on cities, providing a cheap, flexible labor pool for newly established industry.

The sweatshops I saw that day, filled with people who a few years earlier would have been planting corn, were one of the faces of neoliberalism that defined the economic landscape I was traveling through. Guatemala, like many countries across the global south at the time, was part of the "Washington Consensus," a partnership with American-based financial institutions like the World Bank and the International Monetary Fund. These bodies granted loans only on the conditions of fiscal austerity, privatization, and the opening up of local economies to unfettered global trade. This resulted in such dismal economic performance that the 1980s became known as the "lost decade" in Latin America, although economists continue to debate how successful the model was in countries like Chile and El Salvador. In many countries, including those called successes by some, military dictators forced these policies on unwilling populations. In elections Latin Americans have rarely supported politicians who openly advocate neoliberal policies, yet the whole region ended up with them.

Neoliberal reforms may well have attracted foreign direct investments and created jobs in the maquiladoras I saw out of the bus window on that first day in Latin America. But Guatemala's income distribution and human development index were among the worst in the hemisphere. Only the rich minority was in a position to benefit from these policies. The poor were left with no labor protections or social safety nets, and few options besides jobs that didn't pay a living wage. The sweatshops provided jobs, but they didn't look like the kind of place I could imagine working in. They reminded me of prisons.

After we eventually escaped the sprawling outskirts of the capital, the only roadside buildings that interrupted the passing garbage-strewn rural landscape were little roadside tiendas. Each store was painted top to bottom with either Coke or Pepsi advertisements, depending on which of the two soft drink giants had bought the owner paint and agreed to make regular deliveries. Coke and Pepsi products—sodas, bottled water, and juices—are virtually the only affordable drinks in a country where little if any water from public sources is potable. The acid and the sugar in the soda, together with limited access to dentists, left even young children's teeth rotten, while adults had more metal caps than I had seen anywhere outside rap videos.

As passengers got on and off the bus, different people sat down next to me for an hour or so at a time. Although I couldn't communicate with them verbally, kindness and sympathy were often apparent in their eyes and smiles. Several of them told me *cuídate*, "be careful," but I couldn't tell what they were warning me about. The word *ladrón* was whispered on more than one occasion, with particular emphasis. When I finally looked it up in the mini-dictionary I kept in one of my various vest pockets, I was dismayed to learn it meant *thief*. Of course! As the only foreigner on the bus I was sure to be a target, I realized, panic-stricken. But who were the thieves? And what was I supposed to do to foil them?

I tried to sleep but was unable to doze off. I was anxious and uncomfortable. Maybe, it occurred to me, we gringos have made life too easy for ourselves. The Guatemalans around me seemed to have an amazing capacity for discomfort. While the bus rattled and bounced over terrible roads, kids slept on the dirty floor and women stood or sat for hours in positions so awkward that I couldn't have maintained them for ten minutes. No one else appeared to mind the large bugs that appeared on the insides of the windows and roof as the sun went down. Hygiene and personal space were quickly taking on whole new meanings for me.

As one of the few people with a functional seat, I felt embarrassed and self-conscious about my aching back and the fact that it made me uncomfortable when random kids draped themselves across my legs without so much as a glance in my direction before they fell asleep. Apparently an empty lap looked to them much the way an empty seat looked to me. Occasionally the vehicle jostled to a stop at some indistinguishable spot on the road and a woman, often clutching a baby, would wake the kid on my knees and lead them off the bus. My eyes followed them as they set out along narrow mountain roads or forest paths, until they disappeared in the dark.

The paved road became a bumpy dirt track, and a thick mist descended outside the windows of the bus. I heard birds and bugs in the night but my eyes were useless in the pitch black under cloud cover: night had fallen with the suddenness and finality of a black velvet curtain. At one point a couple of loud bangs pierced the silence of the jungle and the bus stopped suddenly: I snapped to attention with nervous thoughts of gunshots from armed bandits, or guerrilla hold-

overs from the country's civil war. But the loud reports turned out
to be only the engine backfiring. The driver announced a temporary
breakdown but assured us that it would just be *cinco minutos más*
as his assistant attacked the engine with a wrench. Twenty minutes
later he was back onboard trying to calm the passengers, demanding
another *momentito*. Once we got going again the remainder of the
ride was uneventful and I dozed.

I got off in Santa Elena, Petén, around 3 A.M. A five-hundred-yard-
long dirt embankment connected the twin cities of Santa Elena and
San Benito on the shores of the lake to the island town of Flores,
the state capital. My *Let's Go* guidebook explained that a short walk
would take me from Santa Elena's bus station across the land bridge
to Flores. But I was frightened of walking anywhere at night, especially with my bags, which, to my relief and surprise, had made it all
the way. I jumped in the first taxi I saw and told the driver: *"Voy a
Flores. Hotel. Barato. Por favor."* I had practiced the phrases for the
last hour of the ride and they were successful. Just a minute or two
later we pulled up in front of a small hostel called La Canoa and the
driver pounded on the wooden gate until he woke the young boy on
the night shift. I splurged on a room with its own private cold water
shower for $5.80 a night. Before going to bed I wrote in my journal
and marked down every quetzal I had spent that day—15 on food, 40
on the hotel, and 120 on transportation. I concluded that my first bus
trip in Latin America was overall okay. In eleven hours I had covered
a little more than one hundred miles.

In San Andrés, Doña Eugenia and Delia made me acutely aware that
the solidarity with the poor and downtrodden of the world that pre-
vailed in my own family, and already shaped my political outlook,
was not necessarily shared by the poor and downtrodden themselves.
During my time in San Andrés, I regularly sought conversation about
the tragic history that decades of brutal civil war, unleashed by a
United States–supported coup, had visited on the country. But whenever I tried initiating discussion about President Jacobo Arbenz and

the role of the CIA in overthrowing him back in 1954, my host family and their friends seemed uninterested. Their silence puzzled me at first: Why weren't they as eager as I to criticize imperialism in general and United States foreign policy in Latin America in particular?

In retrospect I know that the people I spent time with in San Andrés probably didn't feel they had been directly affected by any United States intervention in their country. They knew little of the radical political history and theory that I had been immersed in growing up. Many in the town aspired to a consumer lifestyle like the ones they saw on television. Delia loved to watch Mexican *telenovelas*, soap operas, and was constantly pestering me to tell her about life in *El Norte*. What kind of car did my family drive? How much did my camera cost? How many dollars could a babysitter earn in a week? And a maid? Doña Eugenia's primary concern appeared to be ensuring that Delia was a *virgencita* when she finally married. She gossiped and fussed over what the neighbors said about her and her daughter all day long—Doña Eugenia accompanied Delia to the town dance until the last song of the night so there would be no chatter about whether Delia spent too much time dancing with Hector or Luis, or whether her skirt was too short.

My hosts were also surprisingly preoccupied with the material hardships of their daily lives. Doña Eugenia complained regularly about the local mayor's failure to provide running water for their casa. Although San Andrés had a pipe system, it didn't deliver any water during the months I lived there. A truck occasionally brought lake water up to the more remote houses like the one I was staying in, which was a long steep climb up the hill from the lakeshore, past where the paved street ended and the dirt road began. But its rare appearances meant that rainwater was a more reliable source of life's most basic necessity. According to several locals, tax money went to maintaining some local politicians' houses and cars rather than the town's pump.

When I first heard about the mayor's evident dereliction of his duty to keep the faucets running, I got fired up and suggested we should go to the police, organize a protest, gather signatures on a petition, or meet with the international organizations based in nearby Flores. My hosts and their friends were amused by my ignorance of the way things worked. They explained the lack of running water with a shrug of the shoulders and a simple one-word answer: *corrupción*. And so I quickly abandoned my efforts at rabble-rousing and, like everyone else, got used to manually filling the tank in the yard with rainwater before taking a cold shower or washing my clothes by hand. It didn't take much for me to stop shaving.

I was on my own so I could reinvent myself however I chose, but traveling solo highlights the difference between being lonely and being alone. On the road I'm rarely alone.

My first and best friend in San Andrés, Juan, worked as an assistant to the director of the language school where I studied every day. A short, mustached mestizo—as mixed-race Guatemalans call themselves—he showed me around during my first days in town speaking Spanish slowly so that I could understand what he was explaining. In the evenings he and his buddies would take me along while they hung around outside one of the town's churches to see which girls looked the cutest as they came out after service. When it came to finding girls Juan was ecumenical: he was as happy to spot chicas outside his mom's *iglesia católica* as in front of the town's Mormon or evangelical churches; for a small town San Andrés seemed to have a lot of churches: I counted at least fourteen just in the part of town between my house and the school. Although he knew the best places to find local talent, Juan preferred gringas he met through the language school and was determined to be the first man from the town to love his way into a green card.

Often, sitting in a bar—simple cement-floored stores that sold beer and little else—sipping Gallo beers, or after taking a swim in the lake, we would wind up talking about how he might get entry into the United States. I soon realized how little I knew about obtaining a visa or sneaking into *El Norte* illegally. It was easy for me to offer a place to stay and help finding a job if he ever made it to the United States, but what he really needed was a way to get there. And he wasn't the only one. Lots of Guatemalans wanted me to help them leave their country for mine. I thought the income the language school provided for the town would help prevent people from migrating, but it seemed the more money people had, and the more access they had to *norteños,* the keener they were to depart.

The large house across the street from Doña Eugenia's belonged to Juan's aunt, Rosario, who had previously worked as one of Eco-Escuela's administrators. But Rosario didn't live there anymore. She had moved to the suburbs of Washington, D.C., where she worked as an undocumented housekeeper, sending money home to her husband and three kids. The money arrived every month via Western Union, which took a 10 percent cut for the transfer. The amount received was often further reduced by losses on the currency exchange because Western Union accepted Rosario's dollars in Washington but paid her family with local quetzals.

United States trade policy allowed multinational companies to invest their capital in free trade zones throughout Central America with virtually no taxes or tariffs. Meanwhile hardworking migrants like Rosario ended up paying high fees to send their families enough for the basic necessities. Not that this seemed to dissuade anyone. As many as one thousand migrants a week from across Central America set out from Santa Elena, Petén, for the Mexican border, just a four-hour bus ride away on a little used and—more important for the migrants—little policed road. Guatemala is Central America's gateway to Mexico, which is, in turn, the entry point to the United States. The view from my window in Doña Eugenia's casa across to her neighbor's house made it easy to understand the motivation for this tide of migrants. Thanks to Rosario's support, her family had built a new room on their house, and bought a big screen color television, as well as a bicycle for each person in the family; Doña Eugenia's house hadn't been upgraded in years.

Rosario's family also ate meat at almost every meal, something I envied. Although Doña Eugenia used the income my stay generated to supplement the family's larder, I had the appetite of a small army and there was rarely enough to eat, and almost never any meat. I took to filling up on the one thing that was generally in large supply: handmade corn tortillas. I didn't invent this strategy for quelling hunger; indeed most poor Guatemalans had the same approach. Corn was the one staple that was affordable and regularly available—especially in rural areas where almost every family had someone working on a nearby milpa who could provide the raw material without ever going into the cash economy. A milpa is literally a plot of corn but often refers to a field where farmers plant as many as a dozen crops at once—beans, squash, corn, chiles, and more. The beans use the corn stalks as climbing frames, and return the favor by fixing nitrogen into the soil, which helps fertilize the corn. In our case, it was Doña Eugenia's aging, stooped father who worked the family milpa. He wore black rubber knee-high boots, without socks, to walk five miles each way to his work.

After a week or so I realized that, aside from monotony, there was a more serious problem with my staving off hunger with endless tortillas. There was a protein shortage in my diet. We ate cereal or mush for breakfast, vegetable soup and rice for lunch, and tostadas or tortillas as the core part of dinner with a head of cabbage thrown in for variety. While cabbage is rich in vitamins and minerals, it is also described on nutritional websites as "ideal for weight loss." The black beans were tasty and nutritious but appeared on the table infrequently. The little meat we had was generally tough and unappetizing. High-quality meat was being produced locally, often on land that had been cleared of jungle using slash-and-burn techniques, with all the attendant environmental problems. But this was too expensive for locals by far and was shipped to Guatemala City—or more often to the United States. Only scraps and diseased cows were butchered and sold locally. It was a situation I would run into over and over again throughout Latin America.

After a month at Dona Eugenia's I was becoming increasingly concerned about malnourishment. I was only eighteen, after all, and probably still growing to adult size; yet I could see my body progressively shrinking. Days passed and my stomach ached with hunger. I tried to comfort myself by reflecting that I was at least experiencing a mild version of what many local people were going through, but I felt increasingly miserable about the situation. Of course, I could have supplemented my meals at home by visiting the local restaurants or stores. But I was determined to keep track of every quetzal and not to spend money unless I absolutely had to since my tuition to the school included "room and board." The money I had with me—$500 in traveler's checks and $150 in cash stashed in one of the recesses of my hiking bag under the bed—had been earned on summer jobs waiting tables, working on an assembly line at a South Chicago factory, and building houses in Vermont, all for close to minimum wage. Consequently my budget was a real factor in determining how long I would be able to travel. But I also wanted to live with my host family and not above them by treating myself to luxuries they couldn't have.

The lack of protein was an abiding problem, but I had other preoccupations too. I had become involved with a local young woman to whom Juan had introduced me. Flor had been the town beauty queen until she got pregnant out of wedlock and was stripped of her crown. By the time I met her she had a chubby fourteen-month-old daughter. It seemed like all the women my age were either married or had children. Flor and I were together for most of the time that I lived in San Andrés, though small-town gossip eventually caused us to part ways. If I close my eyes and concentrate, I can still hear her saying, in her slow, Guatemalan drawl, *pueblo pequeño, infierno grande,* a small town can be a big hell. Frustratingly, for me at least, our relationship never got much beyond the odd kiss and cuddle. Partly this was a result of a lack of privacy but I also felt some uneasiness about misleading Flor. I knew I was in Guatemala for only a limited time and that the gaping differences between us made the possibility of a long-term relationship unlikely. She knew it too. A good-bye letter she wrote me said, "I believed you would be a good husband for me and for my daughter a good father. But it isn't possible; we live in two different worlds."

Our involvement, while doing wonders for my Spanish language skills, made me aware of the challenges of cross-cultural romances. There is often something inherently exploitive about such relationships as both people project another culture and identity onto the other. Yet cross-cultural relationships present challenges that often make them more rewarding than the simpler, closer to home variety. Individuals' and families' culturally determined expectations can put unexpected pressures on relationships even years after they begin. When I returned to San Andrés six months after my original visit, Juan told me that the father of Flor's daughter had reentered the picture and she had moved with him to Belize where, reportedly, she was pregnant again.

As time passed I gradually became used to the slow, daily routine in San Andrés. The roosters were far better than any alarm clock when it came to waking early. Once the sun was up I climbed out of bed to brush my teeth in the garden and eat breakfast before heading down the hill toward the language school. I would often come across dead bugs the size of the palm of my hand in the streets that the bright lights in town lured out of the nearby jungle. I had one-on-one classes all morning, studying verb tenses, learning the difference between *por* and *para,* or just working on conversation skills. After school I usually managed to squeeze in a few games of Ping-Pong against Juan and the teachers from the school on a homemade table in front of the police station before heading up the hill to lunch with Delia and Doña Eugenia.

After an hour-long post-lunch siesta that most people in town observed I would meet the school's community service coordinator, Don Gabriel, a sinewy fifty-year-old with twenty grandchildren and counting. He ran the school's various projects, from planting trees to maintaining a nature trail. The community service program had been one of the reasons I chose to study at Eco-Escuela. I soon realized, however, that while the work he assigned was designed to help me feel positive about my contribution to the community, it actually achieved little that was useful for the town or its inhabitants. None of the local people I met showed much interest in whether the nature trail we worked on was maintained. While I spent many afternoons picking up garbage, it was impossible to keep up with everyone else who was busy dropping it. There were no garbage cans to encourage them to do anything else—the mayor would probably get to that right after he fixed the water system. Eventually I started spending fewer after-noons with Don Gabriel, and struggled to find other ways to engage usefully as an outsider.

If it was one of the days when a heavy, warm rain fell, turning the lake an angry gray and reducing the streets to mud tracks, I would stay home and help Doña Eugenia fill every bucket, pot, and pan in the house with water for later use in washing dishes and taking show-ers. I took responsibility for my own laundry and after dinner would often insist that Delia let me do the washing up. None of this was easy in a society where machismo was a harsh reality of everyday life. When the boys in the neighborhood saw me in the yard washing my own clothes by hand they thought it was hilarious. I could get away with it only because I was an outsider. When I was out with Juan and the guys they would regularly grab my lats, the upper back just behind my armpit, and tell me they were checking on how much sex I had been having lately. I had no idea what they were talking about until I slowly realized that they thought only of sex in the missionary posi-tion where the lats got a good workout. As little as I knew about sex, I felt sorry for the men, and much sorrier for the women who had to put up with them.

After dinner and the dishes it was time to go hang out with the guys on the basketball court in front of the tienda where Flor worked the night shift selling Gallo beer, chewing gum, candy, and chips. Most evenings the streetlights were switched off by 10 P.M. but I would stay out late talking to Flor as she rocked her daughter to sleep in a ham-mock hung from the walls of the little shack. After we kissed good night, my walk home took me past the one bar in town that was guar-anteed to have a small but raucous crowd. The wooden building, with music blaring late into the night, had no name. People referred to it simply as *El Bar*. This establishment was different from the cantinas, which were more reputable places that sold beer only and closed early. Here hard liquor and sex were available, for a fee. It was open until the roosters began their early morning reveille. I never went in.

cᴗcᴗcᴗ

Although I had gone to Guatemala to live and study in San Andrés, I caught the backpacker's travel bug almost immediately and used the weekends to explore the area on jungle camping trips and visits to the Mayan ruins at Tikal or Belize's Caribbean coast. My traveling companions on these trips were a couple of gringos who showed up at the language school a few weeks after I started. Max was a tattooed Irish American who grew up in Boston. With him at Eco-Escuela was his friend Sarah, an expert at packing light. There was nothing super-fluous in her bag and by washing a few items of clothing at bedtime and letting them air dry overnight, she kept her bag to half the size of mine. They were both students at Prescott College in Arizona and had already completed their National Outdoor Leadership School (NOLS) training: he in Chilean Patagonia, and she in the Rockies. I was in awe. As the youngest member of the trio I felt a constant need to prove myself, and so ended up concentrating intently on walking faster, climbing higher, and eating more banana pancakes for break-fast than anyone else. I looked up to Max, and over the several trips we took together he was kind enough to teach a few of the basics of international budget travel: keep your money and passport on you at all times; pack only what you can carry comfortably on your back for several miles; and never accept the first price money changers offer at border crossings, because there is always a cheaper way to do it.

After completing their stint at the school, Max and Sarah had to travel up to Cancún to catch a flight home. I had never been to Mexico and was looking for an adventure and a bit of relief from the claustrophobia of the *pueblo pequeño*. We agreed that I would accompany them and take a week off from school. Once we got to Tabasco province, they would head north to Yucatán and on to Can-cún while I would return to Guatemala via Chiapas. So it was that Max, Sarah, and I crossed Lake Petén Itza in a *lancha* like the one that carried me to the town on my first day. This time I sat farther forward to avoid the fumes, noise, and lines that came with sitting in the rear of the boat. Once we arrived in Santa Elena, we walked to the open space that doubled as market and coach terminal. We wandered through throngs of people, cars, and food stalls. The buses created their own minimarkets for cheap imports from China and locally produced street food. Everywhere there was traffic, a bus stop, a terminal, or a crossing, scores of men, women, and children descended on the buses, almost out of nowhere, to sell magic wallets, erasable pens, handheld fans, sewing kits, pocketknives, hairclips, sunglasses, crucifixes, combination pliers, ratchets, Spider-Man plastic cups, or jumbo sidewalk chalk. A steady flow of food merchants offered rapidly melting ice cream cones, salted nuts, pork rinds, boiled corn on the cob, sodas in plastic bags with straws, fried plantains, *chicha, buñuelos, empanadas, granizadas,* or any other unnamed local specialty imaginable. Often on long bus rides the only meal options are delivered by a vendor wrapped in yesterday's newspaper. A strong stomach becomes imperative. In Santa Elena's bus station market we bought some avocados and limes, a tomato, and some corn chips. Eventually we boarded a colorfully painted converted school bus headed for the border crossing into Mexico at Bethel. It was safe to assume that many of the other passengers were traveling to Mexico to head farther north, in search of the American Dream.

Somewhere along the dust-choked Guatemalan road between Santa Elena and Bethel was where I confirmed that I preferred traveling around the slow, bone-rattling way: by bus, with ordinary people. The bus we were riding in had been repainted in bright reds and blues. The inside was colorful too; the seats had springs popping out of the upholstery, and the floor was caked with dirt and garbage. Chickens, some tied in bunches and others wandering loose, squawked noisily. Bouncing along a road to a place I had never been, and would likely never go back to, suddenly felt exciting, liberating even. The four-hour ride cost $3.67 and set a nearly inflation-proof standard that would hold true throughout my trips around Latin America: when riding on a "chicken bus" only an inexperienced gringo would pay much more than a dollar an hour.

As we rode into western Petén I noticed on my map that our route, along a small dirt road, bordered the Maya Biosphere Reserve. But throughout the journey, in what was supposed to be protected rain forest and jungle, I saw numerous cows and corn fields or milpas.

The farming activity made me skeptical about claims I'd read on the Internet that this was the "largest continuous tract of forest in Latin America outside the Amazon." Black smoke rising in the distance signaled still more territory being razed for pasture. Clearing the land like this might help Guatemala export more beef to raise foreign currency to service its debts, but it also meant the destruction of ancient tropical forest and the attendant release of greenhouse gases and species extinction. It made me sad to see it and I couldn't help but wonder how much of the beef being reared was going to end up on my friends' dinner tables back home in Chicago.

Toward the end of the ride I began talking to the boy sitting next to me. His name was Yoni Alexander and he was wearing threadbare work pants and a button-down shirt that was so big it made him look even younger than his fourteen years. His mom or sister had sewn something resembling a Nike Swoosh onto the front of the baseball hat that was pulled down low, hiding his young face. Yoni explained that he was going to live with his sister's family in Mexico. She was twenty-one and already had six kids. He planned on working with his brother-in-law, who traded cattle on the Mexico-Guatemala border. I realized that Yoni couldn't read and that he had no money at all. It seemed a terribly precarious way to travel, but I was just beginning to discover life on the road in Latin America. I slowly came to understand what Mark Twain meant when he wrote that "travel is fatal to prejudice, bigotry and narrow-mindedness." Traveling in Guatemala was intensely uncomfortable, both physically and emotionally, but I learned things from it that school could never teach me: how people actually live outside the United States, the difference between "need" and "want," the value of privacy, the luxury of space, the capacity of the human body to tolerate lack of hygiene and physical discomfort.

We eventually arrived in Bethel on the border with Mexico with Yoni now very much in tow. The rest of the passengers faded into the shadows as soon as we arrived and the four of us had to figure out what to do. We decided to spend the night there and cross to Mexico the next day in a *colectivo* boat—the nautical equivalent of a shared taxi. Yoni was going to hang around until his brother-in-law showed up to collect him. I asked where he was going to sleep and eat since he had no money, and he shrugged and said *"con la gente."* I admired his chutzpah and, filled with the romance of travel, hoped that someday I might be able to live with the people in the same way. But for the time being I invited Yoni to come with us to a cheap-looking hotel we had spotted. It turned out that the Hotel Fronterizo could only offer us outdoor hammocks, no beds. After the usual haggling over every quetzal, which by this point I had learned to relish, we finally agreed on $4.40 per person for a hammock and a mosquito net. Yoni didn't have any money but the owner agreed that he could sleep on an old mattress on the ground near us for free. For dinner, Max made tasty guacamole using my knife and a plastic bag. Yoni had some old corn tortillas and a juicy, sweet melon with him. Although improvised, the food was delicious and, after a cold shower, we all fell asleep under the stars with the roar of howler monkeys in the woods all around us.

The next morning the chorus of monkeys had been replaced by that of birds. Yoni seemed to be able tell the name of each bird from its call, and he spent a long time trying, unsuccessfully, to get me to recognize the difference between a violaceous trogon and a keel-billed toucan. After buying our tickets for the *colectivo* from the boat's skipper we said good-bye to Yoni and headed to a house that had a crude sign advertising breakfast. It was inexpensive but tasty: scrambled eggs, black beans, fried sweet plantains, fresh orange juice, and the omnipresent corn tortillas. Then we headed to the immigration office to get our exit stamps. Entering and exiting Guatemala was supposed to be free, but it never was. On each of the ten occasions that I crossed the border during my first stint there I paid a different fee. A one-room wooden shack passed for an immigration office and the taciturn functionary who sat inside it looked like he could use another cup of coffee and a new posting. Staring unblinkingly at us over his poorly trimmed salt-and-pepper mustache, he told us the exit stamp would cost $5 each. His manner made it obvious that he was confident he would prevail in any disagreement: he was *oficialisimo* after all. The calculation was simple: we were desperate to get out of town and on to the scenic Mayan ruins and hippie camps in southern Mexico near Palenque. My traveling companions had a plane to catch in Cancún, and I had friends of friends to meet in Chiapas who were working in solidarity with the Zapatistas. He was as unyielding as a prison wall. There was no way we were going back to Santa Elena along the same bumpy, dusty road. This was the opposite of the gringo wild card, the downside to being an obvious outsider. We protested feebly, but handed over our quetzals.

Exit visas in hand, we headed down to the Usumacinta River, stretching for some six hundred miles and forming the border with Mexico in much of western Petén. The winding river, whether viewed from the banks or a map, is a natural dividing line that appears almost preordained. The muddy water and its wide course feel timeless, impartial. The river gives the national boundary a legitimacy missing at the arbitrary straight line frontiers negotiated in smoky private clubs and war-room treaties.

The *lancha* had a brightly painted wooden hull that leaked freely but, driven by a Suzuki outboard motor, moved surprisingly fast through the river's swirling water. Aside from the three of us gringos, the boat carried an Argentine couple, also backpackers, and several local ranch hands in cowboy boots and hats. There were a few other young men on the boat—not backpackers—who looked like they had been on the road for a while, perhaps from farther south than Guatemala. The boat carried us past military installations built into the banks of the river with sandbags and the biggest guns I had ever seen. Political borders exude a certain tension, and this one was no exception. The barbed wire and heavily armed adolescents in fatigues and helmets served to put us all on edge but when we disembarked at the Corozal border crossing in Mexico, we did not even find an immigration office. At the time this was not an official border crossing—just a military checkpoint in a wild frontier zone known for smuggling, trafficking, and lawlessness. In the years that followed, the military border guards would yield power to rapidly growing armed gangs of traffickers and the towns on either side would swell to support extensive smuggling operations. Since my crossing that day in March 1999, the border on this lonely stretch of the Usumacinta River has become one of the most heavily trafficked routes on the long, dangerous underground railroad that Central American migrants follow on their way to *El Norte*. I continued my trip into Mexico, through Chiapas and back to Guatemala via a different, more commonly used crossing in the south that took me through the Guatemalan highlands and back to the capital city. From there I repeated my original journey to San Andrés for three more weeks of language school before heading home to Chicago.

My own trip back to *El Norte* by airplane, at the end of my first stay in Guatemala, was, in comparison to the pilgrimage of most Latin American migrants, short and comfortable. But emotionally I found it wrenching. Before boarding the plane I contemplated throwing my ticket away and heading south on my own, going against the flow of northward-bound migrants, to disappear in the subcontinent. I craved adventure; I felt I needed more time to discover both the place and myself. Most of all, I was worried that going back to Chicago would erase what I had already learned, and undo the growth that felt so tangible. Words seemed insufficient for articulating exactly how my time away had changed me—language skills, a love for travel, newfound confidence, a more complex worldview, a better ability to be self-critical. Perhaps, even then, I knew that I had changed less than I liked to think I had, and that realization made me hesitant to return home; the thought that I would easily slip back into my old happy but narrow self was troubling.

While I returned to the United States laden with woven Mayan tunics, hand-knit pants, colorful bedspreads, and indigenous wall hangings, many of the Guatemalans on the plane were carrying steaming boxes of Pollo Campero fried chicken—apparently unaware that it was freely available north of the border and likely to be confiscated by customs officials in the airport. No matter, the stench of hot fat remained with us until we landed. On touchdown the Guatemalans all applauded. I joined in, despite my sadness at what already felt like a premature departure from Latin America.

I was back in Chicago with a bushy beard and a newfound confidence in speaking Spanish, though I still had a thick gringo accent. When I went to visit my friends, still immersed in their senior year of high school, I dressed in handwoven Mayan pants and a blue and white wide-armed, open-chest embroidered shirt. Just as I had stood out in my photojournalist vest in the Guatemala City bus station, I was glaringly out of place in the school halls filled with clean-shaven boys in Polo shirts and Girbaud jeans. But I was determined not to forget Guatemala, and I felt the need to demonstrate how I had grown close to those I had left behind. I had changed inside and I wanted people to know it. It was perhaps a month after I returned before I got out my old razor.

A picture on my mom's fridge from September 1999 shows me with a freshly shaven face, a clean white shirt from Banana Republic, and a conservative red "jacquard paisley" Brooks Brothers tie. I look just like any other conservative young college freshman. The beard and the indigenous garb had gone, but one of my first stops on arriving at college was to the study abroad office: I wanted to apply for funding to go south again. I was two years ahead of my college's study abroad application deadline but, to my great excitement, I was just in time to apply for a Rotary International Ambassadorial Scholarship, which, in 2001, sent me to Chile.

Chicago Boys

September 11, 2001, was a big day in Chile because it was the anniversary of General Augusto Pinochet's 1973 coup against the democratically elected, left-leaning government of Salvador Allende. Protests, often violent, occur every year on this day.

There had been rumors that classes might be canceled, but I couldn't be sure. So I decided to get down to the campus of the Universidad de Chile in Santiago, where I was studying for a year, to see what was happening. For 300 pesos (45 cents) the bus carried me along mostly empty, wide, industrial streets. We passed the National Stadium, run-down and ominous; like so much of Santiago, it seemed to hold secrets that it wouldn't easily divulge to an outsider, or perhaps even to the younger generation of Chileans. In front, the gray statue of a naked man was evidently meant to evoke Grecian athleticism but instead reminded me of the thousands of people who had been raped and tortured inside the stadium's walls during the first weeks of Pinochet's dictatorship. In the distance, I could see the majestic snowcapped peaks of the Andes, just visible through the suffocating smog that plagues the Chilean capital. The Spanish colonialists' penchant for building cities in mountain valleys kept enemies out for the first couple of centuries, and exhaust fumes trapped in ever since.

After a fifteen-minute ride I got off the bus a few blocks from my school at the Pedagogical Campus, so called because it focused on teacher training and education. I later learned that Santiago taxi drivers jokingly call the *pedagógico* the *piedragógico*—*piedra* means rock in Spanish—because of the missiles that fly out of the school grounds during frequent protests. The walls of the campus were covered with political art and graffiti. One mural portrayed protesters carrying large photographs, some of their missing loved ones, others of General Pinochet with the world *culpable* (guilty) written across his face. Another, in front of the library, covered an entire wall and showed a scantily clad Mapuche Indian warrior woman spearing the throat of an eagle wrapped in a Stars-and-Stripes flag and with blindfolded, bleeding peasants gripped in its talons. Slogans demanding the release of all political prisoners were spray-painted on every available surface.

The most detailed mural was a scene of police battling masked protesters in the streets. But on that cool September morning, I was soon aware that the scene painted on the wall was also unfolding in real life where I got off the bus. My campus had become a staging ground for a day-long battle between student protesters and the police. By the time I got there around 10 A.M., classes had already been canceled and there was no way to get inside the school gates. Through the perimeter fence I could see young people in masks running around erecting barricades and spraying more graffiti on walls saying things like *Yankee go home!* And *Pinochet Asesino* (Pinochet [is a] murderer). A few were distributing leaflets calling for Pinochet to be stripped of immunity, demanding that he be tried for his crimes of torture, executions, and disappearances even though he had stepped down in favor of democratic elections nearly a decade earlier. In the middle of the main avenue running past the campus was a wide pile of tires and garbage. I watched protesters drench the rubbish in gasoline and send the intersection up in flames. Traffic backed up and black smoke clouded the already filthy sky.

The police, or *Carabineros* as they are formally called in Chile, are one of the branches of the military. They soon showed up in numbers, aiming to restore order and open the avenue. Motorcycle units, armored personnel carriers, and *guanacos* rumbled by. *Guanacos* are the *Carabineros'* water tanks, named after a species related to the llama that is known for its spitting. The *guanacos* shot powerful jets of water onto the pile of burning garbage and then continued toward the university, blasting water over the fence as they went and causing the masked protesters inside to retreat into the heart of the campus.

I took cover behind a lamppost, kitty-corner from the main entrance where the armored personnel carriers were unloading. Fear mixed with excitement as I prepared to watch my first-ever violent face-off between protesters and police. I took my camera out and made sure I had film loaded. Then I pulled the straps of my backpack so tight they hurt—if I had to run I didn't want the bag getting in the way.

As soon as the *guanaco* passed, students came running back to the edge of campus and began hurling rocks and yelling *"Pacos culiados!"* (Fucking pigs!). A handful launched Molotov cocktails, assembled from beer bottles filled with gasoline, over the fence at the *pacos*. The protesters had evidently filled their backpacks with such missiles for the occasion, instead of their normal schoolbooks. Armored riot police dressed in olive green, with body shields and gas cannons, lined up just out of range of the rocks and fired back what seemed like endless rounds of tear gas. The *guanaco* lumbered back to blast more water. This time the students were ready and used scatter techniques to distract the gunner. As I watched from across the street, I saw the powerful water jet knock over a couple of protesters who stayed too long near the fence. Meanwhile, others approached from different angles throwing rocks and homemade bombs. One masked protester, who I thought I recognized from a third period class on the history of guerrilla warfare in Latin America, sprinted toward the fence and hurled a rock into the middle of the armored police. Although it bounced harmlessly off their shields, it showed them they were not out of range and forced them to back up several yards.

Masked protesters chanted *"Fuera de Chile, Colombia, y Argentina, fuera el yanqui de America Latina"* (Out of Chile, Colombia, and Argentina, Yankee get out of Latin America) and *"No queremos y no nos da la gana ser una nueva colonia norteamericana"* (We don't want to be nor feel like being a new North American colony). Of course it felt a bit awkward hearing my classmates—others of whom

I now recognized through their bandannas and face masks—shouting these chants. After all, I was a gringo in Latin America.

The *guanaco* and the protesters took turns on the offensive. When the *guanaco* passed one part of the campus fence, the protesters scattered and regrouped elsewhere to hurl their missiles, thus drawing the *guanaco* to a new area. They raced around, back and forth in a bizarre dance of fire, water, rocks, and gas. Just when it was starting to get repetitive, a Molotov cocktail exploded on the windshield of a police vehicle, right in front of me. I watched another volley of tear gas canisters fly through the air in tight, low arcs leaving a trail of smoke behind them. I heard them land with a thud inside the school gates. A rock whizzed by within a few inches of my head and the students started throwing the still smoking tear gas canisters back out of the campus. As the gas drifted toward me I decided to make a break for it and relocate to safer ground. To get upwind, out of the line of fire, I had to run through dense tear gas. The black fumes burned my eyes and throat.

Finally, I found a patch of grass where I could sit down at a safe distance. I struggled to stop myself rubbing my eyes because I had been told that the chemicals in the gas get on your hands too. I checked my cell phone to see what time it was—almost noon—and noticed that I had several missed calls and a text. The message was from a friend of mine from California studying abroad in Chile. It said simply: "Turn on TV now." Before I had time to try to make sense of this, the phone rang. It was my mom, Bernardine, calling from Chicago. Great, I thought, I can tell her about my first tear gas experience and maybe she can give me some tips from her protest experiences during the civil rights and antiwar movements in the 1960s. But, uncharacteristically for someone usually a model of calm patience, she interrupted me almost as soon as I started talking. "Chesa, honey." I could immediately detect anxiety in her voice, "Haven't you heard about the awful tragedy? Hijacked planes crashed into the World Trade Center and the Pentagon." Immersed as I was in the drama around me, it took a while for the gravity of what had happened so far away to sink in. Then my mom told me she had to go. All of a sudden I felt very alone on the cold streets. Exhaustion washed over me and I wanted to go back to my apartment. The protests and the police were still blocking traffic around the campus and the buses weren't running so I began to walk. I trudged along the wide avenues, reflecting on the events of the morning.

The ferocity of the protesters' confrontation with the police in the face of overwhelming odds was certainly daring. And I could understand the antipathy of the students toward *Carabineros* who had actively supported the previous military dictatorship. But what exactly were the protests and the violence expected to achieve? The protesters couldn't possibly hope to inflict any real damage on well-prepared, heavily armored units. And anyway, what would be accomplished by hurting the police officers, most of whom probably hadn't even been serving when Pinochet's military rule ended? The whole thing had the air of a well-rehearsed theater performance, I told myself, hoping that my preference for nonviolence was strategic and principled, not simply cowardly.

I opened the door to the apartment and found my two roommates, Franco and Alfonzo, already home. I'd only been living with them for five weeks by that point, and was not sure how they would react to that day's events in Santiago or in New York and Washington. I soon found out and the discovery was to profoundly shape my understanding of the gap between perceptions of the world in the North and South of the Americas.

When I first arrived in Chile, through a friend of my uncle's, I had met a local family that lived about two hours south of Santiago in a small city called Rancagua. The matriarch of the household insisted I call her Auntie Helen and adopted me as an honorary member of her family, perhaps to serve as a surrogate for her only son, who was just beginning a study abroad experience in the United States. Though I lived in Santiago, I would frequently visit on weekends and holidays. It was through my relationship with this family that I first began to learn about Chilean culture.

Auntie Helen was proudly middle-class and conventional. The furniture in her house was draped with handmade lace doilies. Crucifixes were on prominent display in different rooms. She wore a spotless apron when preparing my lunches and was unflagging in her efforts to help me find a "good Chilean girlfriend." And yet, for all her cultural conservatism Auntie Helen was in that rarest of Chilean social categories: a never-married middle-aged mom. She told me that her pregnancy had been planned, by her at least, and that the father of her son had been heartbroken when she told him she had no intention of going down the aisle. At age forty-five, after twenty years of work as an engineer for a water filtration plant, she had retired on a pension to spend more time with her son and her abundant nieces and nephews. She came from a big family with siblings spread around the country.

Though she was no fan of Pinochet, I was soon to discover that other members of Auntie Helen's family were. Later that year I traveled down to Chile's austral extremes to hike through national parks filled with glacial lakes and eternal ice fields. Auntie Helen arranged for me to meet her brother Fernando, a retired air force pilot who lived in Patagonia. He generously invited me and my traveling companion to a typical Chilean *asado,* or barbecue. He hosted us at his spacious house, well insulated against Patagonia's powerful winds, and decorated with plush carpets and photos of him in full uniform and stiff military posture. A big screen television took up a prominent place in the living room; its remote controls were covered in plastic on a table next to the easy chair. After several glasses of wine Fernando began talking boisterously about the failings of the Allende government and the effectiveness of Pinochet's economic reforms. He told us that he had been sent up in a fighter jet on the morning of September 11, 1973. "I thought it was a regular training operation," he recounted excitedly. "But then they gave me coordinates to bomb. I had no idea that the numbers on the screen pinpointed La Moneda national palace until I had already fired. I'm a patriot, and I didn't want to bomb the palace, but Allende was going to turn our country over to the Soviets if someone didn't stop him."

It was during my first few weeks in Chile while exploring Rancagua with Auntie Helen's nieces and nephews that I began to pick up the basics of the dense particularities of choppy, slang-riddled Chilean Spanish. The language I bumped into headfirst when I arrived in Chile in July 2001 was a far cry from the slower, more straightforward Guatemalan Spanish that had been my preparation for this first trip to South America. Chilean was so fast and had so many words not used elsewhere in Spanish-speaking countries that I bought and relied on a Chilean-English dictionary called *How to Survive in the Chilean Jungle.* With the book as a support I threw myself into learning by talking with Auntie Helen and her family or, later, my friends on campus. Once I went into a restaurant and tried to order a tortilla with frijoles. The waitress looked confused but eventually came back with an omelet: in Chile there are no Mexican or Guatemalan style tortillas and the word for beans is *porotos.*

Cooking was a favorite pastime for Auntie Helen. I was disappointed to learn that Chile's geography doesn't lend itself to plantain cultivation but there were plenty of other tasty treats to make up for the absence of my favorite Latin American food. Auntie Helen introduced me to Chilean *empanadas de pino*—soft baked dough on the outside filled with two parts onion, one part ground beef, and chunks of hard-boiled egg and the odd raisin or olive thrown in for flavor—which quickly become a staple of my diet. She also prepared a delicious *pastel de choclo,* a sort of corn-based chicken pot pie. And within a few weeks of my arrival, Auntie Helen must have fed me more *palta*—Chilean for avocado—than I had eaten in my previous twenty-one years.

I traveled out of Santiago almost every weekend, either to Auntie Helen's house, a few more hours south to the small coastal town where she had grown up and where her mother, my *"abuela"* lived, or farther afield to explore Chile's natural beauty solo. If I had a few extra days I would jump on a bus for a twenty-four-hour ride north to Antofagasta in the Atacama Desert, or ten hours south to Temuco in the lakes district. It was on a Chilean TurBus *Semi-Cama* that I first experienced the joys of a full-size padded leg rest. I found bus travel so comfortable that, whenever possible, I planned weekend trips that would allow for an overnight ride on both ends: it saved me time and money, and often the TurBuses were cleaner and more comfortable than cheap hotels.

It was only a matter of weeks before I learned to appreciate the country's travel infrastructure and public transportation system. At 2,700 miles long—farther even than New York City to San Diego—and just 150 miles across at its widest, Chile requires only one central highway, the Pan-American. This main artery is maintained in excellent condition, from the vast stretches of the Atacama Desert in the north, down to the windswept Patagonian plains in the south. In a few areas, where sheer Andean peaks meet the Pacific Ocean, the highway detours across the Andes into neighboring Argentina. Without fail the buses in Chile compared favorably in service, comfort, and cleanliness with the Greyhounds I rode throughout New England during my first two years of college. And what a contrast the Chilean buses were with the Central American chicken buses where I had spent so many bumpy hours.

When I was in Guatemala, it surprised me that there were not more car crashes given the state of the buses and roads in the region, and the cavalier attitude of many of the drivers. Generally I tried to sit in the back of the bus whenever possible so that I wouldn't have to watch in terror as we passed another vehicle while taking a blind turn at full speed, or while the driver chatted to a female passenger and whipped the bus around like a bumper car. But that was all a different Latin America from Chile, where transportation infrastructure and government regulation were both thoroughly developed.

The bus service inside Santiago was, like the city's metro system, first-rate. As an enthusiast of this means of transport, I spent many hours learning the capricious routes of its frequent yellow and black vehicles. Later that year I even wrote a paper for a class on the history of Santiago arguing that the public buses were the glue that held together what otherwise would have been dozens of different cities. In my research I discovered that Santiago residents spend an average of four years of their lives riding the city's fourteen thousand public buses called *micros*—the city's public transportation system has since been overhauled. In the mornings, the *micros* carry workers from poor *poblaciones* to work in the wealthier neighborhoods' malls and commercial districts. It was in one of these wealthy districts that I lived during my first month in Santiago.

A Rotary International scholarship had initially set me up with a home-stay in an elite neighborhood called Las Condes, tucked up against the foothills of the Andes. My host, señora Maribel, lived on Los Militares street, lined with elegant middle-class homes. Most mornings, while the Mapuche Indian maid Rayen served us breakfast, Maribel lectured me about how silly the communists and rabble-rousers were to have gotten in the way of what she regarded as Pinochet's solid economic plans. One day, shortly after I arrived, over a breakfast of cornflakes and fresh fruit, she began a tirade about all the crime in Santiago (actually it is one of the safest capital cities in Latin America). She told me how there were lots of bank robberies and she just couldn't understand "what kind of people would do that sort of thing." It occurred to me that I could have told her about my parents but that might have spoiled her breakfast.

Maribel regularly insulted Rayen, who had been with her for some twenty years, even when she was within earshot. The Mapuche have a proud but tragic history as one of the few indigenous peoples never fully conquered or integrated into the Spanish colony. Their fight for survival against the pressures of the modern Chilean state continues to this day. But Maribel's maid was of a different strain. She seemed to have been all too well trained for her position—she rarely showed irritation or complained and appeared genuinely to look up to Maribel. She wasn't the last Latin American house servant I came across who had learned to please the *jefe* by wearing her lack of education and subservience like a scar on her forehead.

Maribel's house was within walking distance of two massive shopping malls offering the latest models of Apple computers, Nokia mobile communications, and Zara brand European fashion. The neighborhood was peopled with men wearing polo shirts tucked tight into well-pressed chinos while the women wore dark Chanel glasses and high heels. More than a few of those I passed on the street had eyes that were bluer than even a gringo like me. Las Condes was nothing like the Chile I had envisioned while listening to my parents talk about the country's tumultuous political history. Its bustling consumer culture was more closely modeled on the one I had left behind in the United States. The people I met in Las Condes seemed to lead a life that revolved around consumption of foreign brands and styles. Their focus on the United States, Europe, and international trends suggested that some of them wanted to be something other than Chilean. Were they ashamed of their culture? I wondered. Did they see their freedom and future in another way of life?

Santiago's elite had more stories of vacations in Miami than in their own spectacular Patagonia or Andean mountain valleys. Victor Jara, one of Chile's most popular folk musicians, had once sung "The rich were always foreigners, let them go to Miami with their aunts . . . I will stay to sing with the workers." In 1973, he was tortured and killed in the National Stadium by Pinochet's soldiers. Legend has it that they broke all of his fingers and then gave him a guitar and ordered him to play. He scratched out a tune and they gunned him down as he sang his last socialist hymn.

When Maribel found out I was staying in Chile for a full year, her eyes opened wide and she eagerly offered to let me stay on with her the whole time for *un buen descuento,* a good discount. I realized, despite her neighborhood and class identity, Maribel was far from rich. The income a boarder like me could provide her was much needed to support her pension. But I hadn't gone to Chile to live with an overbearing host mother or to resettle in an upper-class Americanized neighborhood. I decided I had to move.

I asked a friend who was tutoring me in Spanish to help me write out a poster announcing my search for an apartment. The teacher made me do the initial draft in Spanish and I wrote: "*Apartamento querido: Americano estudiante mirando una habitación cerca de campus Macul.*" When I saw my teacher holding back a laugh I knew I had messed up. She explained that I had written "Dear apartment:

American student watching a room near Macul campus" and helped me correct it. I added my cell phone number and set off to put up copies around the campus where I would shortly be studying. I got a few phone calls and looked at as many apartments. I decided to pick the cheapest of the lot, despite my generous monthly stipend from Rotary International.

I could have easily afforded a luxurious apartment in the wealthy districts but I didn't want to hide behind security guards, electric gates, or class barriers in my interactions with people in the countries I explored. Too many gringos, I thought to myself, come down to Latin America and spend their dollars in rich neighborhoods, on foreign or local elite-owned businesses, and in so doing isolate themselves from the ugly reality of poverty and inequality, and a neocolonial legacy. Bringing my spending power to rich neighborhoods probably wouldn't do much for the people that most needed it, while spending my money in poor communities would direct resources against their normal flow. I decided that rather than spending lots of money on things like rent or shopping—which would generally benefit the local economic elite—I would indulge my thrifty side and try to live among the working people. My standard of living would suffer but my daily expenses would filter into a poor neighborhood. Plus, I reasoned, the money I saved on rent would allow for more travel throughout Chile—a luxury it took me a while to realize was totally unavailable to my neighbors. I wasn't sure quite what my lifestyle choices would mean in practice but I intended to find out.

And so, a few weeks before classes started, I moved down from the hills into the smog and clutter of central Santiago. Going "up" or "down" in Santiago refers not to north or south, but rather to altitude, and thus air quality, and social class. If someone announces that they are going to *subir* it means going up toward the mountains, and simultaneously up to the higher-class sectors of the city above the smog. For me, moving down was a simple affair: early one Saturday morning I lugged my hiking backpack and a small duffel bag from Maribel's house to the bus stop. She had steeled herself for my departure ever since she overheard me on the phone planning to visit another apartment so our good-bye was as painless as it was brief. Yellow and black *micros* passed at all hours: in the morning they were full on the ride up as they carried people from the poorer parts of the city to their jobs. In the afternoons they ran full on the way down, as people returned home.

I moved in the morning to be sure to have plenty of room for my luggage on the bus. As the 641 carried me down from Las Condes, street vendors climbed aboard offering soliloquies on the merits of the magic pen, the reversible bill fold, or my favorite Super 8 chocolate-covered wafers. With my overstuffed bags, bushy beard, and Patagonia brand fleece vest I was self-conscious of standing out as a foreigner. One of my Chilean friends later told me she could always spot gringos even before they opened their mouths to butcher her language, because they dressed for daily life in the city as though they were on an Andean safari. But the feeling of being out of place soon dissipated as the lurch, bounce, and grumble of the bus made me feel comfortable. I watched the city passing by outside the window.

The bus roared down the colorful, commercial avenues of Las Condes and Providencia neighborhoods, or *comunas* as they are called in Santiago. Like most of Santiago's wealthier *comunas*, the streets I saw that day were clean and well paved. The commercial districts boasted massive malls and shopping complexes with bright signs and advertisements on billboards. Even once we turned off the main avenue near the Los Leones metro stop there were expensive furniture shops, restaurants catering to businesspeople on lunch break, and new cars parked on the streets in the shade of large trees.

Next, the bus passed through a quiet residential district on the border between Providencia and Nuñoa, the sprawling *comuna* I was moving to. Nuñoa is one of those neighborhoods that bridge the gap between rich and poor. On its northeast side, where my bus first entered, there were upscale supermarkets, corner stores, Catholic day schools, petite green parks, and five-story apartment buildings with doormen, two-bedroom units, and shared swimming pools. But my new house was on the other side of Nuñoa, to the southwest, where the city sank well below the smog cover. My destination was farther down Avenida Grecia, with its gray industrial zones, constant bus and truck traffic, and cramped cement apartment complexes. I was moving into the Villa Olímpica projects surrounding the National Stadium. A thirty-five-minute journey, the bus transported me into an entirely different world.

My new home, on a street named after Plato, was on the working-class side of a mixed neighborhood. The building I lived in was part of an ugly four-story concrete box—*bloque* in Spanish—housing project that encompassed hundreds of similar apartments in every direction. Our unit was sparsely decorated with furniture that looked like it had come from a dump. It turned out it had. There were as many broken windows as there were locks on the door. Until my housemates saw my sign on campus, the room I would call home for that semester and beyond had been used for storage; it was the size of a large walk-in closet. But $50 per month for rent was low enough for me to feel like I was living in solidarity with the working class. Later, I realized that, decrepit as it was, this was still, by Chilean standards, middle-class housing. The really poor Chileans lived either in the countryside or on the outskirts of the city, as is the case all over Latin America.

My housemates were both film students and had an appropriately bohemian demeanor. Alfonzo was from the southern university town of Concepción. I soon learned that his whole family identified themselves as socialist. He was married but never wore his wedding ring and his wife and daughter lived in Concepción with his mother. His wife came to visit sometimes but they seemed to spend most of their time yelling and her visits always ended prematurely. In another country they might have gotten separated more formally, but at the time Chile had no provisions for legal divorce.

A native of Santiago, Franco's long greasy hair and thick beard that reached to his stomach perfectly matched his tattered secondhand clothes. It later emerged that he, in fact, came from a conservative upper-middle-class family, but that he had cut off contact with them. Before studying film he embarked on a short but lucrative career as a model for Movistar cell phone service and Almacen Paris department store, among other big Chilean companies. Apparently under all that hair was a handsome, chiseled face.

During the many months I lived with Alfonzo and Franco, neither made any attempt to clean their rooms, much less the bathroom, the living room, or the kitchen. Cooking on our camping stove was hindered by the fact that there was only one bare bulb in the kitchen and another empty socket. When I decided to buy a new bulb so I could see the food I was stirring, my roommates protested, complaining that it would cause the electric bill to go up. When I asked why we each had to buy our own toilet paper and take up precious counter space in the bathroom with three separate rolls, Franco explained that Alfonzo used too much toilet paper blowing his perpetually runny nose. Eventually I learned that it was Alfonzo's mom who was the absentee landlord who refused to fix the broken windows or put a head on the shower spigot. But no matter. During my first several weeks in the apartment I was happy to be in Nuñoa, away from the ritzy shopping centers of Las Condes, immersing myself instead in the day-to-day lives of ordinary Chileans.

When I walked in the door to the apartment on September 11, 2001, I learned that my roommates too had spent the day at protests. Franco had been in front of La Moneda, the national palace, outside of which stood a massive statue of Allende, stepping forward boldly with his left foot. Alfonzo had been at a protest in the national cemetery where the ex-president was buried. They had been tear-gassed as well, and were with crowds that broke a few shop windows at the downtown McDonald's. But it was nothing new or remarkable for them. Now they were glued to the television watching the news from the United States, interspersed with local reports on the protests in Santiago and around the country.

The short phone call with my mom had not been sufficient to drive home the true significance of the day's attacks in New York, my city of birth. Initially, the images of the fire and smoke in lower Manhattan five thousand miles away, even the fact of the large-scale civilian deaths, seemed as distant as the conflagration of the protests in Santiago was immediate. But then I began to get dozens of calls and text messages from Chilean friends expressing their concern for my family back home. Was anyone I knew hurt? Did I need anything? How did I feel?

The truth is I didn't know how I was supposed to feel: sad from arbitrary death, scared of random violence, angry at the perpetrators, patriotic behind the flag, hopeful for improvements in United States foreign policy? I registered each of these things to some degree. The images of people jumping from the World Trade Center upper floors, holding hands, were devastating. I realized that people in New York, including my friends and family, were frantic—without electricity or cell phone service, panicked about loved ones, uncertain of the next hour. In tumultuous times experience has taught me to take emotional cues, to share my feelings—whether joy and happiness or tragedy and heartbreak—with those around me, whom I love. But on that evening, in my drab apartment, I found myself in an emotional vacuum.

Ricardo Lagos, the president of Chile, appeared on the TV at a press conference. Nominally a socialist, Lagos had made little effort to hold the former General Augusto Pinochet accountable for his years as dictator and was actively pursuing free trade deals with the United States, the European Union, China, and anywhere else he could.* That night on television he sent condolences to the families directly affected by the attacks and expressed solidarity with the people of New York and Washington. He called September 11 "a sad day for humanity."

To my surprise, my roommates soon made it clear that they had a quite different perspective. Over dinner, after checking to make sure no one in my family was hurt, Alfonzo speculated that "perhaps the

---

*A couple of years later, when Chile had a temporary seat on the United Nations Security Council, Lagos courageously stood up to pressure from the administration of George W. Bush and refused to support a resolution authorizing war in Iraq despite the fact that the U.S.-Chile Free Trade Agreement was up for a vote in the U.S. Congress.

attack would be a wake-up call to the U.S. government not to meddle in other countries' business." He thought that the United States had the attacks coming to it after all its interventions in Latin America and around the globe. My other roommate, Franco, was even less restrained. He actually celebrated the attack and praised Osama bin Laden for giving Americans "a taste of their own medicine." He hoped that perhaps the attack would spark the downfall of U.S. imperialism. In describing what had happened to the Twin Towers, he employed an old Chilean saying, *"Cada cosa cae por su propio peso"* (Everything falls under its own weight). It took me a while to understand the meaning of the pun and when I did I found myself shocked at the apparent callousness with which he was treating such an enormous loss of life. After all, though we didn't know the precise figures yet, almost exactly the same number had been killed in the United States that day as are believed to have been killed under the entire length of Pinochet's seventeen-year reign.

That night, as I lay in bed, feeling sad and alone, images of the burning towers played on repeat in my mind. As much as I cherished growing up in multiple worlds, living abroad, I realized that trying to come to terms with what had happened to my country from Chile was going to present real challenges. It would be especially difficult given the perspectives my roommates espoused.

The next day, on the morning of September 12, when I walked in the open gates to my university, janitors were patiently cleaning up piles of burned refuse and scrubbing ineffectually at the prior day's graffiti. The campus, typically dirty and run-down, looked particularly bedraggled. The signs of yesterday's battle were everywhere; I even noticed a number of tear gas canisters lying in the grass alongside the library. As I climbed up the wide, winding staircase to my twentieth-century Latin American history classroom, I saw that the wall had been plastered with posters. Next to one of the dozen murals of Che Guevara that littered the campus, a picture of desperately malnourished African children had writing beneath it that said:

ALSO ON SEPTEMBER 11, 2001, 35,615 CHILDREN DIED OF HUNGER

Victims:	35,615
Place:	poor countries of the world
Special editions on TV:	zero
Articles in the paper:	zero
Messages from the President:	zero
Convocations of crisis groups:	zero
Protests in solidarity:	zero
Minutes of silence:	zero
Commemorations of the victims:	zero
Social forums organized:	zero
Messages from the Pope:	zero
The markets:	not bad
The euro:	strengthening
Level of alert:	zero
Mobilization of the army:	none
Hypothesis about the identity of the criminals:	none
Probable perpetrators of the crime:	rich countries

There were dozens of these posters. Someone, probably from a different faction of campus radicals than those who made the original, had systematically blacked out "rich countries" and written "neoliberalism." Someone else had then come along and added "transnational capitalism."

I looked around to make sure no one was watching and pulled one of the posters down and stuffed it into my bag. I figured it would speak volumes to my friends back in the United States about how Chilean students on my campus regarded the events of September 11. I continued up to the second floor, wondering if my class would espouse the same radical views as my housemates had the night before.

On entering room 209, I was surprised to find most of the twenty chairs occupied—generally less than half the students turned up to my classes, a pattern that was apparently repeated across the university. I took an empty seat behind one of my classmates named Miguel, whom

I had known since the beginning of the semester in Santiago. When I showed up the first day he asked me where I was from. *"Soy americano"* (I'm American), I responded cheerily, to which he replied, *"Yo también"* (Me too). It took me a minute to understand that anyone from the Americas—North, Central, or South—might be *americano*. In Spanish there is a more precise word to describe the nationality of people from the United States—*estadounidense,* from the Estados Unidos, the same way someone from Chile is a *chileno*. Once I understood my faux pas, we had a laugh about it and had been on good terms ever since.

From my seat I noticed a backpack in the aisle next to Miguel. It was covered in political patches sewn on by hand. It occurred to me that one of the masked protesters I'd seen throwing rocks yesterday had carried the same bag, or at least one very like it. Before I could dwell on this further, our lecturer for the day, Professor Luis Vitale, walked in.

"Bienvenidos estudiantes," he said, welcoming us to another Latin American history class. A frail, elderly man, he walked slowly to a metal armchair supported on one arm by a young woman student and leaning with his free hand on a cane. He sat down gingerly and prepared to commence his lecture but was halted by an interruption from the back of the classroom. One of the students blurted out a question as to whether, in light of yesterday's attacks, United States global hegemony was about to collapse. "We are in history class, where we study the past," Vitale answered slowly, looking pensive as he often did. "Historians are not known for their prescience. Yesterday is the past, let's start there and work our way backward." As he talked I stared at his face. His skin was pale and hung slackly from his jaw, testament to his nearly eighty years. He sported a thin mustache and his hair was slicked straight back with gel.

When I first saw him at the beginning of the year, Professor Vitale's advanced age had led me to wonder if he was not perhaps a spent force who might be better off in retirement. But I was soon to realize that he was still a heavyweight on campus with extraordinary reserves of energy and enthusiasm. He had taught at more than eight universities in six countries and had published nearly seventy books; when any of them appeared on our syllabus, he encouraged us to get photocopies rather than pay full price for originals. His writing used a Marxist framework to analyze Latin American history through topics like indigenous rights, gender equality, labor struggles, social movements, colonialism, and imperialism.

"We are honored with the presence of an *estadounidense* in our class this semester," he continued, calling everyone's attention to me and making my cheeks flush red. "Chesa, was anyone in your family, any of your friends, lost in yesterday's attacks?" The combination of my roommates' comments the night before, the signs around campus, and my being so far from home had left me feeling defensive and too eager to please. Instead of thanking him for asking and telling the class I was lucky, that I didn't personally know anyone who was killed or even injured, I stammered, "No, I don't really know the people that work in the Pentagon or the Twin Towers." It was true at the time, but two years later, after I graduated from college, my friends and classmates flocked to Wall Street and government jobs inside the Beltway. My answer immediately felt juvenile and cowardly.

"*Bien,*" Vitale said, without making it clear if he was referring just to the "no" at the beginning of my answer, or the declaration that followed it as well. "It's tragic whenever innocent people lose their lives, as far too many did yesterday in the United States. We still don't know much about those who organized the attacks, or what their goals were. We are told that they hated the United States, or at least its economic, political, and military establishment." Vitale asked the class to think about what might have caused the terrorists to direct their anger at the United States, to try to understand their motivation even if we couldn't begin to understand their means. Then, as was customary in class, he lit a cigarette and took a deep pull.

"As historians of the Americas we must remember," he continued, "that political violence and terrorism is hardly unprecedented. Terror has been unleashed throughout Latin American history as a result of dictatorial regimes that all too often had the support of colonial or neocolonial powers, including the United States government." Vitale explained that in certain cases policies supporting dictatorships led to blowback, as exemplified by an earlier terrorist attack in Washington, D.C., in September 1976. That year Pinochet's secret police used a car bomb to assassinate Orlando Letelier, a former Chilean ambassador to the United States and a minister in Allende's cabinet. Also killed in the blast was Letelier's aide, Ronni Moffitt, a United States citizen. "The case of Chile is instructive, not the least because of the date September 11."

The students sitting around me in class, even those who hadn't participated in the protests the day before, didn't need to be reminded of the details of their country's September 11, of how or why Salvador Allende's government was toppled in a military rebellion. They knew all too well that in the seventeen years that followed the 1973 coup, Pinochet enforced his power with summary executions, thousands of disappearances, and torture, that his government drove nearly 10 percent of the country into exile. Many of them had parents or other family members among the more than 100,000 detained, killed, or exiled. The government had set up impromptu concentration camps and torture chambers all over the country, including one in the National Stadium where an estimated forty thousand people were held.

"Twenty-eight years ago today," Professor Vitale went on, *"fui desaparecido."* The words, literally translated, meant "I was disappeared." Thanks to decades of Latin American political violence in which there have been countless *desaparecidos,* Spanish language and culture have a word for which there exists no equivalent in English. "Disappeared" used in this way exists only as a linguistic import from Latin America's political tragedies.

"In the year that followed the coup," Vitale enunciated each word slowly, "I was held in nine different concentration camps, including the Estadio Nacional." There was no ashtray for the professor and my eyes fixed on the lengthening ash that balanced precariously at the tip of his cigarette as his words cast a pall around the room. He described the pain of having electric shocks administered to his testicles, the madness water torture inspires, the trauma of sleep deprivation and dog attacks. He talked of the suffering of women prisoners who had cigarettes extinguished on their bodies before being gang-raped. He told us that for many of the prisoners, the most agonizing torture came from just sitting in their cells listening to the screams of others. Pinochet's torture masters had been surprisingly versatile and creative in the ways they imposed their power on hapless detainees. For example, one of the worst techniques he had witnessed was when women were strapped down topless in a cold room, and soldiers stood over them repeatedly flicking their nipples with their index fingers for hours on end. Then there was the "submarine" where prisoners were forcibly submerged in tubs of urine and feces for several minutes at a time, over and over until they passed out.

As Vitale conveyed the macabre scenes, time seemed to stand still, even as the minute hand of the clock on the wall behind him turned nearly full circle. His voice was calm and flat but I couldn't help but notice that his eyes were wet. His hand trembled slightly and the accumulated ash on his third, or was it his fourth? cigarette fell to the floor.

Despite what he suffered, Vitale said, he was lucky. He endured extreme physical abuse and psychological trauma, but eventually he escaped. "More than a year after my arrest, on November 28, 1974, thanks to national and international pressure for my release, a huge outpouring of solidarity from many countries, I managed to escape to exile in Europe, Cuba, and Venezuela. My comrades in the concentration camps who were less well known, who didn't have an international contingent supporting them, had little chance of escape." In Pinochet's systematic efforts to destroy the Chilean left, Vitale told us, the military disposed of many disappeared progressives by taking them out over the Pacific Ocean in helicopters and throwing them to their deaths. Others were hog-tied and dropped into craters of active volcanoes.

As I sat there in his class, I recognized that this old frail man was not exaggerating. When Chile's first elected government since Allende took power in 1990, it set up a National Commission on Truth and Reconciliation to investigate the deaths during the Pinochet years.

The final report blamed Pinochet for a total of 3,197 deaths and tens of thousands of documented cases of torture. Many Chilean military officials implicated in the coup, torture, and human rights abuses were trained at the United States School of the Americas at Fort Benning, Georgia. Even though I wasn't born at the time of the atrocities, I felt connected to them, and somehow implicated. My guilt by association with the government of my country seemed all the more intense because of the way Vitale narrated the history, making explicit the connection between the United States government and Pinochet. Was the eagle on the crest of my navy blue passport the same one crushing peasants in its talons as the Mapuche warrior woman counterattacked in the mural outside the campus library? I got the feeling that Vitale's lecture was directed solely at me—surely he expected the Chilean students to already know what he was telling us.

He explained that "with the democratically elected government overthrown and the entire left being killed or exiled, Pinochet quickly rewrote the constitution and dismantled the socialist economic policies of his predecessor. There was no more free milk in schools, or subsidies for bread. He privatized nationalized industries like banking and copper." The sweeping economic reforms Pinochet's government implemented made Chile into the testing ground for what became known as neoliberal economic policies, which became the norm throughout the region during the following two decades. Having returned to politics and policies again, Vitale regained his composure and dried his eyes. He reminded the class that "Chile's new economic model was developed with high-level advising from a team of economists, known as the Chicago Boys" because they had studied at the University of Chicago under Milton Friedman. In 1982, reflecting on his experience of watching theory become policy in Chile and beyond, Friedman wrote, "Only a crisis—actual or perceived—produces real change. When that crisis occurs, the actions that are taken depend on the ideas that are lying around. That, I believe, is our basic function: to develop alternatives to existing policies, to keep them alive and available until the politically impossible becomes politically inevitable." Thanks to the Chilean Chicago Boys whom he trained in the years prior to the 1973 coup, Friedman fulfilled his self-described basic function and provided policies in anticipation of the crisis: a few months before the coup the Chicago Boys drafted a confidential economic plan known as *El Ladrillo,* the brick, because of its thickness. *El Ladrillo* was on the desks of the leaders of Pinochet's military junta on September 12, 1973, the same day Vitale was disappeared. The new policies focused on free trade, deregulation, privatization, cutbacks in social spending, and the liberalization of capital flows. Milton Friedman himself dubbed it "the miracle of Chile," a phrase that supporters of these policies have popularized.

"We even have a Chicago boy among us today, don't we, Chesa?" Vitale said, jokingly. Vitale knew that I'd grown up in Chicago and meant no harm with his comment, but he didn't know that I'd studied at the University of Chicago private school from first through twelfth grade. As I sat there in Professor Vitale's class, I reflected on my life and realized I was more of a Chicago Boy than I wanted to admit, certainly than I wanted the people sitting around me that day to know.

Pinochet's coup and the downfall of Chile's democratic socialist experiment had represented a victory for United States imperialism and corporate profits—presumably the United States economy had benefited, as had, at least indirectly, gringos like me. It was hard not to feel a sense of shame for the role the United States government and the CIA had played in supporting the Pinochet dictatorship during most of its seventeen years. But I took solace from the fact that my family, unlike most other study abroad students I knew in Chile, had taken action in support of Chilean democracy, against the coup and their own government's disgraceful role in it.

My mother Kathy's father, Leonard, was a founding partner of a law firm that defended the Allende administration after it nationalized United States–owned copper mines. The litigation was pending when Pinochet's coup toppled the democratic government. My grandfather's firm acquired Chile as a client largely on the strength of its long-standing relationship with the Cuban government. Over

a mojito in a hotel lobby in Old Havana, long after my grandfather's
death, I learned about his work in Cuba from Luis Martínez, the former head of the Cuban national airline, Cubana de Aviación, and a
high-ranking official in the Ministry of Transportation. We sat sipping the sweet minty drinks that reportedly had Hemingway hooked
from his first taste. Our small wooden table had a sign on it with a
cigar circled and crossed out in red: no smoking. The table next to
ours, however, was apparently in the smoking section and dense cigar
smoke hung over our conversation. Luis had gray hair but was fit and
energetic. He had great respect for my grandfather, he told me. Back
when he was running the airline, my grandfather had saved one of
their planes. It had flown into New York to bring Cuban diplomats
to a United Nations meeting, but the United States and Cuba were in
the midst of diplomatic and legal feuds. The authorities in New York
decided not to allow the plane, one of the precious few in Cuba's
commercial fleet at the time, to return to Havana. The Cubans hired
my grandfather for the case and he managed to obtain a midnight
order allowing the plane's departure. With the authorization in hand
he raced to the airport and the plane was able to take off that night,
before a new block could be placed against it.

My interest in the stories about my grandfather's work in Cuba
must have been evident because Luis didn't stop talking. "For example," he went on in nearly perfect, unaccented English, "there was
the case of a cargo boat loaded with sugar. The vessel left a Cuban
seaport for North American harbors before the Revolution had
claimed victory but it arrived at its destination after Batista fled the
island. The *estadounidenses* who received the boat determined not to
pay for the sugar or allow the ship to return to Cuba. Your grandfather litigated the case for us." He explained that when Cuba began
nationalizing large landholdings and factories, many of which had
United States citizens for owners, there was an immense amount of
legal work to sort out the mess. Grandpa Leonard's firm handled
much of it.

Eventually the cigar smoke hanging over our "no smoking" section of the room became too much for me to bear and I rose to leave.

Luis gave me a parting gift that he had received from my grandfather forty years earlier: a slightly worn first edition copy of a book called *The Theoretical System of Karl Marx,* by Louis Boudin, my great-great-uncle.

Louis and Leonard had been lawyers, fighting their battles in defense of civil liberties, labor organizers, and Third World governments in the courtroom, but my four parents took to the streets when the Allende government fell. In the aftermath of the coup there were protests in solidarity with Chilean democracy in countries around the world, including the United States. Some of the protests involved more than marches and chants. Bombs exploded in International Telephone and Telegraph's offices in Italy and Switzerland—the United States–owned company had extensive holdings in Chile and provided financial support to coup plotters. The Weather Underground also protested targeting ITT's Latin America division corporate office. In their press release explaining why they had chosen this target, the group wrote, "Without the machinations of ITT and U.S. government [the coup in Chile] would not have happened. In spite of their insolent denials they stand indicted by their own words and deeds. The blood of thousands of people is on their hands." The declaration went on to detail evidence of United States government and corporate intervention, including an indictment of corporate greed in Chile: "ITT and the two other major investors in Chile, Anaconda and Kennecott copper companies, robbed the people of their subsistence. Chile is a country with a great wealth of natural resources but her people are very poor. Her wealth has been extracted by these giant multinational corporations in the form of exorbitant profits. ITT has assets there amounting to more than $200 million. Over the last forty years Anaconda and Kennecott have taken more than $4 billion in profits from Chilean copper."

On the first-year anniversary of the coup, on September 11, 1974, while Vitale was still being tortured in concentration camps, the Weather Underground again struck, sabotaging one of Anaconda Copper's offices in Oakland. In September 1975, just months after Milton Friedman met personally with Pinochet, the group took responsibility for a small nighttime explosion at Kennecott Copper's offices in Salt Lake City. Consistent with the group's strict policy of not targeting human life, none of these protests killed or injured anyone, though of course with this type of action the risk of something going tragically wrong is always present.

The violence of September 11, both in New York and in Santiago, prompted me to reflect on my family history more closely than I ever had before. Certainly violence is illegitimate when it targets civilians or intends to cause generalized or widespread fear, but my parents never did either of those. I recognized that there are cases for where armed struggle is a legitimate tool for social and political change in the face of much greater, more highly organized force. For example, when the Founding Fathers rose in arms against English monarchical oppression they were not the terrorists they were accused of being at the time and would, perhaps, be remembered as if the Revolutionary War had been a failure. My classmates in Chile would have regarded the Weather Underground's use of nonlethal force against property as more than justified during the months and years their parents and families were being tortured or killed under the Pinochet regime. But there is a key difference between understanding and supporting. While they all opposed Pinochet, they represented a range of political perspectives and ideologies, many of them nonviolent, just as the myriad groups protesting the United States' role in supporting Pinochet had employed diverse tactics during the 1970s.

Though I could only consider the issue abstractly, removed by three decades from the circumstances that surrounded the decisions my parents made, I couldn't imagine myself taking similar risks.

But if I had differences with my parents concerning use of tactics, it was clear they were correct in understanding the crucial role of the United States in backing Pinochet. The full extent of this support wouldn't be made public until 2000, a year before I traveled to Chile for the first time. In that year the CIA released a report titled "CIA Activities in Chile." Many of the most damning documents had been censored or withheld, but enough information was revealed to prove that the United States government supported the coup.

∽∽∽

"Sí, soy de Chicago," I answered Vitale's question, yes, I'm from Chicago. "But I'm not a Chicago Boy and in my family we fight against imperialism." Someone on the other side of the room chortled back, "You sure don't fight imperialism too effectively," giving rise to a few chuckles from the students before Vitale called the class to order. *"Está bien Chesa,"* Vitale answered me. That's good, Chesa. "You see class," he went on, now with a small pile of cigarette stubs on the floor in front of him, "the United States may be an imperial government but it has produced historic freedom fighters and anti-imperialists from the Haymarket martyrs to Malcolm X and beyond. Your protests, like the one yesterday or the ones every Fourth of July when you burn the United States flag, may be for a just cause. But don't let hubris or nationalist bravado lead you astray: allies inside *el imperio* have an essential role to play in any process of global change and should not be scorned." I realized at this point that his lecture had not primarily been directed at me, as I'd previously thought in a rather self-centered way. He was talking to Miguel, sitting next to me, and the rest of the students too. "If history teaches us anything about the Bush family and the right wing in the United States, yesterday's tragedy will be used as a cruel excuse for war and military exertion of hegemony. *Estadounidenses* have a crucial role to play in resistance movements in the years to come. Thank you, class dismissed."

The other students filed out of class talking with noisy excitement about the lecture. I lingered behind, hoping for a word with Vitale in private. I wanted to thank him for sharing his traumatic personal experience, for being generous with me in what could have easily been a hostile atmosphere. But before I could say a word, Vitale took my hand and said, *"Gracias, hermano,* it was *muy importante* for these students to have you here for today's lecture. I hope you didn't mind me calling attention to you to make a point about internationalism and the dual tragedy that our peoples share on September 11." I was stunned into silence: Was he really thanking me, calling me brother? His lack of bitterness and vision were inspiring examples, all the more so in light of what he had suffered at the hands of torturers using techniques learned in my country.

As I walked into the mostly deserted hallway, I noticed Miguel standing by himself near the stairs. When he saw me he blurted out *"Oye gringo."* Listen up gringo, "I've been waiting for you. *Los compañeros* are gonna smoke a joint and drink some beer on the soccer field and then grab lunch. Why don't you come with us?" I had been hoping to break into a social group on campus all semester but I wasn't sure what Miguel and his *compañeros* had in mind for me. He must have sensed my reservations because before I could answer he added, "Don't worry, it's true, we hate your government. But you probably do too. We know how to distinguish between the government and the people. We're gonna call you the anti-gringo. *Vamos anti-gringo!"*

By the time my first semester ended I had made a wide range of friends. Some, like Miguel, I would stay in touch with for years to come. But in December school let out for a three-month summer vacation—in the Southern Hemisphere the seasons are reversed—and I hit the road to explore South America beyond Chile's borders.

Crisis of Currencies

y first journey to Buenos Aires required a series of unglamorous and interminable bus rides. Over the previous three weeks of my summer vacation from school in Chile, I had spent more than 150 hours on buses: festive Brazilian sleepers, dusty Paraguayan vehicles converted from school use, sleek Uruguayan people carriers with Mercedes engines and full meal service on board.

My friends thought I was crazy to spend so much of my time on buses. But for me they had come to represent freedom of movement, new horizons, adventure, the ability to pick up and go, to disconnect when life got complicated or just boring. Part of the point of travel was to appreciate the passage of time—quite the opposite of time spent, for example, in prison where passing time quickly is an imperative, every minute on the road counts and should be dragged out, savored. I could have flown to Buenos Aires in a few hours rather than spending days on the road and breaking the journey at half a dozen cities and towns along the way as I had done. But without those long bus rides how was I to appreciate the distances, the changing geography between the Amazon and the coast, the mountains and the plains? Airplane travel predisposes us to superficial, compartmentalized knowledge of a country, while land travel forces us, often uncomfortably, into contact with more everyday realities.

Latin American buses could never be described as boring. In Guatemala and other parts of Central America, when buses broke down, ran out of gas, or took the passengers on arbitrary detours, it was rarely regarded as a big deal. I've seen bus drivers call in at a store to buy a beer before getting on the road. Once, in Honduras, the driver stopped an hour into a three-hour itinerary so he could visit at his girlfriend's house for forty-five minutes, leaving those of us on board to sweat in the afternoon heat. Throughout Central America, it was common practice for buses to wait in the terminal until all the seats were occupied, collect the fare from everyone on board, and only then drive to the gas station to fill up before the journey. In El Salvador, I was on a bus so packed with people that the driver asked us to duck as we drove past the police station in order to avoid getting pulled over (it didn't work—there were too many people standing in the aisle and we were stopped). And once, on a winding road in the Guatemalan highlands, the bus I was on crashed into another driving in the opposite direction. Luckily no one was hurt, and we kept going as though nothing had happened.

Though I had seen some crazy things in my bus adventures in Central America, my trips across South America added greatly to the list. If memory serves, it was in Bolivia that a pair of drivers on an overnight ride took turns alternating behind the wheel and sleeping on a roll-up mattress inside the luggage compartments underneath the bus. All across Peru I made bets with other passengers about whether the movies—badly dubbed and played at full volume day and night—would feature Steven Seagal or Chuck Norris; somehow one of them always appeared. In Brazil the long-haul buses—the most prolonged ride that summer was fifty-five hours—would stop for meals at private bus terminals where passengers could pay for food by weight, patronize stores selling toiletries, porn magazines, phone cards, and fresh-squeezed juices made from fruits I'd never heard of like *açaí, graviola,* or *caju.* Across the region bathrooms in stations had little old women in front who charged 10 cents for three squares of toilet paper. Some of the terminals had showers for rent and brothels in the back—mainly, I was told, for the drivers, who practically lived on the road. In Brazil, Ecuador, and Paraguay the air-conditioning on buses nice enough to have it was turned up so high that the unprepared traveler would nearly freeze. Coming from the beach I once had to put on every article of clothing in my bag to stop shivering. It seemed unnecessarily cold and other passengers had come prepared with blankets and wool hats. When I asked the driver to turn the air-conditioning down a bit he told me company policy required it be on full strength, "so that passengers paying for our services, including air-conditioning, get what they pay for."

Finally, with my summer vacation from the Universidad de Chile coming to an end, I arrived in Argentina's Baroque capital city. It was February 2002 and I was on summer vacation during my junior year abroad. The urban center I found was nothing like the one described in guidebooks and travel literature. Businesses across the city had boarded up their windows, and protesters had riddled every available surface with graffiti and posters condemning the government and the International Monetary Fund. The people were demanding *que se vayan todos*—that all the corrupt, incompetent politicians and international financiers get lost. Argentina was in the midst of a major financial crisis to which no end was in sight.

I had planned on staying with a gringa friend living in Buenos Aires for her junior year abroad, but when I got off the bus and found a public phone, I couldn't get her to answer. It was already late afternoon and I began to worry about where I would sleep that night. I didn't want to shell out for a bed in a fleabag hostel if I could avoid it, so I passed a couple of hours walking around the city carrying my valuables in a small knapsack on my chest and lugging my big hiking bag on my back. I had gotten dropped off on the bank of the Río de la Plata, the Silver River, the estuary of the Uruguay and Paraná rivers, and which separates Argentina from Uruguay. Spanish colonialists named it optimistically, and as it turned out erroneously, because they believed they would find mineral deposits in its muddy waters.

Following the riverbank along wide, European-style avenues and boulevards, I started out heading south. The streets were lined with beautiful buildings, testimony to Buenos Aires's preference for graceful European-inspired architecture. I followed the massive twelve-lane Avenida 9 de Julio, named for Argentina's independence day, July 9,

1816, which Argentines boast is the largest avenue in the world. Eventually I came to the confluence of several large thoroughfares near the center of the city where a protest was being held. Across the street from me was the Plaza de Mayo, which faced the Casa Rosada, Argentina's White House. I had heard of the Plaza de Mayo, because it was there that the mothers and grandmothers of the disappeared students and leftists from the military's Dirty War in the 1970s organized weekly protests against immunity for the murderers and kidnappers and demanded to know what had happened to the bodies of their loved ones. But the group of maybe one hundred people I saw holding signs and chanting were not the Mothers of the Plaza de Mayo, they were an eclectic mix of Argentine middle-class citizens of all ages and styles. They were demanding to be allowed to withdraw money from their bank accounts. A few of the banks I'd passed on my walk had their windows boarded up but it wasn't clear to me at that point why people couldn't just go to the bank and get their money.

Every twenty minutes or so I stopped at a phone and tried the number I had copied down from my friend's e-mail, but to no avail—it went straight to voice mail every time. When it started to get dark the boarded-up windows in the commercial district seemed more ominous, the abandoned residential streets foreboding. I decided to swallow my pride and open my wallet for a bed in a backpacker's hostel. I wandered the small side streets in the gray San Telmo district full of bars and traditional restaurants. San Telmo is sandwiched between the city's commercial and administrative center and the colorful, touristy working-class district called La Boca. Pictured on many Argentine postcards, La Boca was traditionally home to immigrant Italian dockworkers. San Telmo is full of antique shops, cobblestoned streets, and more than its share of churches. Plenty of the colonial style buildings sport terraces overlooking the streets below. In the last few minutes of daylight I saw a sign hanging from one of the terraces advertising a Hostal Internacional.

The Israeli behind the counter in the lobby, Gideon, was less than a year out of his obligatory military service back home and had the sculpted body to prove it. But he wasn't just another traveler; he was living in Buenos Aires with Rachel, his Jewish Argentine girlfriend, and working at the hostel while organizing all kinds of travel services and activities on the side. After he showed me to my shared dorm room he invited me to join him, Rachel, and some others from the hostel for a night on the town.

Despite the crisis, or perhaps because of it, the city's nightlife was jumping as people looked for ways to decompress and forget about the awful reality that surrounded them. We went dancing in a mansion converted to a multistory disco that blasted old-school rock like it was 1987. It's hard to avoid the pleasure of fulfilled stereotypes on first arriving in a new country, and the Argentines renowned mullet haircuts, sported at the disco by men and women alike, fit the part nicely. Once Gideon and Rachel realized that I spoke Spanish, they disappeared, leaving me with a couple of monolingual English backpackers who were desperate to meet Argentine women. There were lots of young women in the club but the Brits didn't speak enough Spanish to even attempt introductions. We took turns buying rounds of rum and coke until I offered to help them do more than just stare at the passing *minas,* as attractive women are called in both Argentina and Chile. I positioned myself near sofas on the balcony above the dance floor with the Brits lurking nearby. Whenever a group of two or three women passed I would beg their pardon and ask if any of them spoke English. If they said yes—and far more answered in the affirmative than actually could carry on a conversation—I signaled the Brits to join in. For a dull pickup line it worked surprisingly well and pretty soon we were all chatting away.

I ended up talking with two who didn't speak enough English to get past hello with the Brits. I relished the romantic Argentine dialect with which Diana, a slender *morena* (brunette), and her friend Francisca, an athletic *rubia* (blonde), talked to me. Unlike the rough Chilean Spanish I had grown accustomed to, people in Buenos Aires spoke a slower, more rhythmic language with a distinct Italian influence. They said *bárbaro* for cool and addressed each other with *vos* instead of the normal *tú* form of the second person singular. *Yo,* Spanish for I, was pronounced *show,* and in fact any y or ll was enunciated as *sh*. They also called one another *che*, the way friends back home said "dude." Their linguistic mannerisms reminded me that Ernesto "Che" Guevara was himself Argentine. I soon began trying to mimic the girls' accent and incorporate their slang into my vocabulary. They didn't seem to mind and Diana even gave me her number and told me to call her soon.

The next morning after waking up late I discovered I had spent all my local currency on the night out. I headed into the city to buy some pesos with the hundred-dollar bills I had stashed in my money belt. There were lots of banks downtown, but I realized immediately that it was going to take a very long time to get into any of them. Every bank and *casa de cambio* in Buenos Aires had an immense line of people outside it. The run on banks at the outset of the crisis had only slowed when banks froze people's assets. Now, a few weeks into the crisis, Argentines were allowed to withdraw just small amounts of money at a time and had to endure epic lines to do so.

Eventually, a block or two away from the entrance to a Citibank, I found the end of a line and took my place behind dozens and dozens of taciturn, formerly middle-class Argentines. Rick, another tourist from the United States, fell in behind me. For the Argentines, the lines and the economic crisis meant standing by helplessly while their economy and their life savings evaporated. But for Rick and me, trading dollars for pesos, the wait in line actually increased the amount of money we received. A couple weeks earlier we would have gotten exactly one peso for every dollar, but that morning, after more than an hour in line, I got 2.06 pesos per dollar and Rick, immediately behind me in line, got 2.08. "This is great," he said smiling, trying to be cheerful in the midst of a sea of crisis and depression. The gringo wild card does it again, I thought to myself.

Later that afternoon, the rate climbed above 2.20 per dollar. The peso, which for a decade had been pegged one for one to the dollar, would eventually collapse to four to one. Meanwhile, under pressure from the IMF, the government had cut jobs and social spending, and put in place a policy that denied Argentine families the right to access their savings.

I walked around the city, taking in the museums and the historic architecture, and trying to make sense of the history to which I was bearing witness. The protesters in the streets and the graffiti they left behind were clear on one thing at least: *que se vayan todos,* that the government go. But there didn't seem to be any concrete proposals for how to get out of the disaster. As a tourist I faced the impossible challenge of trying to enjoy a culturally rich city that was imploding, of trying to live morally in the midst of crisis. There was no escaping the poverty and desperation, the signs of it were everywhere: children sleeping on streets, garage sales where an entire house had been emptied out and labeled with price tags. And there was the tragic beauty of professional dancers performing exquisite tangos in the street for tips.

Back in the hostel, I found Rachel and Gideon sharing a drink together in the lobby. They invited me to join them for a plastic cup of cheap Cabernet. They had met, they told me, on the magical Inca trail to Machu Picchu while backpacking through Peru. Gideon was sufficiently smitten to follow Rachel back to Buenos Aires. Now they were living together and planning to get married. "We're moving to Israel," Gideon announced, "where the economy isn't in shambles." I wanted to know more about the economy—what had caused the crisis? I asked. What did it mean to have an economy in crisis anyway? Rachel offered to fill me in on the basics.

The Argentine military dictatorship from 1976 to 1983 ran up the national debt on the Dirty War against the country's political left, a range of never finished development projects, and the failed Falkland Islands War with the United Kingdom (in Argentina, the same islands are called the Malvinas). In 1982, under the dictatorship, Harvard-educated Domingo Cavallo was named head of the Central Bank and set up a policy that allowed private companies to transfer their debt to the state. By 1989 the government was unable to continue servicing the debt, inflation spiraled out of control to an annual rate of 3,000 percent, and President Raúl Alfonsín resigned six months before ending his term. That same year Carlos Menem was elected president after a populist campaign in which he suggested he would raise salaries, increase social spending, and ignore the mandates of Argentina's foreign creditors. After taking office he did an immediate about-face and began to work closely with the IMF to open the economy to foreign investment, prioritize foreign debt payments over social spending, deregulate labor, and privatize most state-owned industries. It was a classic example of the imposition of neoliberalism. Government land, telephone, energy, and water utilities were all sold off, often in deals that later turned out to have been riddled with kickbacks, bribes, and corruption—no terrible surprise in Argentina, a country where corruption is a way of life. Much of the money generated from the deals was used to pay foreign creditors but the debt continued to spiral out of control.

In early 1991, with the encouragement of Domingo Cavallo, then minister of economy, and in consultation with the IMF, President Menem fixed the value of the Argentine currency to the value of the dollar. In order to secure this "convertibility," under which any citizen could trade their local currency for dollars at the fixed rate, the Central Bank had to keep as many dollars in reserves as the amount of cash in circulation. If this strategy was to work in the long run, the Argentine economy would have to be competitive enough to sustain such a strong currency and generate sufficient gains in productivity to offset export losses due to the relatively high cost of their exports on global markets. This measure succeeded in curbing runaway inflation, guaranteeing price stability, and restoring domestic confidence in the Argentine currency, all of which generated short-term economic growth. As the country climbed out of the 1989 economic crisis, Argentines began to travel abroad, buy imported goods, and take out dollar-denominated loans at low interest rates. But because the country as a whole exported too little and imported too much there simply wasn't enough foreign currency to finance the interest on the massive foreign debt or to maintain the reserves to underwrite the pegged currency. Throughout the 1990s, even after it became apparent that Argentina couldn't handle its burgeoning foreign debt or maintain the pegged currency scheme, the IMF continued to pump money into the country, allowing the debt to soar. Pressure from the middle class, the IMF, and the United States Treasury forced the government to maintain one-to-one convertibility long after it was obviously unsustainable. By 2001 the total national debt was 50 percent of GDP, including more than $30 billion due in 2002 alone.

As Rachel explained the economic history to me, facts that probably every literate Argentine had become well acquainted with in the weeks since the crisis began, two thoughts raced across my mind. First, I realized that when I started traveling in Latin America, in January 1999, virtually every Latin American country was solidly in the neoliberal fold of the Washington Consensus policy model. Now, three years later, in the streets of Buenos Aires, I was watching the model collapse. Certainly, part of the problem had been Argentine consumption habits, but the United States could hardly take the high road in criticizing another country for consuming more than its share of the resources, or for unsustainable trade deficits.

Second, I started thinking about my first year in college when, in the wake of the Battle in Seattle, the anti–World Trade Organization protests of November 30, 1999, I got involved in the anti-globalization movement. I worked enthusiastically to recruit other students on my campus for a protest in Washington, D.C., against the IMF, the World Bank, and other international financial institutions. I wanted to take action in solidarity with the global poor and marginalized, those sectors of society that Nobel Prize–winning economist Joseph Stiglitz would later call "discontents" in his bestselling book *Globalization and Its Discontents*.

Charles, my roommate at the time, had grown up in the wealthy suburbs of Washington as the son of two career World Bankers who believed in the bank's stated mission of alleviating global poverty. I asked him to come along and protest neoliberal economic policies. He responded by pointing out that my computer's spell check didn't even recognize "neoliberal" as a word. What, precisely, were the policies that I opposed, he wanted to know. His question infuriated me. I told him that hundreds of millions of people across Latin America and beyond understood the word and the policies it summarized perfectly—it had defined their lives and undermined their sovereignty for decades by transferring decision-making power and policy autonomy to Washington-based creditors, away from national elected officials. But Charles wouldn't give in so easily. The World Bank, he explained, with patience and an annoying apparent mastery of detail, is a for-profit bank that makes loans for development projects to poor countries with the stated goal of reducing poverty; at times those loans carry macroeconomic policy contingencies. The IMF, on the other hand, monitors global economic and financial developments, lends money to countries with balance-of-payment difficulties, and provides technical assistance, but with no poverty reduction or development mandate. Or, as Charles put it, "the IMF is simply a cartel of central banks that are out there to do whatever it takes to maintain the status quo of currency stability. The IMF is for the greater good as long as it is for its own good. The World Bank is trying to improve the planet, within the terms of its mandate. There is a big difference." Charles agreed that both institutions had made costly mistakes but was upset that I insisted on lumping them together. I went off to the protest without him, but I was confused. Perhaps I *was* just blindly following the latest progressive counter-cultural protest fad. Perhaps all international financial institutions weren't *that* bad after all. Now my conversation with Rachel and Gideon, indeed my entire visit to Argentina, was allowing me to see things more clearly, from outside Washington's box. If only Charles were here, I thought, he would witness for himself the nature of the impact of the policies that the major international financial institutions had encouraged Argentina to implement.

In Buenos Aires, I could observe the effects of the crisis all around me. The hardest hit among the middle class went from being well-paid professionals with savings and retirement plans to living on the street. I watched entire families teaming up to work through garbage piles more efficiently: the father and the oldest child, perhaps twelve or fourteen, would wade deep into the piles of bags to systematically search for cardboard, tin, glass, or anything of value that might have made its way into the trash. The middle kids, eight or ten years old, would relay the finds between the refuse and the mother, who held the little ones close and kept watch over the cart they used to transport their worldly possessions and salvaged recyclables. Street children, abandoned and alone, were omnipresent, hustling, sleeping, begging, crying. In a testament to the infinite creativity of the desperate, I saw a hunched old man on one street offering to rent the use of his scale for ten centavos to passersby who wanted to know their weight. This was the kind of thing that might have passed for normal in Peru or Ecuador, but not in Argentina, at least not until the crisis. Eventually statistics would corroborate what I witnessed on the ground: of Argentina's population of 37 million, more than 21 million, or 58 percent, fell below the official poverty line; 7.5 million or 20 percent couldn't afford basic nutrition.

After a few days of trying I finally got through to my gringa study abroad contact. It turned out she didn't have any extra space for me to stay. She apologized for having missed me when I arrived; she had been at the beach for the weekend with a friend and had turned off her phone. But they were back now; did I want to spend the day with them? I did. The crisis all around me was beginning to feel overwhelming. Perhaps a day with a couple of gringas would provide a bit of a distraction.

We met in the mid-morning for cappuccinos and *media-lunas*, literally half-moons, delicious mini-croissants that are staple breakfast fare in Buenos Aires, at least for those who can afford them. We caught up on our mutual friends and compared notes on what we'd seen of the crisis around us, without ever getting below the surface of events. The girls told me that their afternoon plan was to go shoe shopping. It was, they gushed enthusiastically, not only the best half-off sale ever, but also a great way to pump dollars into the economy and help small businesses avoid bankruptcy. Everyone had to do their part, they insisted. And so we set off, down wide pedestrian avenues lined with shop windows filled with signs advertising discounts of 40, 50, and even 70 percent. Most shops were empty and understaffed but the streets were populated with beggars, people in lines at the occasional bank, and others going about their business. The service in the stores we visited was first-class, unsurprisingly as we were pretty much the only customers. With no desire to weigh my backpack down with new purchases, I had a tough job resisting the attentions of enthusiastic sales clerks. I soon wished I was doing something, anything, else.

Between boutiques we stopped to watch a spectacular tango show on a pedestrian-only street called Florida in the center of the city. The dance was captivating. The couple dressed to perfection—he in a sharp black suit and she in a short red skirt with black stockings—the steps syncopated expertly with each other and the music. But I found myself unable to focus. Behind the crowd that had gathered to watch the show, hunched up against the brick wall of a building, were four kids, faces smudged with dirt, feet black from walking barefoot. They were far from the first street kids I had seen, indeed such youngsters were everywhere, but the interaction of this particular group, with the older ones evidently looking after those who were younger, caught my attention. I told my gringa friends I would call them later and sidled over to the wall.

Squatting down, I introduced myself to the eldest of the group, who, I soon discovered, was Alicia and was fourteen. I could tell she was at first a little suspicious of my attention, but after I reassured her that I meant no harm she introduced me to her brothers and sisters: Juan, eleven; María, five; and Natalia, one. I asked Alicia about their family and day-to-day survival strategies: she never met her dad; her mom's factory job evaporated in the months before the crisis; no family or friends would take in the whole family; Mom headed off to find work a week earlier and never came back; the kids were getting used to sleeping on the streets and begging for food. As she talked, I thought about how I might help them. My Chilean roommate, Franco, had argued that any kind of charity was inherently counterproductive because it discouraged the poor and oppressed from taking revolutionary action. I asked him what sort of revolutionary action he envisaged. Half smiling, he replied that it was better for the poor to steal your wallet than pretend to be thankful for your loose change. I wasn't about to encourage Alicia's little group to start stealing but

Franco's admonition of the futility and tokenism of handing over a few coins stuck in my mind. What to do? In the end I asked the kids to follow me to a nearby grocery store. There we picked out pasta, canned tuna, fruit, toilet paper, and other basic products. I spent $12, which bought them about as much as they could carry and then we said our good-byes.

As I stood alone in the street, watching the little band disappear amid the traffic and wondering what to do next, I realized I had made a mistake. I was glad to have been able to help desperate kids caught up in the middle of a national crisis. But in seeking to feel better about my role as a crisis tourist, I had created a relationship that wasn't healthy for any of us. Travelers do have some responsibilities to the people and places they pass through but those obligations—to treat people respectfully, to keep an open mind, to be a good guest, to honestly convey what they see and hear to their compatriots back home—can't simply be replaced with random charity. I was unwittingly playing the role of a typical tourist—mobile and rich—ignorantly and narcissistically dropping in on the inert poor. I couldn't have a meaningful conversation with the kids because they were inevitably eager to tell me what they thought I wanted to hear. And what I'd bought for them seemed entirely arbitrary. It hadn't even occurred to me that it might be difficult for street kids to cook pasta or to open cans. And why those kids and not any of the thousands of others living on the edge all around me? I don't know what the kids thought about it. I guess they were happy to have something, anything. But it didn't make me feel any better.

I didn't know what to do next. I wandered around for a bit feeling confused and alone. I decided to call the number Diana had given me in the nightclub on my first evening in the city. She sounded pleased to hear from me and we set up a double date with Francisca and her boyfriend.

The next evening I caught a commuter train to the suburb where Diana and her friends lived north of Buenos Aires along the banks of the Río de la Plata. The view from the window of the rattling train looked out onto green trees and simple periurban homes not so unlike the South Chicago suburbs I had to drive through on my way to summer jobs during high school. Diana picked me up in the old Ford she shared with her mom and brother. It had been difficult to see what she really looked like in the disco with its flashing lights. Now I noticed for the first time that her eyes looked sad. She wore dangling earrings and tight jeans with a green halter top.

She drove us to pick up Francisca and her boyfriend, who was muscular and handsome, wearing a stylish leather jacket and pressed jeans, I couldn't help but feel intimidated. He leaned in confidently to greet me with a kiss on the cheek, something I learned was common among Argentine men. We headed to a local bar and took turns buying rounds of Quilmes cerveza. Our conversation wandered around the globe, through politics, culture, and romance, the things young people talk about when drinking beer and playing pool. When we left the bar we found that the side of Diana's car had been smashed in. The side mirror was knocked off and the passenger door wouldn't open. There was no note or any indication of where the culprit had gone. She announced that she had to get a police report in order to make an insurance claim and the three Argentines took out their wallets and started assembling a pile of cash. I wanted to know what was going on. Diana stopped counting bills and said in a tone of voice that left little doubt about the foul mood she was now in, "*Tenemos que juntar plata para pagar un soborno.* That's how it works in our country." They had to get money together for a bribe.

I soon learned that corruption in Argentina wasn't just limited to the petty, mundane tasks like a police report. The Menem era privatization schemes had been riddled with bribes, kickbacks, and tax evasion; money laundering and illegal, unlisted corporate accounts were widespread. Tax fraud and capital flight through illegal bank accounts contributed to the disappearance of funds that otherwise might have slowed or moderated the crisis. Investigations, arrests, allegations, and lawsuits reached the highest levels of Argentine government and key stakeholders in the global financial system. For example, ex-President Menem was placed under house arrest while being investigated for illegal arms deals, money transfers, and possession of Swiss bank accounts containing state funds. Clearstream, a Europe-based global supplier of "post-trading" financial services, a sort of bank for banks, was accused of facilitating illegal capital flight from Argentina in the weeks before the crisis. According to the as yet unsubstantiated allegations, Clearstream maintained a series of unpublished accounts that its clients, including Citigroup and many Argentine corporations holding private Argentine debt, used to get their assets out of the country while the peso was still pegged to the dollar. In 2008 Citigroup settled a lengthy federal investigation into its accounting of Argentine bonds during the crisis. Whether the allegations of fraud were true or not, Argentines knew their country was deeply corrupt and in the midst of the crisis they suspected the worst from their leaders and the international financial community. That night at the police station Diana didn't have much choice but to participate in petty corruption and pay the police officers the equivalent of $8. But it was large-scale economic dishonesty that had taken its toll on millions of Argentines like her.

Over the next few days I spent most of my time with Diana and her friends. Francisca invited me to crash on her couch instead of the grimy hostel where I had been staying. She had been earning her living as a model but once the crisis started, advertising budgets were quickly reduced and she hadn't worked in weeks. I ate lunch with her family one day and with Diana's neighbor the next. The neighbor was a pensioner, struggling to survive on a reduced monthly income. While she stirred a simple red sauce for pasta, she explained bitterly that her state pension had been guaranteed until a few months earlier. In December 2001, as the crisis loomed, the Argentine government under President Fernando de la Rúa reached out to the IMF for support. In exchange, the IMF demanded more and more fiscal austerity measures. State pensions, salaries, unemployment benefits, and other social spending all got slashed. The IMF insisted that the Argentine government end subsidies to the poorest provinces, put in place protections for private corporations, facilitate foreign capital acquiring bankrupt local firms, and halt an investigation of senior bank officials accused of smuggling dollars abroad. It may have been generous to transnational corporate interests, but for people like Diana's neighbor it was nothing short of a disaster.

I was pleased to be making friends and getting to know the local scene. But I was also overwhelmed by the generosity of so many people in the midst of an economic catastrophe. My insistence that I contribute something was always refused: none of them ever expected me to pay or asked me for anything besides friendship in return for their food, shelter, companionship, and time. It was a generosity all the more profound because of their economic circumstances, an example to inspire kindness and humanity in the worst of times.

As I got to know Diana a bit better, I learned more about how the crisis had impacted her personally. She owned and ran a small computer shop with her brother and took me there one evening to get a bit of privacy and to talk. The small space on the ground level of an apartment building had a pull-down metal gate in front of a picture window storefront. One side of the room had stations set up like an Internet café, and the counter displayed new and used computer components. The public space was carpeted and had fluorescent lights overhead. The back of the shop, where her brother did his repairs, was a disorganized mess of tools and parts strewn everywhere.

Before the crisis, Diana told me, the shop had been doing well. She and her brother were on their way to purchasing their store space and to paying off the loans they had used to get started. Though the peso was pegged to the dollar, they had decided to accept lower interest rates and keep all their revenue and savings in dollar-denominated accounts with international banks. "It just felt safer at the time," Diana explained. But when the crisis loomed, companies and savers began pulling their money from banks. Her brother had wanted to take out their money too. "I told him to stick to repairing the computers and let me handle the finances," she said bitterly. They didn't participate in the mass withdrawals.

As much as $1 billion per day had fled the banking system in early December 2001. To prevent a total run on the Central Bank and under pressure from the IMF, Domingo Cavallo, the same economy minister who developed the fixed convertibility scheme in the first place back in 1991, created a legal *corralito,* or little fence, to limit withdrawals. The *corralito* left Diana's and millions of other Argentines' savings trapped in failing banks. Unemployment climbed to above 18 percent and, in accordance with its agreement with the IMF, the government announced budget cuts of more than 20 percent for the following year, at the expense of yet more jobs and basic social services to people like Diana's neighbor.

The IMF-mandated policy changes and budget cuts were not well received. In response, Diana told me, masses of people took to the streets in protests called *cacerolazos* (banging pots and pans). Soon, protests included property destruction, often directed at banks, foreign companies, and hallmark multinationals like McDonald's and Coca-Cola. That explained why I had seen so many buildings in the downtown area boarded up.

"Then," Diana went on, "the political instability got really out of hand; over twenty people died in riots." After participating in the *cacerolazos* she had hid at home with her mom during the most violent protests and kept abreast of the developments via local news. On December 20, 2001, President de la Rúa resigned, and abandoned the presidential palace in a helicopter as protesters fought through police barricades and clouds of tear gas below. In the ten days that followed, the country went through five nominal heads of state. When Argentine politicians realized that the foundation of their economy, the one-to-one exchange rate for the dollar, wasn't sustainable, no one wanted to take responsibility for devaluation and the crisis that it would unleash. In early 2002, under pressure from the IMF, President Eduardo Duhalde issued a decree mandating *pesificación,* or forced conversion of bank accounts denominated in dollars into pesos at a rate of 1.4, significantly more than the official pegged rate but far less than the value the market would support if the peso were allowed to trade freely. Then, with people prevented by law from accessing their savings, the government let the currency float and stopped paying its debt. The Argentine government default on $155 billion was the largest sovereign debt default in history. As Diana explained, it was clear that through its policies and pressure the IMF had ensured that the economic burden of the crash would, as usual, fall on the poor.

While there were a variety of extraneous factors, including a strengthening of the dollar and Argentine corruption and consumption patterns, the IMF had guided Argentina's economic policy right into a major national crisis. Why would the IMF do such a thing? True, the IMF and the administration of George W. Bush wanted to make their economic poster child a success, which helps explain why they kept pumping money in when it should have been obvious that disaster was imminent. But the IMF also represents the interests of its financial backers and foreign bondholders. The longer the IMF convinced the Argentine finance ministers and presidents to blindly defend the fixed exchange rate, the more creditors' losses were mitigated and corrupt corporations were able to get their investments out as dollars. Although the media described emergency IMF loans as bailouts, it was the largely foreign bankers and bondholders who were being bailed out at the expense of people like Diana.

"When the government put in place the *corralito* and mandated *pesificación*, it essentially allowed foreign bankers and bondholders to steal from me and my business," she continued. "All of a sudden our debt burden more than doubled and at the same time the government prevented us from accessing our money and forced us to convert our dollars into pesos that were in the process of collapsing." Her money had been forcibly converted to pesos at a rate significantly worse than the market rate; she would have to accept the market rate to get her dollars back in order to finance her business's debt. Her savings had been converted from dollars to pesos but her debt had not. And of course, in the throes of the crisis no one was spending money on their computers. Diana's revenue stream dried up. It was just a matter of time before she and her brother filed for bankruptcy. The same thing was happening to businesses across the country, and to the government itself. She was already making plans to get a visa to go to Italy where she had distant cousins. It was, she said, her only hope. Even if her visa came through, the plane ticket to Europe would cost her several times what it would have cost just weeks earlier and the *corralito* would make it tough for her to get enough money out of her account to cover the fare. As I left Diana that evening, I struggled futilely for a way to express my sympathy, to imagine a way to be of some use. It was an impossible situation.

Crisis or no, my summer vacation was coming to an end and the next day I had to catch a double-decker bus for the twenty-four-hour ride across the pampas and over the Andes to Santiago for my second semester of classes at the Universidad de Chile. On my last night in Buenos Aires, Diana and Francisca took me out to an Irish pub; there really is one in every city. After the pub scene started to die down in the wee hours of the morning, Francisca headed for home and Diana drove me to the bus station for a tearful good-bye. I never did find out whether she made it to Italy. But back in Chile and then later when I returned to college in the United States, I made a point of keeping up on developments in Argentina.

Defenders of the neoliberal free trade model would blame the crisis on Argentina's irresponsible fiscal policy and "rigid labor laws and strong union pressures," which prevented reduction in production costs that the country "needed to become competitive" internationally. According to this perspective, Menem's free market policies were not the cause of, or even a contributing factor to, the crisis. The real tragedy, according to this argument, wasn't so much Argentina's suffering but rather that other emerging markets would "misinterpret" the Argentine experience and move away from pro–free trade policies. Argentina had been a neoliberal model for the IMF and if the Washington Consensus couldn't work there it wasn't likely to work anywhere.

Argentina's voters certainly seemed to draw that conclusion. In May 2003, Néstor Kirchner, a left-leaning Peronist, was sworn in as president. His election came after former President Menem withdrew from a reelection bid amid accusations of corruption and culpability for the crisis. Kirchner faced the immense challenge of renegotiating the country's foreign debt with the IMF and other international lenders as well as improving government transparency and accountability. His leftist program promised an increase in social spending, but the country's creditors would hear nothing of that, certainly not until their interest payments were guaranteed. The government encouraged domestic production of previously imported goods, a strategy known as import substitution, to improve the balance of trade. It also made credit lines available for local corporations, aggressively improved tax collection, and set aside large amounts of money for social spending while controlling other budget items.

Argentine factory workers began taking over their bankrupt companies, starting up cooperatives to keep the assembly lines operating. Shoemakers, pasta factories, electronic assembly lines, and printing presses that had been written off by their owners were all taken over by workers who insisted they could be run profitably. In most cases the government gave short-term permits to workers to get the businesses operating again, though some were forced to barricade themselves inside their workplaces and fight off police efforts to evict them.

Argentina managed to return quickly to economic growth. From 2003 to 2006 the economy grew more than 8 percent per year, making it one of the fastest expanding economies in Latin America. Inflation accompanied the growth but was nowhere near the levels at the peak of the crisis, and wages rose faster than prices. Since Kirchner took office, more than eight million Argentines have managed to pull themselves above the poverty line. These gains owe little to the support of the international financial community and much to Kirchner's tough heterodox economic strategy.

In his first year in office, Kirchner negotiated hard with international creditors and won an agreement to reschedule $84 billion in debt over three years on favorable terms. In early 2005, the government initiated a bond exchange to restructure another $80 billion of private debt. At the end of 2005, following Brazil's example just two days earlier, Kirchner announced the cancellation of Argentina's debt to the IMF with a single payment of $9.8 billion—the country had other outstanding debts but the IMF would no longer have any leverage over domestic policy. Not only did Argentina win its independence from political control of the IMF, but the country also saved

$842 million in interest payments. Venezuela, under President Hugo Chávez, purchased more than $3 billion of Argentina's debt, helping give Kirchner the financial breathing room to stand firm in his negotiations with foreign creditors and ultimately to pay off the IMF.

In March 2007, President Bush organized a highly publicized Latin America tour to try to combat President Chávez's growing influence and to shore up his government's collapsing prestige in the region. Chávez organized a counter-tour, following Bush and leading anti-imperialist protests and rallies in cities near Bush's planned stops. Like much of the Bush administration's Latin America policy, the U.S. president's tour backfired badly. While in Montevideo, the capital of Uruguay, he encountered massive protests and hostile questions, while President Chávez, on the opposite bank of the river in Buenos Aires, was hailed as a hero by still larger crowds.

Under Kirchner, Argentine foreign policy shifted from closely following U.S. instructions, to an independent regional focus. Kirchner joined Chávez and Brazil's president, Luiz Inácio Lula da Silva, known simply as Lula, in rejecting Bush's Free Trade Area of the Americas, preferring instead to focus on Mercosur, the Southern Cone's regional trade alliance, and other subregional integration initiatives and trade deals. With windfall oil profits in Venezuela, independently minded leaders like Kirchner winning elections across the region, and the economic weight of Brazil, the influence of the IMF fell to an all-time low in Latin America. A cornerstone of the neoliberal Washington Consensus had collapsed. With financial backing from Venezuela and burgeoning social movements across the Americas, Argentina had evidently decided not to buy back into the currency of the Washington Consensus.

Kirchner proved to be such a popular president that in December 2007, his wife, Cristina Fernández de Kirchner, was elected to succeed him, the first-ever woman to hold the post. Since taking office she has struggled with an unmanageable deficit, accelerating inflation, and widespread protests over her agricultural tax policy. But when she was elected the country was still basking in the optimism of rapid recovery.

In 2007, less than a year before Cristina Kirchner's switch from first lady to first *presidenta,* I went back to Buenos Aires. The city showed no signs of the economic crisis I had witnessed on my previous visit. The peso had settled at about three to the dollar, and the city had become a center for expatriates looking to live in a happening town for a fraction of the cost of a New York or London. I was spoiled for choices as to where to stay, ending up with a friend near the upscale new shopping district that after the crisis had been rechristened Palermo Soho. But friends from my first trip, during the crisis, Diana and Francisca, Gideon and Rachel, were nowhere to be found. I tried asking around at the hostel where I had stayed on my first trip but no one there had heard of Gideon or Rachel. I went back to Diana's neighborhood and looked for her computer shop but it had been replaced with a store selling handbags and the woman behind the counter had no idea who or where Diana was.

Although the country certainly still had plenty of people living in poverty, the face of Buenos Aires had changed dramatically since the crisis. Walking around the city I saw expensive steakhouses, chic cafés, and upscale wine bars all bustling with customers on weekday afternoons. Some new Argentine friends took me to a meal where I ate a succulent steak, and fresh pasta so perfect I might easily have been in Tuscany. We washed it all down with a Malbec wine produced from vineyards in the foothills of the Andes that are irrigated by ice-fed streams. Best of all, the Argentines announced, the wine and the food were produced right there in Argentina so I could applaud my consumer ethics—supporting the import substitution policy to help the economy recover from the crisis. Argentines rarely sat down to dinner until after 10 P.M., so an ambitious eater could make time for four meals in the day. The nightlife I remembered from 2001 was, if anything, more active and the mullets and the 1980s music were still going strong. New commercial districts had sprung up, and the consumer economy was buzzing.

One day, while walking around downtown Buenos Aires, I found myself on Florida Street, on the same pedestrian street corner where six years earlier I had met the street kids and bought them groceries.

The street performers, dancing the tango for tips, were nowhere to be seen. The avenue was lined with brightly lit, bustling fashion boutiques selling the latest in formal but comfortable footwear, and one-of-a-kind designer furniture. My awkward efforts to provide direct charity came to mind and I realized there were no longer hordes of homeless children as there had been my first time in Buenos Aires. It made me feel better but I couldn't help but wonder what had become of Alicia and her family of little ones.

Into the Amazon

The oversized cloth hammock would be my bed for nearly a week on the *Estrela da Amazona,* a two-hundred-foot riverboat that plied the wide, dark waters of the Amazon River from the mouth at Belém to the capital of Amazon state, Manaus. I strung my new bed on the open-air lower deck, helped by a member of the crew whose biceps were as big as my thighs and whose missing front tooth made his well-meaning smile seem, to me at least, a bit ominous. Perhaps it was just that I was nervous about the adventure that lay ahead of me. It was late at night in January of 2002, and I was taking advantage of a long summer vacation from school in Chile to travel into the unknown.

As I waited for the boat to take on cargo and leave Belém I couldn't spot a single other tourist onboard. Ports and border towns tend toward the dangerous, and being the only foreigner on a cargo boat about to head up the Amazon in the dead of night, I couldn't help but feel a little anxious. Sitting in my newly strung bed I felt sweat beading on my forehead. Other passengers were setting up their hammocks on all sides, awfully close it seemed. I saw would-be thieves and assailants everywhere.

My mind began to race. What if another passenger decided to throw me over the side of the ship? Who would help me? Certainly it would be impossible to swim across the miles of murky water to shore, especially as there were island-sized clumps of dirt and trees floating on the surface and piranha and candirú, a tiny parasitic relative of the catfish that is reputed to swim up openings like the anus or urethra, beneath it.

I was sure I didn't want to be the typical tourist who goes to the global south only to disappear into luxury hotels and elite white neighborhoods that may well be geographically removed but are culturally contiguous extensions of the United States or Europe. But had I gone too far in trying to embody Kapuscinski's "authentic traveler," prepared to "pay the reckoning with your health, if not your life"?

When I thought no one was looking at the gringo—as though it were possible to do anything in that tiny space crammed with over a hundred people without anyone noticing—I took my cash, tickets, passport, camera, Walkman, and sunglasses and put them in the various pockets of my photojournalist vest, which I planned to use as a now very lumpy pillow. I pulled Geoffrey O'Connor's *Amazon Journal: Dispatches from a Vanishing Frontier* out of my travel backpack, in the hopes that it would teach me a thing or two about the region I was to boat through and perhaps soothe my wilder fears. Before settling down to read, I tried to adjust my hammock height so that, as a further security precaution, my butt could rest gently on my big hiking bag as I slept. I undid the simple, strong slipknot the crew member had tied and attempted to retie it with a bit more slack. After several minutes of increasingly frustrated fumbling I had only succeeded in turning the thick twine into a rat's nest of impossible-to-undo knots. A tall man about my age who later introduced himself as Morilo had set up right next to me and was relaxing in his hammock, watching me make a fool of myself. With a chuckle he jumped up and, after telling me to *"presta atenção"*—pay attention—he gave a couple of deft flicks of his wrists, and firmly tied my hammock up at the perfect height.

A few minutes later our boat pulled out into the mighty Amazon, just up from the mouth. The scale of the Amazon is hard to grasp. Oceangoing vessels can travel up it from the Atlantic to Iquitos, Peru, the furthest inland deepwater port on earth, some 2,300 miles from the river's mouth. Fifteen thousand tributaries flow into it, making its volume greater than the next eight largest rivers combined. During the rainy season nearly seven million cubic feet of water flow from the mouth of the Amazon every day, and it carries nearly one fifth of all the freshwater worldwide. As a result "potable" water can be drawn from the ocean when land is not even in sight, and the salinity of seawater is significantly reduced a hundred miles offshore. The estuary where we were beginning our journey is over two hundred miles wide and is freckled with fluvial islands—one as large as Switzerland. These islands are formed from silt that is carried for thousands of miles by the river from its 2.7 million square mile basin, an area that covers 40 percent of South America.

With the sound of the water racing by us, and the soft rocking of my hammock, I should have been able to fall asleep immediately. Instead my anxiety made it impossible to relax. Every time I heard one of the hundreds of people on deck make a sound or get out of their hammock to go to the bathroom I jumped up to make sure nothing was wrong. It wasn't until late in the night that I began drifting in and out of an uneasy sleep.

I woke on my first morning aboard to feel the *Estrela da Amazona* rocking my hammock gently as it beat its way against the current of the impossibly wide, muddy river. As the sun rose the banks emerged only as a thin green line on the horizon. Most people were still asleep and I decided to take the opportunity provided by the relative quiet to explore the blue and white painted steel-hulled boat, now rusty with age. I discovered that the lower deck where I had slept was located right above a hold filled with onions, canned food, powdered milk, motorcycles, and other cargo bound for Manaus's two million inhabitants. My hammock was one of nearly a hundred strung up every which way, often overlapping at different heights and occupying every inch of free space. The floor area under the hammocks was strewn with various types of bags, sacks, and bundles. Many people appeared to be traveling with all of their life's belongings. The side of the boat was open to the elements with the river racing swiftly by only a couple feet below. The white guardrail at about thigh height had hooks so a plastic tarpaulin could be tied down during daily rainstorms. There was a small kitchen at the stern and steep metal stair-cases leading to the deck above on either side at the bow.

I climbed up, holding tightly on to the handrail as I was still trying to get my river legs. The middle deck above was also open-air, with as many hammocks as down below, but here crammed into a much smaller space. Just looking at all the *redes,* as Brazilians call them, made me feel claustrophobic. On one side of this deck were cabins for the captain and passengers who could afford to pay a bit more. A cabin provided privacy and security but, as I was told gleefully by my companions out in the open, had the disadvantage of trapping occupants in the event of the boat sinking, as a fair number of riverboats do. The far end of the middle deck was dedicated to a tiny mess hall with metal benches anchored to the floor in a manner that reminded me of my parents' prisons. Here, meals of rice, beans, noodles, and meat were served in shifts, shuttled up from the kitchen below on a dilapidated dumbwaiter. Next to the mess hall were the showers and the bathrooms, and a row of sinks looking out onto the Amazon. The cramped metal showers and sinks had running water pumped straight out of the river, while the toilets and garbage, in a form of recycling I tried not to spend much time thinking about, dumped straight into it. I always felt dirtier after a shower than before.

The top deck was mainly for storage of a few lifeboats that looked as though they had seen better days. One could take sun there, or sit in the shade and play dominoes, checkers, or chess. A tiny café opened at night blasting out forró music, a kind of sensual country-western two-step. Customers could buy sandwiches, soda, and Antarctica beer. (Beer served at the equator sounds more appealing if it's named for the colder regions; Venezuelans drink Polar Ice.)

Next to the café a massive water-purifying machine provided drinking water. Only after it was too late would I learn that the machine filtered but did not sterilize the bacteria-ridden riverwater. I have a strong stomach but on *Estrela da Amazona,* for the first time in my travels, I became seriously ill. Judging by the state of the bathrooms I was one among many. It was all the crew could do to plunge the toilets and keep them stocked with paper.

The channel thinned as we worked our way upriver and occasionally the captain would navigate a stretch close to one of the shores.
For several hours at a time the boat was no more than a hundred yards
away from the bank and I got a close-up view of the extraordinary
jungle, which extends over 1.6 million square miles, roughly six times
the size of Texas, and represents over half of the planet's remaining
rain forest. It is home to an astonishing variety of species, thousands
of birds and mammals and 2.5 million of insects. Up to two thousand
species of insects can be found on a single tree. In recent years slash-
and-burn agriculture has been taking a toll on the Amazon, and today
deforestation in the basin clears about eleven thousand square miles
a year, an area roughly the size of Connecticut. One quarter of greenhouse gases generated by human activity comes from burning tropical
forests.

Greater Amazonia was once home to more than one thousand
separate tribes and nations of indigenous people; today only around
two hundred remain. Most of the people I saw living on the banks of
the main branch of the Amazon were relatively recent settlers or fron-
tiersmen with some indigenous ancestry. Indigenous peoples still living according to their traditional ways of life could only be found on
smaller, more isolated tributaries where big boats couldn't pass. From
the upper deck of *Estrela da Amazona* I saw hundreds of small dugout
canoes, traditional indigenous vessels, plying the muddy waters. I saw
one small boy, entirely naked and no more than five years old, cap-
taining a tiny piece of wood on the mighty river by himself.

A number of canoes raced out toward our boat, their occupants
paddling furiously to stay alongside while they begged from the passengers, who, with the generosity one often finds among people who
have very little themselves, would throw them odd hand-me-downs
or scraps of food in plastic bags. The class and cultural divide between
the people in the canoes living in isolated rural homesteads and the
mixed race, Westernized people on the boat mostly heading for larger
towns and cities along the river was tangible. The passengers on the
boat with me didn't have much money—otherwise they would have
flown from Belém to Manaus in three hours instead of spending five

days on the boat—but the settlers and indigenous people lived almost entirely outside the cash economy and were eager to beg for charity or sell what little they had.

Some dugout canoes tied up to the boat and men climbed onboard to sell freshwater shrimp, hearts of palm, and Brazil nuts. I bought a bag of nuts and had a raucous time trying to crack them open with my newfound shipmates. Farther upriver vendors sold fresh açai juice, a deep reddish purple Amazon palm fruit that, several years later, would appear on Jamba Juice menus across the United States as a health food extolled for its antioxidants, protein, fiber, and high mineral content.

In the afternoons, when the skies parted, I learned that Amazonian rainstorms were warmer, cleaner, and higher pressure than the dirty riverwater showers. Rain or shine, looking out from the top deck became one of my favorite pastimes. We crossed paths with dozens of rickety boats loaded to the point of collapse with cattle, prompting me to wonder how many acres of forest had been burned to make room for those cows to graze. From my vantage point on the top deck I also caught glimpses of six-foot-long pink freshwater dolphins, which reportedly have as much as 40 percent more brain capacity than humans. Also swimming alongside the boat was a huge snake—probably not an anaconda, which tend to prefer shallower, slower water, but terrifying nonetheless. Aside from the occasional wildlife and sporadic houses visible right on the riverbank, the view from the boat was a monotonous green line of trees on the horizon. But whenever looking out from the deck got boring, there was plenty of excitement inside the boat to keep me entertained.

By the end of the first day I had too many friends to count and kept meeting more people all the time. A newly married couple in a massive hammock on my left never seemed to go anywhere and kept an eye on my stuff when I went for meals or out on the upper deck. Then there was Morilo almost touching my hammock on the other side. Daniela was toward the middle and behind me with three of her seven kids on their way to reunite with the father and the rest of the family. A group of people, mainly young women and children, followed me around persistently. Many of them had never been photographed before and lined up to have me take a picture of them.

One day while I was relaxing in my hammock, a lanky nine-year-old girl with a wide grin appeared and confidently handed me a neatly folded piece of paper. The note was from the girl's mom, Lara Ribeiro. In bubbly, cursive letters she announced that she wanted to meet with me. Would I go and introduce myself? I mustered my courage and followed the bearer of the note to the other side of the deck. To my immense delight it turned out that Lara was both beautiful and, it was soon evident, great fun. We fell into a lengthy conversation, with me straining my rough Portuguese to its limits. I soon discovered that at age sixteen, before finishing high school, Lara had gotten pregnant with a man ten years her senior whom she subsequently married. Five years later she was mother to three kids. By her third birth she had come to hate her husband and had her tubes tied without consulting him. When I met her, Lara was twenty-four years old and moving with her three kids to start over in Manaus, where a number of her siblings had already settled. She had a deeply endearing combination of the maturity necessarily derived from being a responsible mother at a young age, and the fun-loving playfulness of a woman who had missed out on much of her adolescence.

Our boat continued upriver stopping at island towns and the occasional city. Lara and I sat together at meals in the galley. We took her kids for walks around dirty, humid ports and watched impossibly strong men hauling boxes in and out of the hold whenever the boat stopped to load or unload cargo. As the days passed I became frustrated with the lack of privacy and my inability to communicate articulately. My Portuguese was improving—it's so similar to Spanish that I simply replaced the Spanish sounds and words with Portuguese ones, and made it up when I wasn't sure—but I was a young adult trying to express my complex ideas and emotions with the vocabulary and grammar of a child. I wanted to get to know Lara but the subtleties of what she tried to communicate to me were all too often lost because I had no linguistic context in which to interpret her words. My Portuguese was an embarrassment and it didn't make me any less self-conscious to have people listening in whenever we talked.

Lack of privacy wasn't just limited to interactions with Lara, but also to everything on the boat. None of the locks on the bathrooms or showers worked so I often had people walk in on me at awkward moments. I had to shave at the sinks without a mirror and in front of the hundred people who were in line for breakfast. Trying to find a quiet space to read or write in my journal was a lost cause. It began to feel like there was never a single moment in the day where I had privacy: someone was watching me at all times. I felt sorry for myself. Lara, on the other hand, took it all in stride.

One night, after I was asleep, Morilo nudged my hammock to show me that he was getting a blow job from Daniela, whose kids were asleep only a few feet away. A couple days later, Morilo started drinking cachaça, a clear sugarcane-based hard alcohol that is a Brazilian favorite, and gambling with other drunks. When he was losing he approached me in a corner of the deck, breath reeking of alcohol, and insisted that I lend him a few dollars to help him get out of the hole. I had little faith that he would ever pay me back but all of a sudden the fears I had the first night on the boat came racing back— what if he held a grudge and "accidentally" knocked me into the river at night? After consulting with Lara, I decided that five reals was a relatively small price to pay for keeping the peace in my row of hammocks. Of course the money wasn't worth much to me but being bullied into giving a loan, however small, is no fun. As a traveler it is never simple deciding when and how much financial support to give the people one meets. The economic inequalities are so vast that a little help can go a long way. On the other hand, there are far too many people who need help to decide easily who is most worthy or how much to give. More complicated still is the struggle to build honest, equal relationships with people, not just relationships based on financial support. I usually try to keep money totally out of my relationships for as long as possible so that there is a basis for trust and loyalty that has nothing to do with any perceived financial incentives. In the case of Morilo I made an exception but with no intention of maintaining a relationship with him after we got off the boat.

Our last night on the boat, Bible in hand, Morilo led a loud prayer circle of evangelicals on the crowded middle deck. I know I have more than my share of contradictions but I was flabbergasted as I watched him work up a sweat preaching the gospel after his uncouth behavior over the previous few days. With so many people in so little space, pretty much the whole boat had to watch the proselytizing.

The next morning, when the boat arrived in Manaus's massive deepwater port, Lara was dressed to kill in white jeans so tight they looked like they were painted on, a low-cut lime green blouse, and white high heels. I still don't understand how she managed to look that sexy on the dirty, cramped boat. It reminded me of the women, mostly black and Latina, who I'd seen on hundreds of visits to my dad's prisons. After traveling by bus to upstate New York they pop into the bathrooms at the Greyhound station and emerge dressed immaculately. I dress for comfort on prison visits but these women don't get to see their men often and want to make sure they look their best every time. Lara hadn't seen her family in Manaus in years, and was more concerned with arriving in style than in comfort. As it turned out, none of her family members were actually in the port to greet her because riverboats don't have a fixed schedule and their arrival time and even day are unpredictable.

I was eager to get to know Lara in a setting where we didn't have hundreds of eyes and ears following us, where we weren't confined to an overcrowded boat. So, despite having no idea what to expect, when she invited me to stay with her family I immediately agreed. We had to catch a city bus from the port to her house. As in most of Brazil, the public buses in Manaus have a driver and a separate fare collector who operates a turnstile to keep track of how many people get on and make it harder to skim money. We got off the bus in a working-poor neighborhood of Manaus called Santo Agostinho. The neighborhood, sprawling over several small hills, was dirty, crowded, and hot. At the bottom of one of the hills the houses were all made of cheap wood scraps and built over a swampy drainage ditch filled with mosquitoes and raw sewage. On the top of the hill, where Lara's family lived, the houses were simple cement structures and the views of the bright Amazonian sunsets over the city were breathtaking. The downside to the cement houses was that they had metal roofs and turned into veritable ovens during the hot days. The heat made one's sweat-drenched clothes feel as though they were welded on and even breathing became difficult. No one in the neighborhood had air-conditioning. Such modern amenities could only be found in the city's wealthy neighborhoods on the banks of the Amazon.

Lara shared a simple two-bedroom apartment above a minimart, up a flight of cement stairs with peeling paint and behind a rusty steel gate, with her sisters Marcia, Harim, and Deina. The place was crawling with children. In addition to Lara's three kids there were another three of Marcia's and one belonging to Deina, as well as a couple of nieces and nephews. Seven children shared one bed and others alternated between the big bed in the second room, thin mattresses on the floors, the couch, and hammocks. It was an impossible number of people for the space.

Lara and I slept on the floor in the living room, which we shared with a few other people, depending on the night. Usually her nephew slept on a hammock near us, but one night her brother showed up drunk and needed to sleep on the love seat—his wife wouldn't let him in that night because he had boozed away his paycheck. Although sharing a bed with Lara while several of her family members were asleep nearby in the same room made me very self-conscious, the others in the house seemed unaffected by the lack of privacy and space. Far from resenting my arrival, which added yet another body to the melee, I was welcomed with open arms. I couldn't help but feel a little ashamed when I remembered the way my brothers and I would complain about the intrusion when our parents invited friends to stay at our spacious house in Chicago.

On a typical morning in Manaus I woke up at dawn and cuddled with Lara before people started running through the living room getting ready for the day ahead. Eventually we got up, put away our bedding, and took turns in the bathroom with everyone else in the house—the small water closet was steadily occupied all morning. Lara made a big pot of coffee and a batch of tapioca pancakes served with butter and cheese. The food disappeared as soon as it came off the stove and there was nothing approaching a sit-down group meal for what they called *café da manhã*. Even the little kids drank coffee, though diluted with three quarters milk. Meanwhile, Marcia made sure the little ones got dressed and that one of the older kids walked them to school. With most of the children out of the house Marcia set off for work—an hour commute by bus—at a private residence where she provided care for an infirm grandmother.

Helping out where I could with the kids, but mostly just trying not to get in the way, the morning flew by. Before I realized what was happening, it was time for lunch, and someone had come back from the store with supplies. Lara and a few of her nieces were usually around so some took care of the kids while the others prepared rice, beans, stewed beef, and *graviola* juice. There were generally around fifteen people eating at each meal in their house, but there were rarely enough plates or utensils, let alone chairs, for that many. People ate out of Tupperware and sat on the floor. After eating, the nieces cleaned up the kitchen and Lara started washing piles of laundry by hand. Before she had finished, the kids would start coming back from school, hungry, and the cyclone started all over again.

Men in traditional Latin American *machista,* or macho, cultures are supposed to be breadwinners. But, as often as not, the women end up doing all the housework and child care, and pay the bills as well. I had generally thought of myself as anti-*machista*—growing up with two feminist mothers can have that effect—but on my first visit to Manaus I soon slipped into a perfect caricature of a *machista* man. I didn't have a job and the houseful of women rarely let me lift a finger. They cooked and fed me, washed my laundry by hand, even shaved my face and gave me manicures and pedicures. My attempts to help out with the chores didn't make a dent in the immense amount of work it took to keep the house going. Often the most they would let me do was play with the kids. My favorite activity was to take one of the little ones and flip them upside down and over my shoulder. They laughed and giggled, drawing the attention of their siblings, cousins, and neighbors. In no time I would have a line of five or six kids—at least one of whom was far too big for such a game—waiting eagerly for their turn. In this way I got my daily workout.

One day I insisted that they let me help cook lunch and I volunteered to fry the sweet plantains, my favorite dish. Since none of them believed I would be able to handle even that simple chore, Harim was assigned to supervise me. After I had finished cutting up the overripe bananas (with style pointers from Harim) and put the oil on the stove to heat up, Leonardo, one of Lara's nephews, and at fifteen the oldest man in the house, called me aside.

"What are you doing," he whispered in a conspiratorial voice. "I will never have to wash a dish in my life and neither should you."

By this point I spoke Portuguese well enough to understand him but not well enough to enter a serious discussion on the politics of gender so I simply said, *"Mas eu gosto"* (But I like to), and went back to the kitchen. When the oil was hot I clumsily shoveled the thick slices of sweet yellow plantain into the frying pan, sending a burst of scalding oil onto my hand and down my leg. After Harim iced my burns the sisters agreed never to let me near the kitchen again. Only much later would I convince them to let me take charge of cooking a few big family meals.

My relationship with Lara and her family led me to make four separate trips to Manaus over the next five years. The more time I spent with them the more evident were the disparities in the economic realities between me and my hosts. Even as a student on a tight budget, I had more money than they did. I didn't want my relationship with Lara and her family to be based on my wallet. Now looking back on that first trip I realize I was careful with my money to the point of being stingy, while my hosts were infinitely generous with what little they had. It's hard not to feel ashamed of my behavior then. But it reflected a more general problem: when traveling in Latin America it's often hard to ascertain how much people like me for who I am or how much they just like the gringo. Would any North American they happened to meet be as well received or is there something unique in our relationship? So many of my close friends from Brazil, Guatemala, Colombia, and most countries I have visited in Latin America are interested in going to live or work in the United States. I offer my friends a place to stay if they come but it's an empty promise because I know it's nearly impossible for them to get visas or plane tickets. And when I travel to their countries, despite their poverty and my wealth— at least in relative terms—so many people roll out the red carpet and open their homes and their hearts. On some occasions genuine human connections are in play, at other times people are simply trying to size me up and work an angle. There is no way to separate my personality from my nationality in this context and maybe there is no need to— being from the United States is and always will be a core part of who I am, with myriad benefits. I just have to make an effort to reconcile the class and cultural complexities of the relationships I build while on the road the same way I do the linguistic ones.

On one of my many boat trips on the Amazon, heading downriver to Manaus from tributaries in Ecuador and Peru, I passed by a town called San Pablo, Peru. At the time, I happened to be reading Jon Lee Anderson's definitive *Che Guevara: A Revolutionary Life,* so I knew that on his now famous motorcycle journey Che had spent a few weeks working at the San Pablo leper colony. As my boat motored slowly downstream I looked at the distant green shores and could practically hear Che making his farewell speech to the colony staff back in 1952: "Although our insignificance means we can't be spokespeople for such a noble cause, we believe, and after this journey more firmly than ever, that the division of [Latin] America into unstable and illusory nations is completely fictional. We constitute a single mestizo race, which from Mexico to the Magellan Straits bears notable ethnographical similarities. And so, in an attempt to rid myself of the weight of small-minded provincialism, I propose a toast to Peru and to a United Latin America." It was a trip that began Che's politicization as a radical. In years to come he would use stronger language and actions in his attempts to mold the region to meet his vision.

More than three decades after Che died while trying to bring revolution to the region through armed struggle, Latin America appeared to be in the midst of a significant political shift, driven by grassroots social movements and democratic elections. President Chávez had won the presidency of Venezuela on an anti-neoliberal ticket in a landslide election and took office in January 1999, just as I was arriving in Latin America for the first time. Then Brazil, the region's largest, most populous country and economic powerhouse, elected a poor former metalworker turned labor leader named Luiz Inácio Lula da Silva as president. Lula, the leader of the Workers Party (Partido dos Trabalhadores), took office in January 2003 after decisively winning a runoff election against a pro-neoliberal candidate. The prospect of his election had been enough to send tremors through international financial markets and was widely seen as a victory for Latin American integration, and a defeat for Bush's free trade agenda. Although Lula would ultimately disappoint many of those on the traditional Brazilian left with conservative economic policies and good relations with Washington, he did promote social programs, work with other progressive Latin American governments on a range of integration projects, and, using Brazil's economic might, block the implementation of the United States–backed Free Trade Area of the Americas. Lula's support for participatory budgeting initiatives, an affirmative action program for Afro-Brazilians, and antipoverty measures help explain his ongoing popularity.

When I went back to Brazil for the first time after Lula's victory, in May 2003, it was too early to assess his track record in office, but I was excited by the prospect of a country as powerful as Brazil having a progressive, working-class president. I had no idea what Lara and her family would make of his election: we didn't talk much about national or global politics because they were more interested in local day-to-day developments. When I canvassed the house in Manaus as to their views of Lula I discovered a wide range of opinion. One of Lara's nephews, Diego, who was just old enough to have voted for the first time in the election, told me: "Now we have a president who will stand up for Brazil when Bush tries to push us around." Lara was less optimistic: "I don't really know what to expect from him, but I worry that people in other countries won't take him as seriously as our other presidents." Harim's skepticism was still more apparent: "Lula is a big risk for Brazil. People don't know if they can trust him, they don't know if he is prepared to make the hard decisions required to keep the economy functioning."

I was initially surprised at the negative attitudes that seemed to prevail. I wondered how Lula had been elected if even poor Brazilians didn't support him. Of course, class wasn't the only factor in his election, but I also came to realize that those in Lara's family, poor as they were, were significantly better off than Brazil's impoverished masses. Much of Lula's campaigning in his first election was targeted at the country's most destitute, those living on just a dollar or two per day. To me the difference between a dollar a day and five dollars a day at first seemed marginal, but I came to understand that for Brazilians like Lara such differences have enormous implications for quality of life, class identity, and political outlook.

On one of my trips to Manaus, in 2007, I counted seventeen people in Lara's family living in three small adjoining apartments. Of these, only seven were employed, and they earned a total of only about $2,000 per month, or around $4 per person per day. This level of family income placed them well above Brazil's poorest, but it hardly provided for the opportunity to save, invest, or ride out unexpected crises like a lost job or an emergency medical procedure. Brazil has the largest gap between rich and poor of any sizable nation on earth. In Western Europe the richest 20 percent of the population has an income four times greater than the poorest 20 percent, while in the United States the proportion is eight to one. In Brazil, where just 10 percent of the population claims 80 percent of the income, the proportion is thirty-four to one. An estimated one third of the country lives on less than two dollars per day but no emerging market on earth except for China boasts more millionaires. This context helped me understand Lara's family's mixed support for Lula over the years.

The women in Lara's family did all the work because they lived in a *machista* culture, but also because where they grew up there were not many men around to share the work. Lara was one of the elder of seventeen siblings, thirteen of them girls. When their mom died after giving birth to her eleventh child, their dad, Danilo Ribeiro, had one child with a mistress. Within a year he remarried a woman who was younger than several of his kids and who already had two of her own children. Danilo and his second wife then had three more kids together. He raised his bountiful family in rural Pará on one of the state's endless cattle ranches. Pará is one of Brazil's largest states and lies on the northeastern edge of the Amazon basin. Originally covered with tropical rain forest, Pará has been heavily deforested over the last sixty years but it is still only lightly populated.

Like the Ribeiro family, approximately 20 percent of Brazil's nearly 200 million people lives in rural areas, but more than 45 percent of the country's agricultural land is controlled by just one percent of landowners. Income and land inequality spur violence across the face of the earth but in Brazil's Pará the problem is particularly acute because of widespread irregularities in land titling and the near total absence of the state in this frontier region. One of the main reasons that poor people colonized the Amazon is because most of the arable land in the rest of the country has been monopolized by a few wealthy owners. The federal government encouraged landless peasants from other parts of the country to settle the Amazon basin both in order to bring new land under cultivation, and to diffuse tensions in more populous regions. But migration into the Amazon basin generally causes more problems than it solves.

The peasant farmers that clear the land can rarely survive on the same plot for long because once the forest is slashed and burned, the monoculture of crops quickly exhausts the soil and heavy rains erode what's left. Lack of state infrastructure and financing exacerbate the situation. Peasants often give up on one plot and cut down more forest to begin anew. While poor settlers do the work clearing the land, gunmen and wealthy entrepreneurs consolidate huge estates for cattle ranching on the otherwise exhausted soils. With teams of hired guns at their disposal, wealthy absentee landlords evict, enslave, or even kill peasant farmers who get in their way. The BBC reports that in remote parts of Pará as many as ten thousand people are forced to work without compensation or labor rights, often on land for which their enslavers have no clear legal title in the first place. Modern-day slavery in Brazil is generally more subtle than it was two hundred years ago. Landowners will hire foremen to recruit labor in urban or semi-urban areas. Young men, or sometimes entire families, are employed for a tiny signing bonus or simply the promise of good pay, and transported to isolated parts of the state—some ranches in Pará are bigger than small European countries. Once on the inaccessible ranches the duped workers have no rights, no escape, and no recourse.

The patriarch of Lara's family, Danilo Ribeiro, still lives in rural Pará with his second wife and seven of the youngest kids. On one of my visits, Lara explained that her dad managed a large ranch for its absentee owner. I couldn't keep images of paramilitary thugs from passing through my mind—large landowners were known to brutalize and kill peasants whenever labor or land disputes arose. Over the years, as peasants struggled to defend their rights and their land, some organized rural land unions. Then, in 1992, a national organization, the Movimento dos Trabalhadores Rurais Sem Terra (MST, Landless Workers Movement), expanded its political work for agrarian reform from Brazil's southern states into Pará.

The Landless Workers Movement was founded in 1984 with an anti-capitalist platform focusing on peasant rights and radical agrarian reform. The movement started in the southern state of Rio Grande Do Sul with a small group of peasants demanding their own plots of land to raise food for their families. Since then, it has grown into a national movement that boasts more than one million members, and claims to have forced the government to redistribute more than 20 million acres of agricultural land to 350,000 peasant farmers. While the movement focuses on agrarian reform it has a broad political agenda calling for social justice in areas such as health care, education, infrastructure, and finance.

With the slogan "Each and every Landless studying," the MST has forged relationships with universities across Brazil, and with foreign governments such as those of Venezuela and Cuba, to increase popular education in literacy and medical care. Many of its 1,600 government-recognized settlements, across twenty-three Brazilian states, have their own health care centers. Landless Movement schools serve an estimated 160,000 children, and a literacy program has enrolled some thirty thousand adults. The movement draws funding from diverse and creative sources including four hundred farming cooperatives, its own natural medicine line, and sales of literature, baseball caps, and T-shirts. The group also advocates the adoption of cutting-edge agro-ecology and food sovereignty policies, resisting the imposition of genetically modified seeds, and arguing against ethanol production as a destructive monoculture practice that jeopardizes Brazil's domestic food supply. It is an example of one of the many social movements that have revolutionized Latin American politics over the last two decades in the fight against neoliberalism.

President Lula and his Workers Party have deep roots and a shared history with the MST going back to the 1980s. The nascent Landless Movement was one of dozens of groups and social movements that fought against a brutal military dictatorship in the years before the 1985 transition to democracy. A few years before the MST was officially founded, an anti-dictatorship labor coalition under the leadership of Lula and the Brazilian Metalworkers Union founded the Workers Party. During the twenty years he spent campaigning for public office before finally winning the presidency in 2002, Lula openly supported the MST. In the run-up to the 2002 election he consolidated the support of the MST by promising to give land to 400,000 families, and allow 500,000 squatters to acquire formal deeds to the land where they already lived.

But five years later, Lula had broken many of his links with Brazil's poorest communities and, in the process, had put to rest the fears Lara's family expressed on my first visit to Manaus. In 2007, at a Landless Movement settlement in the state of Rio de Janeiro, a lawyer for the group told me that "Lula used to be part of the left, but now he's the head of a bourgeois state. He's running a great government for people with money and a terrible government for people without." Lula has been widely criticized for rushing to the center as soon as he was elected on a left-wing ticket, for maintaining strong relations with the Bush administration, and for betraying the MST. A wide range of the same left-wing coalition groups that supported Lula's election in 2002 became disenchanted with his government in the years that followed.

Disagreements within the left, hardly a problem unique to Brazil, may have also weakened the MST. While most of the left no longer supports Lula, some also criticize the Landless Movement. These include modernizers who claim the organization focuses overmuch on yesteryear's struggles, suggesting that agrarian reform is no longer a key priority in the struggle for social justice. Others, on the far left, argue that the movement isn't revolutionary enough because it fails to call for the abolition of private property, demanding, instead, the redistribution of land to small scale private owners. Still others point out that the MST's roots, as well as most of its activity, are in Brazil's productive southern states, whereas the most unproductive land, landless farmers, and abusive labor conditions are in the north.

The issue of race also creates tensions for the movement. I visited an MST settlement in the state of Rio de Janeiro in July 2007. One of the community's leaders, a white man in his forties named Victor, met me in the city and accompanied me to the settlement. To get there we had to ride two public buses to the end of the line and then hire a motorbike to take us down a long dirt road. The settlement was on a former dairy farm and people had set up makeshift homes out of plywood under the massive hangar the previous owner had built. There weren't many cows left and the settlement had just one small community garden. I noticed that most of the settlers were white and when I asked Victor about the racial dynamics within the MST he told me defensively, "There are poor white farmers too." Indeed, the majority of the MST's leadership is white, leading to criticism from Brazil's *movimento negro*. Victor's settlement demonstrated another problem the movement has faced: years after taking possession of the land they had not established any farms. Most of the community lived on the dole. Many poor Brazilians join the Landless Movement hoping to get a piece of property to call their own but they don't have the skills to farm it effectively, and, even when they do, subdividing the land into small family parcels often limits productivity.

Criticisms notwithstanding, the MST is a prominent example of the radical social movements that have reshaped the politics in Latin America over the last two decades. And yet, it is faced with a dilemma that the left faces in Bolivia, Ecuador, Venezuela, the United States, and beyond. How can a group go from being a radical, fringe social-political movement that relies on grassroots organizing, protests, civil disobedience, and direct action, to becoming a real stakeholder within a democratic system? The MST had become disillusioned with Lula, but how did the people representing the landowners feel about him?

It wasn't until my fifth trip to Brazil in 2007 that I made it to the ranch in Pará that Lara grew up on, and to where she had returned after living five years in Manaus. By then she and I had long since given up trying to make a long-distance romantic relationship work and were just friends. I made the seemingly endless journey from Manaus to a small, dusty town called São Geraldo. After getting off another multiday river trip, the fourteen-hour bus ride took me past fenced cattle ranches, with softly rolling green hills and the odd watering hole cut into bright red soil. A few palms and the occasional old-growth tropical tree stood out like sentries, the only indication that just a few short decades ago Amazon jungle covered the land for hundreds of miles on all sides. Lara's father, Danilo, had migrated to the region in the 1980s, in the frontier heyday when southern Pará was still being cleared of jungle and when landowners were busy consolidating large estates. He found work as the manager for a ranch that would eventually encompass more than six hundred square miles and boast nearly thirty thousand head of cattle. He ran the place for its absentee landlord for over twenty-five years before retiring to a simple but comfortable house in town. It was there that we met for the first time.

Danilo and I had heard a lot about each other over the years and it was a much anticipated get-together. I imagine he was curious to see the gringo that his daughter had fallen in love with and who had already met fourteen of his seventeen kids. Aside from my interest in seeing the roots of the family I had come to love in Manaus, I was also curious to learn about land politics in Pará.

When Lara introduced us, Danilo greeted me with a big smile and a strong handshake, his hands leathered from years of work on the ranch. Thin and sinewy, his face was almost a caricature of itself: a big button nose, several missing teeth, and ears that got wider as they went up. He showed me proudly around his new house, still under construction, and then invited me to sit down on his front porch while his wife went to fry up yucca from their backyard garden and Lara hopped on a motorcycle to buy supplies for a trip to the ranch. After sharpening a fruit knife on a stone in the yard Danilo pulled up a chair and a bowl of oranges. We were both keen to ask questions, but as the host and my senior it was his right to start. A brief silence filled the air while he organized his thoughts and then he began to pepper me with dozens of often entirely unrelated inquiries. Did I like Brazil? How about Pará? Did I eat beans? How were his kids in Manaus getting along? What kind of car was most popular in the United States? How much did my digital camera cost? Did I want to help milk the cows?

I answered as best I could and then it was my turn. I learned that Danilo was proud, as any father would be, to have supported such a large family. He went on to describe his employer, the ranch owner and one of the richest men in Brazil. Danilo managed just one of his three ranches and the big boss also ran a precious and semiprecious stone export business and had other related companies based in Hong Kong, China, and Germany. Danilo was quick to add that his boss had done right by him, helping him pay for the construction of his new house and supporting his purchase of a small ranch in the area for one of his son's families.

When I inquired about the specifics of his work Danilo explained that he had supervised a team of around one hundred men for everything from cattle round-ups, to administering medicine to cows, to periodically burning the property to keep the jungle from creeping back and create ash that helped to fertilize the grass. He casually acknowledged that he didn't pay his hundred-plus ranch hands a living wage. There had been a small settlement of landless peasants on his boss's ranch back in the mid-1990s, he told me, but the problem had been settled peacefully by paying the squatters to vacate. Since then he had been diligent in using all the land so as not to invite further invasions. I had no reason to disbelieve his claims on this front. Certainly there had been a lot of land-related violence in Pará but it had not taken place on every ranch, not even all the big ones.

His young wife came out to the patio with crispy yucca and a steaming bowl of black bean *feijão*. She joined us for the snack and handed me a pile of literature from an evangelical Christian group they belonged to. While I ate she talked about the miracles of Jesus and the need to spread the faith. Danilo appeared only mildly interested in the proselytizing, but did ask if I could help get any of his kids a job in the United States. I tried to steer the conversation back to Brazil, asking Danilo what he thought of President Lula. "I thought he was going to be a terrible president, but once he got into office he turned out to be okay," he said noncommittally. He might have been speaking for much of Brazil's population, at least those sectors that identified with the ruling class.

Over his years in office Lula's moderation may have assuaged Danilo's concerns. But, regionally, the shift to the left was centered on a process more radical than that in Brazil. I had decided to make a trip to Venezuela, to see what President Chávez and the Bolivarian Revolution, named after Venezuela's liberator, Simón Bolívar, would look like on the ground. So after a few days in town and exploring the rolling hills and water holes on the ranch, I said my good-byes and got on a bus heading north.

In the President's Palace

Our jeep pulled up in front of El Tablazo, one of the Venezuelan state oil company petrochemical refineries in the western state of Zulia, and the cameraman jumped out with the digital tape rolling. It was almost dusk and he would only have a few minutes of natural light to capture the industrial complex on film. But natural light from the fading sunset wasn't the main reason we hit the ground running; we didn't have permission to film oil installations.

When I saw an army sentry charging toward us, I knew there would be trouble. I was the locally based fixer and interpreter, hired in Venezuela for ten days' work in late 2006 by the French-American film crew. They were on a multi-continent project, documenting poverty, capitalism, and globalization. As the fixer it was my job to arrange transportation, hotels, meals, interviews, security, communications, and incidentals, but also to obtain permission for shooting exteriors like refineries. Instead of the required paperwork, I had only been able to get ahold of a tape of stock footage from the oil ministry press office. The director who hired me wanted his own footage and he had decided to risk it—all he needed was a few minutes of film to run while the narrator described the oil industry's crucial role in the national economy: oil accounts for approximately 90 percent of export earnings, 50 percent of federal government revenue, and 30 percent of GDP. As the only member of the group who spoke any Spanish, it was my job to head off the soldier.

I jogged toward the rifle-toting sentry waving a file of papers and yelling *"Buenas tardes, señor,"* hoping to distract him for long enough

104

to let the cameraman get his footage. Ignoring me, he headed straight for the tripod and radioed for backup.

"Turn the camera off now," he ordered in Spanish. Rather than interpret what he was saying for the rest of the group—it was clear from the context anyway—I told him everything was fine, "No hay problema, we have the permission of Miraflores Presidential Palace," I insisted. He didn't seem to care and, in any case, I was fudging the details—all I really had was a letter from the palace listing the names and passport numbers of everyone on the crew and saying that we were doing an "important film project." I forced the letter, on official palace stationery, into his hand just as the backup he had called screeched to a halt nearby. The truckful of soldiers unloaded and surrounded us and our jeep. The smaller pickup carrying the head of plant security and his aide pulled over right next to where I was distracting the sentry. The sentry passed the letter to his superior, who, without looking at it, ordered the camera be turned off. The cameraman yelled out, "I got it. Done. Let's get the hell out of here," and started breaking down his tripod. Footage captured, camera away, crew in the jeep; now all I had to do was talk them into letting us drive off.

The head of security ordered the soldiers to watch the camera crew, and told me to get into the cab of his pickup truck. I tried to reassure the crew but secretly I was panicking. My faith in the gringo wild card was being stretched to its limits. The aide, carrying a rifle, got in on the passenger side, leaving me squeezed in the middle as we drove into the industrial plant, now brightly lit against the dark sky. The flames of burning gas waste overhead and the silence in the cab of the truck cast an ominous pall over the interminable drive to the central office. The head of security took my letter from the palace, my passport, and the rest of my faux very important papers into his office and left me in the car with the olive-clad aide and his rifle.

My mind raced. I had read the news reports about gringos getting arrested for taking pictures of oil installations in Venezuela and then being accused of spying for the CIA or the United States military. With tensions between President Chávez and President Bush at an all-time high, the last thing I wanted was to get accidentally caught up in international power politics, to be accused of espionage or put forward as a symbol of Yankee intervention. How had I gotten myself into this mess, and why had I ever thought I was qualified to be a fixer in a politically polarized country that was not my own?

I was still anxiously pondering those questions when the head of security came back into the pickup, handed me my papers, and said simply, "Melinda from Miraflores Palace says hi." The relief enveloped my body like a warm bath: an adviser I knew, albeit peripherally, happened to have answered the palace phone and told security I was a friend, not a spy. The drive out to the film crew felt shorter than the way in. When the head of security parked the car, he said, "Sorry for the trouble but we have to take precautions, you understand. Next time, let the press office know you're coming and we will be happy to arrange a tour of the plant, a boat trip out to the wells, or a helicopter ride for aerial footage; just no more unannounced visits, okay?"

That day, working as a fixer, my connections and friends helped diffuse what might have been a messy situation. I had come a long way since I first arrived in Venezuela with nothing more than a backpack. I had stepped off a bus in the Caracas terminal for the first time on a rainy Tuesday afternoon in November 2004. My expectations of the city I had arrived in came from Professor Vitale, back in Chile. Based on his years in exile in Caracas, he had told our class stories of beach excursions, salsa dancing, and lush green avenues. On my arrival, however, the city seemed to have changed a lot. The Caracas I encountered was congested and dirty. The streets were lined with little stalls selling clothes, food, and random Chinese imports; the buildings were mostly concrete and steel dating back to the 1970s oil boom. It couldn't have been more of a contrast with the places I had spent time over the previous months. Since finishing my year abroad in Chile, I had returned home to finish college, earned a master's degree in England, and then headed back to visit friends in Santiago. From Chile I hit the road heading north. My trip to Caracas from Santiago had covered nearly five thousand miles on boat and bus along a route similar to the one

Che Guevara followed on his motorcycle adventure in 1952. A break from school gave me time to further explore the region.

Life overseas and on the road gave me constant intellectual, cultural, and linguistic stimulation unlike anything I had ever known. I met new, fascinating people all the time. I saw different ways of life, different worlds everywhere I went. Time on the road presented me with continuous opportunities to move between and across social, political, class, and cultural divides that seemed much more rigid when I began to settle down in one place. Travel became the lifeblood of my imagination.

All in all I've crossed more than twenty-five different national borders in South America. The no-man's-lands they mark are always fascinating, spaces where conventional regulations and patterns of behavior break down, where unregulated economies can flourish, where the unexpected and unusual is there to be observed and savored by the curious traveler. The crossing from Peru into Ecuador on the coast is an instructive example. Public transportation only takes the traveler within a few miles of the immigration office. From there it is necessary to either walk or hire a taxi. The driver waits—one fervently hopes—with one's luggage while the traveler goes through a series of lines to obtain an exit visa. The lines are slower than they are long but the immediate environment is enthralling: wanted posters, legislative decrees, and cheap reprints of pictures of the national president adorn the stained walls. Indigenous women with impossibly large bundles come in and out. Men in cheap leather shoes and stained track suits lurk inexplicably. Are they drug enforcement agents or drug traffickers? Are they petty traders waiting for a big break, or hobos hoping for a free ride?

Eventually the front of the line materializes. It later becomes apparent that the exit visa—which may cost a few dollars depending on which immigration officer is on duty—is entirely unnecessary because no one checks passports or even enforces customs operations here. The taxi bearing one's luggage then proceeds, also without any customs inspection, into the netherworld of the border town that has sprung up in between the immigration offices and police checkpoints of the respective countries. The taxi will only take you a few hundred yards however, not all the way to the immigration office on the other side. One then has to gather luggage and belongings and venture, on foot, into the space between.

Virtually every border in Latin America has a strip of land separating the official entry and exit points of neighboring countries. When the border area is rural and isolated, the separation—the gap between legal jurisdictions of either country—can be spectacularly beautiful and liberating. In Patagonia, between Chile and Argentina, the strip of no-man's-land is a vast swath of territory cradled against the Andes and filled with grazing sheep—one can only wonder whom they belong to. Between Belize and Guatemala there is a lazy river with women washing clothes under a bridge that must be crossed on foot—no vehicle traffic allowed. The space between Colombia and Panama is the better part of the Darién Gap, a dense swampy jungle region that covers hundreds of square miles with virtually no roads or formal presence from the government on either side. From Peru into Brazil or Colombia at the triple frontier, a motorboat must be hired to cross the mighty Amazon River.

When, on the other hand, the border crossings are in more densely populated areas, black markets, thieves, gamblers, prostitutes, drug runners, and child laborers fill the space in between. Men armed with pocket calculators—some of them jury-rigged to provide a currency exchange unfavorable to the unwitting traveler—rush about with wads of cash in hand, offering to trade for "the best value." It behooves the traveler to know the official rates and spend time negotiating with several money changers at once. Food stands offer roast chicken, fried yucca, or juicy watermelon. Young boys offer to run errands or shine shoes. Beggars abound. Hustlers offer guide services or discounts on onward bus tickets to whichever destination one can imagine. Navigating my way through these zones is always a challenge that makes the chicken bus waiting to be boarded on the other side feel like a warm safe home.

I had spent the year before my overland trip from Chile up to Venezuela in England, researching internally displaced people in

Colombia. But that master's program discouraged me from doing field research, so it was the only full year I spent without going to Latin America since my first trip to Guatemala in 1999. I missed the region, and its languages, and I was long since ready to trade Britain's bland potatoes for my favorite sweet plantains. The elitism and ivory tower intellectualism that inhabited Oxford's hallowed spires had left me craving a connection to the global south. I greatly appreciated the opportunity to study in England—I had learned, grown, and built a few friendships that would last—but I needed a break before I went back for my second and final year of studies in the old empire.

As I rode north across South America in fall 2004, buses and adventure travel served as portals to worlds I couldn't have even imagined before stepping into them. After all, one of the reasons one travels is to experience the unimaginable. Politically, I already knew I didn't support imperialism or the business-as-usual governments in developing countries that facilitated it, but I didn't have any meaningful experience in a country with an alternative model of government. It was easy to criticize but I wanted to learn how to imagine an alternative. Though I had no way of knowing it when I stepped out of the comfort of the deeply familiar long-distance bus into the Caracas terminal, I had arrived in a country that would captivate my attention for years to come.

At that time I knew only a couple of people in Caracas. One was Marta Harnecker, a Chilean-born journalist, writer, and radical theorist, who had spent much of her life living in Cuba and was then working as an independent journalist, writer, and adviser to President Chávez. She had been the editor of a political journal of the left in Chile during the Allende years and had narrowly escaped the country after Pinochet's coup on September 11, 1973. The other was Marta's husband, Michael Lebowitz. Michael was a Marxist economist and professor from Canada whose unkempt hair and puffy white beard framing a full face might have led the casual observer to confuse him with the photo of Marx on the cover of his award-winning book, *Beyond Capital*.

Once the tropical rain let up my first day in Caracas, I met Michael, Marta, and a couple of friends of theirs who were visiting from Canada for a buffet dinner. Conversation was casual and in English because the Canadians didn't speak Spanish. We chatted about President Hugo Chávez's recent victory in a recall referendum aimed at driving him from office, of labor rights in Canada, and of the ill doings of the Bush administration. Tall and thin with a face that radiated great energy, Marta spoke to me in her first language, Spanish. At one point she asked me to translate what the others around the table were saying. Though it didn't occur to me at the time, I later realized she was testing me.

After dinner, as people were saying their good-byes, Marta asked me if I would be willing to translate into Spanish a working paper Michael had written that she wanted to be able to share with friends in the Chávez administration. It was the first of many occasions when I realized that when Marta asks for something it is very hard to say no.

"*Bueno,*" I said, "but I don't have a computer or anywhere to work."

"No problem. Just come to *mi oficina* around 10 A.M.; I will find you a computer," Marta replied. The idea of translating working papers and learning from Marta and Michael was exciting, but I still had my doubts.

"I don't even know where your office is," I said hesitantly. "Plus, I'm backpacking, I don't have any formal clothes to wear."

"It's in the president's palace, Miraflores," Marta said, an audible edge of annoyance now creeping into her voice. "Anyone can tell you where that is. When you get to the gate, inform the guards that you want to see me and they'll call my office so we can send someone down to get you. Don't worry about your clothes, just don't wear shorts."

The next morning for breakfast I had a glass of passion fruit juice and a Venezuelan empanada, a national favorite, which is a small cornmeal envelope filled with ham and cheese, chicken, ground beef, or whatever other filling the tienda happens to have available, and then deep-fried. I bought a Spanish-English dictionary, just in case my hunch that I was in way over my head was right.

It didn't take long to find Miraflores, a large white building with abundant verandas and balconies and a red shingle roof located in the center of historic Caracas, surrounded by Spanish-style *tasca* restaurants, street vendors, and an assortment of other government buildings and ministries. The palace is located on the side of a hill, and I approached it from the top. The first gate I saw was stylized black wrought iron manned by a handful of uniformed presidential guard soldiers carrying automatic rifles and wearing red berets. Even thinking about approaching them made me self-conscious, and I couldn't help but imagine the treatment a casually dressed foreigner approaching the White House and asking to be taken to the West Wing would receive. When I finally got up the nerve to say, "*Buenos días*, I'm here to see Marta Harnecker, adviser to President Chávez," they informed me that I was at the president's private entrance, and all personnel access was through gate number three, around the corner and down the hill.

Gate three looked a lot less presidential: it was a large entrance into a concrete parking garage that seemed to have been a recent addition to the main nineteenth-century building. There was a steady flow of people and cars going in and out, each being searched by uniformed soldiers. I stood around awkwardly for a few minutes until I got one of the guards to pay attention to me long enough to ask him to call Marta's office. After waiting about ten minutes in the fume-clogged shade, one of Marta's assistants arrived to get me a day pass and escort me through various security checkpoints. It turned out that Marta's office was in the heart of the old palace. The large room had a high painted ceiling and tall wooden doors that led out onto an open-air courtyard garden with a small fountain in the middle. The suite of offices on the other side of the fountain belonged to the chief of staff, a position that changed frequently under Chávez. Supporters claimed the rapid turnover was because no one could keep up with his pace of work, while according to his critics he concentrated his power by creating institutional chaos. Like so much in Venezuela, the reality was probably a combination of the two.

Marta and her team were working frantically, a normal state of affairs as I soon came to realize. But she found time to greet me with a kiss and a few affectionate words, *"Hooooola, ¿cómo estás, mi amor?"* She introduced me to the other people scurrying around the office as the son of political prisoners in the United States. Then, wasting no time, and reminding me she needed it by the end of the day, she set me up at a computer to translate Michael's paper.

The paper was called "Walking on Two Legs: Making Radical Endogenous Development Work." It laid out a development strategy based on a productive economy oriented toward Venezuela's consumption needs rather than the demands of the export market. Though it was written in simple, straightforward language, phrases like "monetary revenue" made me glad I had bought the dictionary. Endogenous development, Michael argued, was a direct rejection of neoliberalism because it would focus on the needs of the Venezuelan people rather than profits or capital. Michael was evidently drawing heavily on Chávez's recent speeches and the new constitution he had introduced. One of Chávez's central themes was that to end poverty, power had to be given to the poor. That simple concept made sense in a revolutionary kind of way, and I wondered why I hadn't heard it articulated so concisely before. Though I still knew little about Venezuelan politics in the Chávez era, it was quickly becoming apparent why so many powerful forces in Venezuela and beyond were trying to undermine his government.

Engrossed as I was with the work, I suddenly realized it had gotten late and that I was ravenous. Marta and her team were still going strong at their computers, but she called the palace kitchen to order food for us. I finished the translation, exhausted, just as our guava juice and ham sandwiches arrived. Marta looked over my work while I ate. She must have been satisfied with the translation because she asked me to come back to the palace early the next morning to interpret at a meeting for Michael, who didn't speak Spanish.

As promised, I showed up at the palace at 8 A.M., dressed as well as my backpack would allow me: hiking boots, black cargo pants, and an old yellow short-sleeved button-down shirt. It was 10 A.M. before the meeting started at the round wooden table in Marta's office. From the warm greetings that were exchanged it was obviously a meeting of friends. Still, I couldn't help but feel nervous. In addition to Michael and Marta, the meeting included Haiman el Troudi, a presidential adviser at the time but soon to be chief of staff, and several other senior people in the govenrment.*

As soon as the meeting started I knew it was going to be a difficult time for me as interpreter. Venezuelan Spanish, which I had only heard for the first time a few days earlier, is fast, choppy, and riddled with slang. Worse still, Haiman, Marta, and the others made constant references to places, people, programs, agencies, and acronyms that I had never heard of, all of which made it impossible to do a decent job simultaneously interpreting their rapid back-and-forth exchanges. At one point I got stuck trying to make sense of a sentence about Misión Vuelvan Caras in Anzoátegui and its relationship to the CVG. I hadn't heard of any of them and became terribly confused. Michael took pity on me and interrupted my incoherent whispered interpretations to explain that Anzoátegui was in fact one of Venezuela's states, that Misión Vuelvan Caras was a new job training program that he was hoping the government could use to help build a social economy, and the CVG stood for Corporación Venezolana de Guayana, a state-owned holding company for heavy industry. As the meeting went on, Michael spent more and more of the time explaining things to me and gave up on being able to participate fully himself.

When proceedings came to a close I was convinced that Marta and Michael wouldn't ask me to interpret again. But, my poor job notwithstanding, Michael turned out to have been pleased to have a native English speaker as an interpreter—even if I had no background

---

*Haiman served for roughly a year as chief of staff before leaving the palace. Marta, Michael, and several other colleagues of theirs left the palace with Haiman and founded a policy think tank called the Centro Internacional Miranda. As of December 2008, Marta and Michael were both in senior positions at the CIM and Haiman had recently been named minister of planning.

in Venezuela—rather than the Venezuelans who didn't speak English particularly well that he was used to depending on. The way he saw it, with me, if nothing else, he could chat quietly and easily when the meetings dragged on.

After the morning stress, I had the afternoon free to try to do errands and get to know a bit of Caracas. One of the people who worked with Marta agreed to help me find someplace to live near the palace. A friend of his had just bought a small place at the entrance to a barrio called La Pastora, a ten-minute walk uphill from gate three. The new owner, Humberto Meza, was a radical journalist and an intellectual. He agreed to let me share his apartment rent-free if I helped out with food and furnishing the empty living room. For an unemployed budget traveler like me, the price and location were right and made me more than willing to tolerate the less than luxurious conditions: the apartment had running water only intermittently and a major roach problem. But over the year I lived with him, Humberto and I spent hundreds of hours talking, sharing ideas, and debating politics, an experience that more than compensated for the shortage of material comfort.

In addition to his political and intellectual tutorials, Humberto weaned me off my Chilean Spanish. *"Epale, ¿cómo está la vaina, chamo?"* he would ask in pure *venezolano*, Hey, what's up man? He also called women *princesa, amor, reina,* or *mami,* a term of affection that was normal in Venezuela but that would have gotten me smacked if I had used it to address a woman in Ecuador or Bolivia. Venezuelans were more sensual than people in other Andean countries, and pretty soon I got used to being called my king, my love, sweetheart, and even *papi,* at the strangest of times. When I asked him what barrio Venezuela's renowned ruling class lived in, he laughed, telling me that only poor people lived in the barrios. In Chilean Spanish, shanties were called poblaciones, and a barrio was just a neighborhood, but in Venezuela it was the other way around.

We lived in a Venezuelan barrio. La Pastora had more than its share of the homeless and drug addicts. On several occasions I saw snatch-and-grabs just down the street from my house. One unfortunate would-be thief, whom I recognized as one of the guys who hung out smoking rocks and sniffing glue in a nearby alley, got caught in the act of stealing a cell phone, a frequent street crime. The angry crowd that gathered beat him severely before the police, evincing no sense of urgency, showed up to arrest him.

This was but a small taste of Venezuela's major problems with insecurity, crime, and failed judicial and prison systems. Caracas is one of the most dangerous cities on earth. A 2005 UNESCO publication reported that in Venezuela a murder occurs every sixty-nine minutes, 9.6 rapes take place every day, and ten people are robbed every hour. No surprise, then, that I heard gunshots from my room most nights. In 2007 more than 13,000 people were killed across Venezuela, or 48 per 100,000 citizens, the second highest rate in the world.

Everyone in Caracas seemed to have a cell phone and Marta encouraged me to get one as well—I later realized it was so she could call me with assignments at all hours, rather than out of concern for my safety or social life—so I headed to Caracas's expansive Sambil mall. I wandered around the massive consumer mecca taking in the scene. It was packed with heavily made-up, silicone-pumped, aspiring Miss Universes and their coiffed, credit card–wielding male counterparts. The chains of Auntie Anne's pretzels, Timberland outdoor wear, McDonald's burgers, and Nike sports gear gave me no hint as to what country I was in. I had been to plenty of malls before so my first trip to Sambil seemed normal enough, though in Venezuela the vast majority of the population is too poor to afford even a simple meal in the mall's food court. If I had been more adept at reading Venezuela's revolutionary context, I might have seen that trip to the mall as political foreshadowing. Chávez's goal of creating a socialist country would inevitably have to confront a consumer culture deeply rooted throughout the political spectrum and across class lines.

As I lay in bed on my first night in my new apartment, I reflected on the job I had started after my whirlwind arrival in Venezuela and felt a tangible sense of excitement. I knew almost nothing about the Chávez government except that it purported to represent power to the people, wealth redistribution, and anti-imperialist global south regionalism, which all seemed like worthy goals to me. I had heard plenty of criticisms of export-oriented neoliberal economies before translating Michael's paper; rarely had they put forward alternative models on a national scale, and they had never, to my knowledge, been seriously debated within the inner circles of a head of state. Of course, breaking out of a deeply entrenched global system of power and policy hegemony wouldn't be easy, even if the alternative policies being put forward were excellent. But Venezuela seemed like the perfect country to try to imagine and implement an alternative system. The country's extensive oil resources—it is the fifth largest exporter globally—and its repeated democratic elections showing continued, widespread support for Chávez's self-proclaimed revolutionary government appeared to give him a solid base from which to experiment with radical policies.

It was hard for me to believe that after just three full days in the country I had already participated in a meeting in the heart of the presidential palace. As I replayed the day's events in my head, I remembered that Marta had introduced me to her friends as the son of "political prisoners in the United States." I wasn't entirely comfortable being introduced in this way; certainly it wouldn't have been one of the first things I told someone about myself. In hindsight, however, I realize that Marta's approach made sense given the context. Venezuelans generally believed, understandably given the evidence that subsequently emerged, that the Bush administration supported a short-lived coup against the Chávez government in 2002. United States–Venezuelan diplomatic relations were deteriorating and a gringo in the palace might be cause for suspicion. Marta herself was a foreigner, albeit one with Chávez's personal confidence, but for her to bring in non-Venezuelans required explanation.

In Chávez's Venezuela it couldn't be easy for *estadounidenses* to gain political access of the sort I had stumbled into. I had found one of few places on the planet where having parents in prison in the United States for politically motivated crimes actually opened doors rather than closed them. I was, in truth, accustomed to more than my share of luck on the road. In all my travels I had never been robbed or assaulted. No nation had ever denied me access at the border: a blue passport with an eagle on the cover could get me just about anywhere. On countless occasions and in countries throughout the region, my white skin and connections had opened doors to free places to sleep or eat, access to private clubs or parties, and generous or preferential treatment by local authorities and distinguished families. I hammed up my gringo accent when dealing with government officials or resolving bureaucratic errands and people invariably gave superior service to me rather than to locals, if for no other reason than to get me out of their hair. My accent and clothes could get me into nightclubs without waiting in line or paying a cover even when far better dressed nationals had long waits. But now, among Venezuela's new political elite, it was my family's radical background that substituted for the usual gringo wild card.

Marta seemed to have translations for me to do every day. Pretty soon I got into a rhythm of long hours spent in her office. I happily ate rushed lunches and dinners in a crowded palace dining hall that served fried sweet plantains with every meal. Rarely would I leave work before dinner. Marta was a demanding boss, but she didn't ask for more than she herself put in. Most of the people I met in the palace were overworked but Marta's drive was legendary, as was Chávez's work ethic. Marta had more than forty years on me so I figured I had no excuse for not being able to keep up with her.

One night I watched her take a call from Chávez himself asking her for a project to be completed for the next day. Marta's whole office went into overdrive. Around 2 A.M. the last of her assistants made his excuses and left Marta and me in the office alone. There wasn't much I could do to help with her urgent work at that point but I decided to stick it out. I would keep her company by picking up my work on a translation of a book of interviews Marta had conducted with Chávez.

The two of us sat in the nearly abandoned palace, typing away. As the hours ticked by, my pace decreased steadily and my eyes got heavier. While in the middle of translating Marta asking Chávez if his government would be able to avoid the fate that befell the Allende government in her native Chile in 1973, I almost fell asleep at my desk. I decided to take a break to walk a few laps around the courtyard outside the office.

The tiled floor reflected the security lights on the roof and a fountain sputtered under the open sky. The windows in the high doors on the offices surrounding the central courtyard were all dark. White pillars framed the passageway surrounding the garden and hallways led off in several directions. Down one corridor was the chief of staff's office; another led to Chávez's personal secretary. There were lone security guards at the entrances to the building and I could see an honor guard carrying a rifle and patrolling the roof above.

The palace felt ominous. Any old deserted building can seem eerie late at night, but my feelings of foreboding intensified as I looked up at the night sky and imagined fighter jets flying overhead. I was frightening myself unnecessarily, adding to the drama of the night, but it wasn't as far-fetched as it might seem. My mind ran over images of Allende's La Moneda palace being bombed.

I wondered about my role as an outsider, as a gringo, in Venezuela's revolutionary process. If my grandfather Leonard had been alive, his legal practice might well have counted the Chávez government among its distinguished and controversial clients. If the coup that briefly toppled Chávez in 2002 had occurred in the 1960s or 1970s, while my parents were young activists, they probably would have protested the State Department or a big oil company. But to my knowledge, none of my forebears had ever had this kind of a window into a radical government. It raised myriad fascinating questions for my understanding of politics in the United States as well. In Chávez's Venezuela, the country—from the poorest barrios to the highest positions in government—was actively discussing how to best put into practice policies that would be relegated to the realm of pure theory in the United States. In most countries, politics is about the art of finding compromises, about what's known to be possible. In Venezuela, I saw politics in action in a whole new way. As Marta put it, politics here was the art of making possible tomorrow what appears impossible today. Venezuela's voters had the audacity to hope for a better system, to imagine that radical alternatives to the Washington Consensus could improve their country. Thinking about it as I strolled around the palace fountain, I understood why I was here: to play my small part in defending a democratic alternative, and to learn along the way.

Working with Marta and Michael did provide constant learning opportunities, from mastering Marta's efficient electronic file management system to watching, from close quarters, the way the government responded to breaking events. At first unsure of my own political take on what was happening, I found inspiration in the commitment and the values of the people around me. And so I stayed. I had planned to visit Venezuela for only a couple of weeks on my backpacking route, but those weeks stretched.

From my computer in Marta's office I took to signing my e-mails to friends and family "in the belly of the revolution." Auntie Helen from Chile, who never forgot a birthday and wrote regularly to check up on me, asked why I was working for someone as radical as Chávez and if I preferred Venezuela to her own dear country. Later, she e-mailed me to announce triumphantly the election of Chile's first-ever woman president, Michelle Bachelet, and proudly reported that exactly half of her cabinet positions had been assigned to women. But when Chávez announced his support for Bolivia's claim to territory lost to Chile in the 1879–1883 War of the Pacific, Auntie Helen, ever the patriot, complained that Chávez talked too much. She was probably right: at the time, according to the Ministry of Information, the president was averaging about forty hours of public speaking per week, including lengthy question-and-answer sessions. His weekly television and radio show called *Aló Presidente* would often run five hours or more. Then there were the daily appearances at inaugurations, press conferences, or whichever locations happened to be in the eye of the media storm at the moment.

A month after my arrival in Venezuela, Caracas hosted an international conference called Artists and Intellectuals in Defense of

Humanity. Nobel laureates, activists, painters, writers, dancers, and organizers from across the globe were invited to participate. Among them was my mom, Bernardine. My time in Venezuela had built my confidence as a translator and I was hired as one of the dozens of interpreters at the conference. It was good to have a break from the office routine and a paid job for a change. And I got to hang out with Mom when my working group wasn't in session.

It was at one of the plenary events for the conference that I first saw Chávez speak. The Teresa Carreño Theater in central Caracas was packed with thousands of red-shirt-wearing chavistas—red being the color of Chávez's political party—by the time my mom and I made it through the security lines into the massive auditorium. The center section had been reserved for participants in the conference and the rest of the seats allocated to various community groups and representatives of social movements from around the country. There were overflow rooms with closed circuit screens for people who didn't fit in the main space. The stage had a podium with an elaborate bouquet of tropical flowers, and a set for the musical act that would follow Chávez's speech. He was expected at 7 P.M. but at eight we were still sitting listening to the buzz of the crowd.

A group of young people behind us from the Francisco de Miranda Popular Front, a chavista youth brigade, began chanting *"Alerta! Alerta! Alerta que camina la espada de Bolívar por America Latina!"* (Be alert, Bolívar's sword is marching through Latin America!) Pretty soon the whole crowd was chanting. Finally the Argentine Nobel Peace Prize recipient from 1980, Adolfo Pérez Esquivel, appeared on the platform to introduce Chávez. He spoke without notes and with slow, carefully enunciated words. "The situation in Venezuela shows that popular mobilization is capable of taking and maintaining power for the people and promoting and defending great transformations in their interests. In this hour of particular danger, we renew our conviction that another world is not only possible but also necessary. We commit to struggle for that other world with more solidarity, unity, and determination; in defense of humanity we reaffirm our certainty that the people will have the last word."

By the time Chávez walked into the theater—from the back entrance that we had used—the roar from the crowd was continuous. We might have been in a soccer stadium or a rock concert. Everyone was on their feet chanting and clapping. Chávez slowly made his way through the crowd, stopping to give a kiss here, having a brief exchange of words there, receiving the occasional handwritten note from a supporter, and embracing a minister or ambassador nearer to the stage. After about twenty minutes he finally made it to the front of the auditorium and took his place behind the podium.

He thanked Pérez Esquivel for his introduction and then mentioned a few prominent visitors he knew were in the crowd: Daniel Ortega (soon to be reelected president of Nicaragua), Ricardo Alarcón (the president of the Cuban National Assembly), various ministers from his own cabinet, Tariq Ali (the Pakistani writer and intellectual), Ignacio Ramonet (the Spanish editor of *Le Monde diplomatique*), Danny Glover (the Hollywood star), Cynthia McKinney (then congresswoman from Georgia), representatives of the national labor union (UNT), the national indigenous federation of Venezuela, and the Bolivarian farmers. On several occasions after he had started on the body of his speech, someone from the audience would yell out another name or a country and he would digress back into acknowledging those who were present.

Chávez began by talking about the significance of the conference, the need to build networks of intellectuals and artists fighting for humanity. He criticized the intellectuals who had announced "the end of history" and the triumph of neoliberalism. He called for the downfall of the Washington Consensus. The crowd interrupted him regularly to chant *"Uh ah, Chávez no se va!"* (Uh ah, Chávez isn't going anywhere!) He would wait for the din to subside, often for several minutes, and then continue: "What has always happened in Latin America and the Caribbean when a people goes out and reclaims the flags of their [liberation] struggles? . . . The military comes and puts down the popular uprising, the popular hope with lead, fire, and bullets." He explained how that is what happened in 1989 in Caracas when the people rose up in protest against a neoliberal structural adjustment package, how that massacre ultimately led to his emergence on the national political scene.

His speaking style was erratic—wandering, switching topics, going off on tangents—yet captivating. He didn't use notes or a teleprompter and relied on sheer charisma to carry the crowd with him on a journey that stretched around the planet (he had just arrived home after a six-country tour), across history (he recounted independence struggles in Venezuela and Haiti), and through political theory (he cited Martí and Trotsky). At one point he shared an anecdote about his daughter María. They were driving through Caracas together and as their motorcade passed under a bridge she saw homeless people camped there and drew his attention to them. "I saw people passing by the homeless as though it was normal, walking by, driving by, each with their own rush, me with mine, you with yours, and we believe we don't even see them. María saw them and told me: 'Papá look at them!' Now, this is a problem we all face." Someone in the audience yelled: "It's the mayor's problem." The mayor of Caracas was not particularly popular at the time but Chávez responded to the interruption saying, "It's not only the mayor's problem, it's yours too, and mine and all of ours."

Since that night in the theater I've watched Luiz Inácio Lula da Silva, the president of Brazil, speak. I've heard how Evo Morales, the president of Bolivia, talks to a crowd; and Rafael Correa, the president of Ecuador. Being at such events always has a profound effect on me. Words on a page cannot capture the contagious energy they inspire. Those in attendance bear the hours of waiting admirably, celebrating their optimism, their newfound connection to state power. For an outsider, it takes strong nerves to stand in the midst of such crowds and endure the ecstatic screaming that greets their leaders' arrivals. But it's only by doing so that one can fully appreciate the political shift the region has lived through since I first traveled to Guatemala in 1999. It is true, perhaps, that Latin America has been home to more than its share of *caudillos*, or strongmen leaders, but when else in the region's history have so many democratically elected, progressive, charismatic leaders been in power at the same time?

ᴄᴕᴄᴕ

Four months after I began working in Miraflores, I switched to a new office, that of Presidential International Relations. The routine of long hours at the computer stayed the same, but my daily responsibilities changed. I was now charged with following media reports on United States–Venezuela relations and Venezuela's role in the international arena generally. This work was closer to my own interests and, I figured, might help get me into a master's program in public policy in Latin America the following year. My new colleagues were closer to my age and, for the most part, welcoming, though I did have to put up with daily banter about my being a CIA agent—payback for the gringo wild card I'd benefited from so often. The people who ran the office approached their assignments with the same tireless passion that Marta did, but over time I came to realize the deep political commitment and long hours of my colleagues in Miraflores were by no means universal among government employees: I happened to have fallen into a group that worked exceptionally hard. Plenty of other people were in the government because it was simply a way to pay the bills or obtain privileges—the government is one of the largest employers in Venezuela and under Chávez its role has increased. New ministries have been founded almost every year while the expansion of social services has brought hundreds of thousands onto the state payroll.

When Marta or Michael wanted me, I took time off from my new office to work with them. Marta coordinated the organization of the Third Annual International Conference in Solidarity with the Bolivarian Revolution. There were topic-specific meetings across the country and participants from around the planet. I traveled out of Caracas with Michael to join the subgroup on labor in the revolution, worker co-management, and the alternative economic model. I was in the interpretation booth for a tense but necessary debate between a new national labor organization and the minister of labor over how to define the role of workers in the rapidly expanding state-run sectors of the economy. What would be the balance of power between the state and labor? Would the government move to establish state-dominated capitalism or to empower workers to control the means of production themselves?

A few months later we traveled to a university town so Michael could speak at a student conference on twenty-first-century socialism. Chávez had been calling for a new socialist model but no one in the government had explained concretely what exactly this new economic system would look like. Michael's speech argued for a humanist vision of socialism, emphasizing the need for a clear sense of what the final goal was before embarking on a new policy experiment. He suggested avoiding a one-size-fits-all policy approach, insisting instead that Venezuela's masses play a leading role in constructing their own brand of socialism. He said socialism can "never be delivered to people from above," and warned against repeating the mistakes of the socialist experiments of the twentieth century. The students inundated him, and me as his interpreter, with questions and requests for further information.*

Trips out of Caracas to conferences, to barrios and community gatherings, were among the highlights of my months in Venezuela, but most of the time I was in the office where, after a while, the long hours and tedium of staring at a computer began to catch up with me. After months living in Venezuela, I felt that I still didn't have enough of a sense of the political process on the ground, of how average Venezuelans understood the changes in their country. In May 2005, my parents, Bill and Bernardine, were invited down to Venezuela and I got a chance to hit the streets.

Bill and Bernardine gave talks to audiences of as many as two hundred people in Caracas and the interior at universities and cultural centers. The groups they spoke to were primed with screenings of the Academy Award–nominated documentary *The Weather Underground*. I interpreted for them throughout the trip, including their public appearances. I had heard them both speak many times before

*The paper he presented was titled "Socialism Does Not Drop from the Sky," and since then tens of thousands of copies have been circulated in Venezuela. Chávez has spoken about it several times on television and recommended that it be widely read.

and had even interpreted for them in Spanish and Portuguese on various occasions, so I knew what to expect of their practical idealism in discussing the opportunities a society offers its children. Their talks included anecdotes about successful community-based struggles for equal education and justice in poor Chicago neighborhoods. The lessons they had learned from 1960s-era freedom schools and protest movements were employed to inform today's struggles, a focus on the present and the future rather than starry-eyed reminiscing about the past. Bill was fond of employing literary allusions in his speeches, wonderful images that were, however, a living nightmare for his interpreter. Try rendering into Spanish without a moment's preparation "Each of us is an entire universe, the one and only who will ever tread this earth, a work-in-progress and an unruly spark of meaning-making energy on a voyage toward infinity" and you'll get the measure of what I was up against. Worse still, he would often surprise me with a quote from Neruda or Márquez in English and leave me to try to simultaneously translate the lyrical language back into its original Spanish.

Regardless of the venue and the focus of the talk, Bernardine and Bill made explicit that they had not come to Venezuela with answers: they knew little about the country and were there to learn from the process, the politics, and especially the people. The response was overwhelming. I spent exhausting hours interpreting questions and answers, and trying to help both of them simultaneously when lines of people rushed the dais after events to shake hands and continue the discussion. We were astonished at the enthusiasm of the crowds' reactions, especially in the interior. The documentary screening certainly played a role: seeing a person on a big screen and then having them appear in the flesh was clearly a thrill for many. But the way the audiences approached my parents, and asked questions about the United States government and its people, indicated that Venezuelans still felt a deep bond to our country politically and culturally, despite the tensions between our governments. An old, wrinkled woman in the Andean state of Táchira wanted to know how people in *Los Estados Unidos* see Venezuela today. A bespectacled teacher from the plains state of Barinas asked if we might be able to establish an exchange program with her school. The Afro-Venezuelan director of education at a juvenile detention center in Caracas hoped we would send native English speakers to teach language classes to his detainees.

People with a highly developed political analysis saw, in the film and in our presence, hopeful examples of internal resistance to *imperialismo norteamericano*. Others simply seemed happy to have people from *El Norte* in their midst affirming their attempts to build a new, different society. I interpreted a question from an old man with a long beard about racism and repression of radical movements within *el imperio*. A young community organizer named Ricardo, with acne scars and skin that revealed his mixed indigenous-African background, wanted to know what we thought of the new social programs known as *misiones*, or missions. We pleaded ignorance and Ricardo invited us to his neighborhood in a rough Caracas barrio known as La Vega to see for ourselves.

On a hot, sunny day in May 2005, Ricardo took Bernardine, Bill, and me on a tour of his barrio. He had a speech impediment that made his barrio slang that much harder to follow. When I set out to learn Spanish I knew I would have to contend with slang and variations from one country to the next, but I had not factored in speech irregularities like Ricardo's and I struggled to keep up with his rapid-fire commentary as we walked through his neighborhood. Tiny flimsy houses made of cardboard and scrap metal tottered up the face of the steep hills. Sewage ran openly through the unpaved streets, festering in the heat of the sun. Chávez, a champion of the poor, had been in office for six years but even basic infrastructure like sanitary drainage was missing in this massive Caracas barrio with nearly a million residents. And yet, wandering around that day, the vast majority of people we met professed deep affection for their president.

Much of the social spending under the Chávez government is being channeled to the country's poorest communities through missions set up to parallel ineffective and often exclusionary government agencies. They provide services such as education, health care, soup kitchens, subsidized grocery stores, indigenous rights advocacy, job training, and homeless shelters. Like everything in Venezuela, the missions are funded by oil sales: tens of billions of dollars have been spent on basic social services. By the time Ricardo invited us to La Vega, seven months into my time in Venezuela, I knew a lot about the missions but hadn't yet seen them in action.

We first visited high school equivalency program Misión Ribas, hosted in an extra room of one of the sturdier houses in the community. The class of fifteen people included young mothers who had been forced to drop out of high school due to unplanned pregnancies, elderly grandparents who, as youngsters, had joined the ranks of child laborers and had never been able to take time off to go back to school, and, it seemed, everyone in between. We observed as the class watched a lesson on videotape. As an educator, Bill was unimpressed by the methodology and the curriculum but applauded the outreach and the goal of inclusion.

Venezuela's minister of education would later explain to us that the government promised to do away with the elitist, exclusionary education policies of the past and to make public education free and universally available. But there were far more classrooms filled with prospective students than teachers to run them. So they compromised quality for quantity and developed a video curriculum that could be implemented with the aid of a volunteer facilitator who needn't be a trained teacher. The new educational missions did not replace the pre-Chávez public and private school systems, which continued functioning as they always had. Rather they were an addition to the education system, designed to meet enormous previously unmet demand. Since their inception, more than three million Venezuelans have enrolled in educational missions that provide teaching at a variety of levels: basic adult literacy, primary school, high school equivalency, and university.

Ricardo knocked on the door of another small house and led us into a living room converted into a medical clinic. A screen divided the room with a few chairs set up on one side as a waiting area. On the other side was an examination table and a wall of medicine cabinets. The small clinic had six people waiting—a young mother with two kids, an old man, and a couple in their twenties or thirties. It was staffed by a bald Cuban doctor wearing a white gown with a stethoscope around his neck. One of the kids had a hacking cough, and the doctor took him behind the screen to conduct a preliminary examination for respiratory illness. Though the community clinic didn't have the ability to take X-rays or develop lab samples, the doctor could order these services. Misión Barrio Adentro, as the health care mission the Chávez administration launched was called, brought over twenty thousand Cuban medical practitioners to Venezuela to provide free service to impoverished communities near their homes. The doctors came as part of a broader bilateral treaty agreement that provided Cuba with discounted oil and Venezuela with medical professionals, sports trainers, teachers, and advisers. The health care program became one of the most popular social initiatives of the Chávez administration. By providing doctors who themselves lived in poor communities, it eliminated the need for the people to travel long distances to overcrowded centralized hospitals. Despite legitimate concerns about the quality of the services provided, the program's popularity speaks for itself: in 2004 Barrio Adentro logged more visits than the entire public and private health care systems combined over the previous five years. As a model for national primary health care it has myriad advantages over the one we depend on in the United States, both in terms of cost-effectiveness and access.

Free health care is a revolutionary, and yet remarkably simple, humanist concept. The health care system in the United States saves money in the short term by reducing demand through making a visit to the doctor expensive. I saw the results of this approach to medicine when I volunteered as a Spanish language interpreter at a Connecticut hospital during my college years: poor people flooded the emergency room with problems that could have been easily treated at an earlier stage but were exacerbated by lack of preventive or early primary attention. Misión Barrio Adentro, in contrast, provides preventive medicine that can deal with illness before it becomes life-threatening or costly to treat. More significantly Venezuela's new approach to health care focuses on the imperative of providing all people with free and easy access to medical practitioners and medicine. The approach in the United States favors corporate profits, legal liability, and first-class health services for a tiny minority of the rich and well insured.

Bernardine, Bill, and I left our first visit to Ricardo's barrio filled with a sense of awe. The programs we had seen demonstrated that an alternative model for caring for people was not only possible but also was being actively constructed. Not only were the missions evidently wildly popular among Venezuela's poor majority, but they also significantly increased quality of life in ways that wouldn't register in statistics showing how many dollars per day the poor lived on: these services were free. Whereas most poverty and quality of life statistics are based on purchasing power and income, here were state services that created a significant social safety net without having any impact on the official numbers published by organizations like the World Bank. Though many people we met had complaints about the sewage, unpaved roads, water shortages, corruption, and bureaucracy, they vociferously insisted that Chávez cared about their community and that his government's programs had empowered them. In hindsight, it's clear that the missions were also a potent organizing tool for community activists like Ricardo, and a huge vote winner for Chávez himself. Ricardo's support for the missions notwithstanding, he was quick to define himself as a revolutionary but not a chavista. "As long as Chávez is working for the people, we will support Chávez," Ricardo said as he walked us to a bus stop on our way out of La Vega. "But if he and his policies begin to ignore us, we will take his power away just as we gave it to him: organizing protests and voting in elections."

Their visit at an end, my parents went home to Chicago while I returned to my daily grind at the office newly inspired and energized. Although interpreting for them had been exhausting, it was reassuring to have them witness Venezuela's revolution in action. The missions and the people in the barrio had likewise strengthened my resolve to stay connected to Venezuela, to find ways to learn from the process that had brought such groundbreaking social programs to an entire country. In the barrios I found the inspiration that I had first experienced when I'd started work in the palace.

Over the ensuing months Ricardo became a trusted friend. I often relied on him to gauge the rapidly changing political climate. I visited La Vega again and went to many other barrios around Caracas as well. Caracas's dozens of unplanned barrios are home to a massive, unsurveyed population and are the source of much of the city's crime as well as its political firmament. I found these visits the best antidote to any tendency to cynicism that young people are often prone to, especially when surrounded by corruption, bureaucracy, and a consumer culture that belies the high-minded socialist rhetoric.

I had arrived in Venezuela as a backpacker, an outside observer, a position and perspective I was accustomed to. But a combination of lucky timing, contacts, and a desire to learn had landed me in a hands-on role. I had found hope in the possibility of an alternative political system, one whose successes and failures seemed to me to provide valuable examples for the rest of the globe. In September 2005 I returned to England and wrote a thesis on Chávez's use of oil in international relations for a master's in public policy. I wasn't surprised to find that the Latin American Centre and international relations community at my university were disapproving of the Bolivarian Revolution, but the intensity of their opposition troubled me. More often than I liked, I found myself speaking as an advocate for the Chávez government. I had plenty of criticisms myself, but the discussions I participated in at my graduate school always seemed to start with the assumption that the revolution would and should fail. I preferred to be critical of the Chávez government in a framework that tried to extract lessons from its accomplishments and shortcomings but recognized what I saw as evident progress based on firsthand experience. I tried to insist on recognizing Venezuela's right to set its own course democratically and peacefully, to make its own mistakes, to invent its own model.

Nonetheless, distance from Venezuela and immersion in an intellectually rigorous and overtly hostile environment made an impact: I felt myself moving away from the role I had taken in my first months in Venezuela. I no longer felt comfortable playing the partisan; the idea of working for the government in any capacity had lost its appeal. Maybe I was getting more conservative with age or maybe the independence of an academic or journalistic framework was simply a more natural fit for me. In September 2006, when I returned to Caracas, it was with the plan to spend more time in the barrios, to have room to be a constructive but also critical voice.

I worked as a freelance journalist, an interpreter, and a think tank researcher with ties to the Ministry of Higher Education. I also started taking jobs as a fixer with foreign journalists visiting Caracas who needed someone on the ground with connections, language skills, and a sense of how to get things done. The job was exciting and it paid well. Most of all, I enjoyed it because it allowed me to play a role, however limited, in shaping the way people outside the country understood Venezuelan politics. It was in this capacity that I would witness firsthand Venezuela's democratic practice in action during the December 2006 presidential election.

Ten Fingers for Chávez

L oud fireworks woke much of Caracas, me included, at 2:30 on the morning of the presidential election, December 3, 2006. The stakes that day were high: the Venezuelan constitution specified that the maximum any president could serve was two six-year terms. Victory would mean Chávez serving a second time. But during his campaign he promised to do away with presidential term limits altogether, allowing for the possibility of him serving in the office for life. This was undoubtedly one of the factors that led the political opposition to participate in the election unlike previous ballots, which had been boycotted. They had even managed, in an uncharacteristic display of unity for Chávez's opponents, to come together behind one candidate, Governor Manuel Rosales. Rosales, like all the heavyweights in the opposition, had supported the short-lived coup against Chávez in 2002.

Going into the election, Chávez had all the benefits of an incumbent riding high on the wave of spending that an oil boom allows. He sought to solidify his democratic credentials with a huge margin of victory—his main campaign symbol emblazoned on T-shirts and posters everywhere featured two hands with the fingers spread wide to represent the ten million votes Chávez hoped to win out of sixteen million registered voters. It was a nearly impossible goal requiring upward of 80 percent of the actual vote.

Rosales, on the other hand, enjoyed nearly unconditional support from the private media and the best international campaign advisers. His response to Chávez's *diez millones* was a campaign slogan presenting himself as the leader of all 26 million Venezuelans, not just one polarized group of them. This claim was undermined when Rosales, in an unguarded moment on live television, described those supporting Chávez as "parasites." Though no serious poll ever put support for Rosales above 40 percent, his most ardent supporters, cut off from the mass of poor people behind the high walls protecting their villas and high rises, were convinced he could win.

I lay in bed for a few minutes listening to the fireworks and reflecting on the two polar-opposite images of Hugo Chávez that existed both inside Venezuela and in international public opinion. One, known to the Venezuelan opposition, global corporate media and its followers, presented *El Comandante* as a power-hungry, authoritarian army officer who used populist rhetoric and high oil revenues to buy cultish loyalty from the uneducated masses but had failed to build a diversified Venezuelan economy even as he gave petrodollars away to allies like Cuba's Fidel Castro and Bolivia's Evo Morales. The other view, held by the majority of Venezuelans and the international left, regarded Hugo as a man of the people, someone who had grown up poor, who directed oil profits into extensive social programs, redistributed wealth, empowered local communities, and challenged the role of the United States. I had come to believe that both of these perspectives held some truth, though I was more sympathetic to the latter.

The cacophony of the fireworks was joined by the loud chanting of political slogans. I got up and looked out my window where I expected to see hundreds of people gathered. Instead, I gazed down upon the same empty strip of pavement that separated my decrepit concrete apartment complex from a series of identical ones on either side. In the gap between two of the prisonlike towers that dominated the view from my window I could see the lights—mostly powered with pirated electricity—coming on in the closely packed brick and zinc shanty homes that crept like snakes up the spine of the hill. The small but violent barrio San Agustín, like most barrios in Venezuela, is a stronghold for chavistas.

✧✧✧✧

I had planned on getting out of the house by 3 A.M. anyway. I was working that day as a guide and an interpreter for a team of documentary filmmakers from the United States and had to make sure they got to see as much of the action as possible. Working with the film crew meant I had a car at my disposal to go wherever the action was, a must on election day.

Jhonny, our six-foot-four, three-hundred-pound driver, had a shiny bald head and a thick bushy mustache. He drove a comfortable Blazer with tinted windows and ample storage for tripods, lights, and sound equipment. He picked me up and we drove across town to the hotel where the film crew was staying. Jhonny was being paid in cash, which suited the filmmakers, who had obtained their local bolivars on the dollar black market. The Chávez administration had put currency control in place to prevent a run on the currency that would lead to hyperinflation and economic instability. The policy succeeded in stemming the outflow of money but it also made it difficult for average Venezuelans to obtain dollars for travel abroad, international purchases, or as a hedge against their own inflation-prone currency. As a result a currency black market flourished with financial firms engaged in the highly profitable business of helping Venezuelans get their money out of the country through legal debt swaps. Customers paid in bolivars to buy a Venezuelan security that traded on a foreign exchange, then sold that security, taking payment in dollars and depositing the money in offshore accounts or buying back their bolivars on the black market for a huge profit. The financial companies also ran parallel black market exchanges. The official, government-controlled exchange rate was 2,150 bolivars to the U.S. dollar. The week before coming down to film, the crew I was working with had wired their money to an offshore bank, and received an exchange rate of 4,000 bolivars per dollar. In this way they got half price on everything they paid for in cash.

Although the black market was rarely prosecuted, I had ethical qualms about using it and anyway earned enough money in bolivars to cover most of my local costs. But I couldn't blame the film crew for choosing not to take a 50 percent hit on currency transactions, especially at a time when Venezuelans were buying computers, televisions, and any other expensive luxury items that would hold or even increase their value because they had to be imported with dollars. Cars, for example, were sold months in advance of their arrival in the country and could be immediately resold for a profit to people who didn't want to wait out the backlog at dealerships. Demand for new cars was up 70 percent year on year in part because the country was flooded with petro-wealth, but also because Venezuelans who worried about holding bolivars preferred to invest—even take out loans for—big-ticket items that would hold their value.

Black market money would prove to be the least of the ethical issues I confronted while employed by foreign media in Venezuela. One team of journalists I worked with interviewed a radical right-wing Venezuelan who had, long before the Chávez era, been president of the national oil company, PDVSA. The information he presented as fact—for example that only about 5 percent of Venezuelans lived in poverty—was so blatantly false that when we walked out of his luxurious office suite at the end of the interview, the producer of the film crew said, "We can't run a word of that. To be ethical and honest we'd have to explain that he's totally loony and if we do that we discredit everything he says so there's no point in including him at all." Yet, when the final report came out, sure enough a clip from the interview was included, containing information that was biased, subjective, and unsubstantiated about President Chávez's intentions to stay in office for life.

Another reporter said to me, "I know this is a crappy piece of reporting, but we've got a plane to catch and the bright side is we've only been in Caracas for five days and managed to file three stories." Working with such reporters made it easy to appreciate why the image of Venezuela that gets transmitted to the outside world is far removed from the reality on the ground. I did my best to improve the quality and focus of reports I worked on, but it was difficult persuading the journalists I worked with to change their initial assumptions and preplanned story lines, written before they even landed in Caracas.

By 4 A.M. Jhonny had dropped me and the film crew in the heart of a large Caracas barrio called El Valle. Pedro, my local contact who was arranging safe passage in an otherwise dangerous neighborhood, had insisted that we show up "the earlier the better" to see the election. He suggested 3 A.M. Since Venezuela is notoriously behind schedule, I took this advice with a pinch of salt. But, sure enough, by the time we arrived, a line of over a hundred people was already waiting in the dark to be among the first to cast their ballots. Venezuelans are accustomed to long waits and usually figure out how to make the most of the time by eating, listening to music, dancing, and flirting.

Since Chávez's political base is the poor, I wasn't surprised to see more than a few people on the main avenue running up into El Valle wearing red shirts (this despite the fact that the National Electoral Council had officially banned wearing political propaganda to the polls). Pedro was waiting to meet us. After showing us around and introducing us to his friends, he had to help set up one of the local polling stations, and so assigned a couple of his *panas* (friends) to keep us out of trouble. Our cameraman was stumbling around in the dark and peering through his lenses while I struggled to interpret for all three members of the film crew at once.

In addition to the lines, there were groups of motorcyclists racing around, lighting rockets and noise bombs—poor people's fireworks— to get stragglers out of bed and mobilized. One motorcycle driver was dressed up in a perfect Che Guevara outfit—wild hair, beret, cigar, and fatigues—and had a radio on his bike blasting "Viva Che!" a famous Cuban song in homage to the revolutionary. Caravans of motorcycles and cars packed with red-flag-waving barrio dwellers passed with horns blaring and a range of rhythmic chants emanating: *"Se queda, se queda, el Comandante se queda"* (He's staying, he's staying, the Commander is staying); *"Son diez, son diez, son diez millones, son diez"* (There are ten, there are ten, there are ten million [votes for Chávez], there are ten); *"No volverán"* ([the oligarchy] will not return); *"Uh ah, Chávez no se va"* (Uh ah, Chávez isn't going anywhere).

Around six, the sun rose over the steep hills of the barrio and street vendors with portable kitchenettes began selling pumpkin and beef stew, coffee, and *arepas*—a Venezuelan staple made from cornmeal hand-molded into a small, thick pancake and then pan-fried and finally cut open and stuffed with anything in the kitchen. Pedro invited us to observe the neighborhood polling station where he was working. State-of-the-art electronic machines were set up in a kindergarten classroom. Pedro and the other local employees of the Electoral Council plugged in the machines, hung curtains, brought in cardboard screens, and sealed ballot boxes while members of the National Guard ensured security at the door. Observers from different political parties were on hand to report any irregularities. International media—like my crew of filmmakers—and the numerous delegations of international observers from around the world, including the Organization of American States and the European Union, had unrestricted access to observe firsthand at polling stations across the country. Everyone, it seemed, wanted this election to be fair, and so all possible safeguards against voter fraud were put in place.

By 7 A.M., *tambores* (drum circles) were beating out Afro-Venezuelan Caribbean rhythms, while trumpets blared reveille. The line for the biggest polling station in the neighborhood, where about six thousand people were expected to vote, was six blocks long and three people deep. The lines continued to grow even after the polling stations were open. We circulated freely in and out of various polling centers in the barrio. The relative efficiency of the process surprised me, given Venezuela's usual penchant for making everything take twice as long as necessary and leaving to tomorrow what could easily be done today.

Once in the polling station, voter IDs were checked off the electoral list. They were fingerprinted electronically and cross-checked against a national database to make sure no one voted more than once. They then got in a new line and were shown, one by one, what the ballot looked like and what to do when they got to the machines. Next, they went into a booth where they made their selection on a touch screen that showed not just names and party affiliations of the candidates but also a high-resolution picture. After voting, the machine printed a paper ballot confirming the name and party chosen, which was deposited in a sealed box. Since this was a newly developed system, fully 55 percent of the polling stations were expected to do manual counts of the paper ballots to verify the electronic results. The voter then signed and fingerprinted the registration list. Finally, as an additional safeguard to make sure no one voted twice, the tip of their pinky finger was stained purple with semipermanent ink.

After checking out several polling stations in the neighborhood we hiked up the hill into the barrio to get a shot of the city in the morning sun. We climbed steeply for ten minutes before our local security escorts told us they couldn't guarantee our safety if we went any farther. While the cameraman scanned the horizon, I took in a vista of two different worlds in the middle of the same city. To the east I could see mostly empty villa neighborhoods, with high gates and walls drowned in flowers. I looked out onto sprawling residential luxuries including private pools, thousands of square feet per person, and spacious garages for BMWs and Mercedeses. But not more than a couple blocks away from the edge of the rich enclaves began a sprawling barrio where hundreds of thousands of people lived on top of one another in shacks and shanties built on hilly, unstable land. Sewage ran openly in the streets, garbage piled high, and many homes were only accessible via steep, narrow dirt trails far removed from the nearest paved road. The two worlds I looked out on were only blocks apart but few people could cross the boundaries separating them.

Around 10 A.M., Jhonny's Blazer drove us through Caracas's eerily abandoned streets to another notorious barrio: 23 de Enero (January 23). This was built in the late 1950s on the orders of then dictator General Marcos Pérez Jiménez, who was as committed to major public works projects as he was to lining his own pockets. He so successfully pandered to oil interests that President Dwight Eisenhower awarded him the Legion of Honor even as he was violently squashing all political opposition in Venezuela. The barrio includes nearly a hundred housing blocks, the largest of which were built to hold 450 families. A network of parks separates the blocks and once provided recreational space for their inhabitants.

Early in 1958, before the middle-class housing could be sold off, the general lost his grip on power amid a riotous uprising in the streets. Pérez Jiménez boarded his private jet, *The Sacred Cow*, his bags stuffed with money, and headed to safe haven in the United States, with a visit en route to his friend Rafael Trujillo, dictator of the Dominican Republic. Along with his position as head of state, Pérez Jiménez abandoned the newly constructed sprawling housing complex to the poor and homeless who had helped drive him out. The squatters that occupied the more than nine thousand apartments and built shanties in the network of parks named their barrio after the day the dictatorship fell.

Today 23 de Enero has a strong political identity. It is to the Venezuelan left what Wrigley Field is to Cubs fans. While violent gangs and traffickers control some of the *superbloques*, others are organized politically. Radical political groups like the Tupamaros have a strong presence and provide security and stability to parts of the complex. The barrio has been a testing ground for many of the Chávez government's social policies, including the *misiones*, and much local power has been transferred to the *consejos comunales* (community councils). 23 de Enero is just blocks from the presidential palace and, back in 2002, during the short-lived coup that temporarily removed President Chávez from power, hundreds of thousands of people from the barrio and others nearby poured down from the hill to surround the palace and demand the return of their president.

Perhaps in gratitude for the loyal support of the barrio, or to create a good photo op for the press, it had been decided that President Chávez would cast his vote at a polling station in a school in 23 de Enero. We went there to film the occasion. As we got closer to the school where the polling station was located, the security was increasingly intense. We were forced to leave Jhonny and our vehicle outside a cordon of soldiers, the first of several, and proceed on foot through the barrio. I figured we would be busy for a few hours and told Jhonny to take the opportunity to go vote himself since he wasn't likely to get another long break. When we eventually arrived at the polling station we found the place mobbed with reporters from dozens of countries. A few photojournalists with more chutzpah than clout had climbed on top of bus stops and kiosks outside the innermost security cordon to get an angle for their photos. Off to the side was a long line of voters who, because of security, wouldn't be able to vote until after Chávez had come and gone.

I had used my contacts to get the film crew on the all access list for the event and had been told to get there by 7 A.M. But I had learned the hard way not to take scheduled times too seriously in Venezuela and I knew Chávez wasn't even due to arrive until 10:30 A.M. So I was not concerned that the crowds in El Valle had delayed our arrival until ten. Imagine my mortification then, when a member of presidential security told me they had already sealed off the school and we would have to stay outside the cordon with the press on top of the bus stops. I could barely bring myself to translate the news for my crew. They were anxious for their own footage of Chávez and I was sure they would be upset with me for losing track of time in El Valle. I realized it would take more than the usual gringo wild card to get me out of this one. After all, there were dozens of foreign correspondents in the same predicament as we were. Luckily I had what Venezuelan's call a *chapa*, a sort of Get Out of Jail Free Card, an ID or document that opens doors and solves problems. This took the form of a signed and sealed letter from the office of Presidential International Relations explaining the political significance of the film we were making. It worked its magic and in a matter of moments we were through the last round of security.

An hour and a half after he was scheduled to arrive, Chávez drove up in a bright red Volkswagen Beetle. He was wearing a matching red shirt. Supporters mobbed him as he exited the car and walked, hand in hand with his daughter, toward the school where he was to vote. I watched from about fifteen feet away as he went through the same voting process we had witnessed over and over again in El Valle, ink stain on the little finger and all. Photographers crammed into every inch of the classroom where he voted—fifth graders wouldn't have tolerated all the pushing and shoving I thought. After emerging, he gave what was, for him, the shortest of press conferences, answering just three questions in half an hour. He then headed off to the palace to wait for the results to come in. He looked exhausted.

I was tired and hungry too, and so I walked the film crew down through the barrio to find a place for lunch. Most everything was closed for the election, and as we got farther and farther away from the presidential security I realized I didn't know my way around—or out of—the sprawling barrio. We didn't have anyone from 23 de Enero guaranteeing our safe passage but we did have a high definition camera worth more than most families in the area earned in a year. Jhonny was nowhere to be seen. When I called him he explained he was stuck in an interminable polling line in Petare, a barrio on the other side of the city. I told him to go ahead and vote, and catch up with us after we'd eaten. Eventually we found an open restaurant. The crew opted for seafood paella while I ordered arroz con pollo and sweet fried plantains on the side. When I asked the waiter for a beer—Venezuelans regularly drink with lunch even on workdays, something one would rarely see in Chile for example—he apologized, telling me there was a dry law in place prohibiting the sale of alcohol on election day. I made do with fresh coconut water.

Jhonny arrived as we were finishing lunch and we raced across town again to a different barrio: La Vega. La Vega is much larger than El Valle, the hills steeper and more sprawling. It extends on all sides up to green, undeveloped hilltops. Periodic mudslides during the rainy season destroy shanties and often kill the families that inhabit them. Ricardo, my friend in La Vega, was there to meet us. He arranged for us to tour the polling stations in the back of a pickup truck, a safer vehicle to be seen in than Jhonny's expensive Blazer, and which had the added advantage of allowing the cameraman to get open-air shots.

Starting around 3 P.M., we spent three hours winding our way through the hills at breakneck speed, turning around at dead ends where the only way to keep going up to the dozens of houses above was on foot. The barrio is so inaccessible that those lucky enough to have jobs in the city center can spend four hours a day commuting to and from work. Even getting groceries is a huge chore, especially for the infirm, elderly, or single mothers. We stopped at a handful of polling stations where the lines were still around the block. By this point millions of Venezuelans had already voted, and at least in La Vega there was a celebratory atmosphere. Despite the dry law, people were drinking, setting up barbecues, and dancing salsa and merengue in the streets. Red shirts, hats, and paraphernalia were everywhere. I even saw a goat dressed in a red shirt.

As we wound our way through streets, the pro-Chávez chants and firework explosions made for a deafening roar. Everywhere we went, people threw up ten fingers to show me and the camera crew where their support lay. On more than one occasion friends of Ricardo's came charging up to our pickup, holding their purple-stained pinkies high, yelling, *"Esto es para Chávez"* (This is for Chávez), and then flipping up their middle fingers, *"Y eso para Rosales"* (And this is for Rosales).

Very occasionally we would come across someone who would indicate their support for Rosales, either through an opposition-blue T-shirt, or by yelling out the Rosales campaign slogan: *"Atrévete"* (Dare to change). These loners' comments were usually met with friendly derision and joking from their neighbors in the streets. As we held on to the side of the truck for dear life, Ricardo outlined his analysis of what was going on in the election: "Eighty percent of Venezuelans are poor," he shouted over the din of the crowds. "Of those 80 percent, nine out of ten votes will be for Chávez. Even if every single Rosales supporter in the higher classes comes out to vote, and even if a couple million chavistas don't vote today, there is no way Chávez can lose. Do the math."

Our pickup climbed to the top of La Vega where the view down into the packed barrio clinging to the hillside was awe-inspiring. The sunset reflected off gray clouds rolling down El Avila, the steep green hill that separates Caracas from the Caribbean coast, as the thunderheads began to open on the city below. We drove back down to where Jhonny had left his car, thanked Ricardo for his help, and headed out of La Vega. When our filming finished, I took the crew for a typical Venezuelan dinner of *pabellón al criollo:* white rice, black beans, stewed, shredded red beef, and yellow fried plantains. Some Venezuelans joke that it is the national dish because its colors represent the racial diversity of the country's ancestors: white Europeans, black Africans, red indigenous people, and, once the races started miscegenating, yellow mestizos.

After eating with the film crew and seeing them safely back to their hotel, I walked over to an opposition-controlled neighborhood near the Chacaito metro station where two Chilean friends I'd met in Caracas, Liza and Pablo, lived. We'd planned on watching the preliminary election results on television together.

Rumors of all sorts, mostly false, were flying via text messages and phone calls: Rosales supporters claimed he was winning 57–43 but that the government was organizing fraud to reverse the results; Chávez supporters said their man had won 72–26 but that Rosales would refuse to recognize the outcome. A friend who worked as a foreign policy adviser in the presidential palace called to tell me that people there were already drinking champagne and celebrating. A gringa friend was at the Rosales campaign headquarters where, apparently, people were also drinking champagne and celebrating. Unable to make much sense of what was happening, we channel-surfed and waited for a clearer picture to emerge.

I had met at least half a dozen Chileans, like Pablo and Liza, who had come to Venezuela to work in solidarity with the Bolivarian Revolution; no doubt they had hopes that it would prove more successful than their own country's short-lived democratic revolution. Many of them had spent decades in exile after Pinochet seized power. The democratic-socialist experiment in their country had lasted only two years before being brutally suppressed and replaced with concentration camps and neoliberal policies. When Chávez first took office in

1999, it was on a platform calling for a frontal attack on neoliberalism, which, as he described it at the time, represents "the road to hell." His election was the first of what would become a series of groundbreaking electoral victories for a new breed of Latin American leftist nationalists. As such it attracted attention and support from radicals and intellectuals around the globe, especially those in Chile.

Pablo's and Liza's four parents had been supporters of the socialist Allende government in Chile. When Pinochet took power in a bloody coup, they were tortured in concentration camps along with tens of thousands of other Chilean leftists. Unlike the thousands who died, Pablo's and Liza's respective parents managed to escape into exile. Liza had grown up in the Soviet Union and Pablo in England. Of course I too have parents who paid a heavy price for their radical politics, and this common experience was undoubtedly part of what drew the three of us together. We hung out in the politically progressive expat scene in Caracas, which some Venezuelans view as an expression of international solidarity and others as political tourism. Venezuelans that dislike the Chávez government often make snide comments about gringos who wear red T-shirts, or dress as hippies, suggesting that it would be better if they spent their time and money on Venezuela's beaches than on playing games in the political system, and that they would never tolerate a government like that of Chávez in their own countries.

While I dozed on the tiled floor with my head against the mattress, my friends lay on their bed. Pablo anxiously flicked through the channels as we waited for election news. I tried to get a few minutes of sleep after an exhausting day but just as I was settling into slumber, the bed shook violently, waking me up. Pablo and Liza had jumped and were yelling at the tops of their voices. "What happened, who won?" I mumbled, my eyes half closed.

"They haven't announced yet," Pablo said.

"So what's all the fuss about?"

"Pinochet has had a major heart attack. He's in critical condition and a priest is on the way to give him his last rites," Liza answered.

She was furious that death might allow the aging general to escape accountability.

"It would be just like the old bastard to get off facing justice— hiding behind his self-created immunity and multimillion-dollar lawyers until the end," Pablo added.

"At least he lived to see a female, socialist survivor of his torture camps get elected to the presidency," I said, trying to comfort them by referring to Michele Bachelet.

Now wide awake, I reflected on the symmetry of Pinochet's rise to power and his imminent death. He had headed up a military regime that brutally tortured and killed thousands in the name of the war on communism. Holding on to dictatorial power for seventeen years had given him plenty of time to impose a wide range of business-friendly policies deregulating and privatizing everything within reach, abolishing the minimum wage, and attacking organized labor: he had turned Chile into a policy testing ground for the region. Although he had successfully dodged conviction, narrowly evading charges in Europe in 1998, he had also lived long enough to watch the region and his own country run nearly full circle. In his last years Pinochet and the economic model he imposed were firmly on the defensive. The regional round of elections in Latin America in 2005–2006 consolidated the new trend. Bachelet, who won the Chilean presidency in 2005, is a single mother, an agnostic, a member of the Socialist Party, and the daughter of a high-ranking member of the Allende government who died while being tortured after Pinochet's coup. In Brazil, a former metalworkers labor leader, President Luiz Inácio (Lula) da Silva of the Workers Party, won reelection in October 2006. A month later Daniel Ortega and the Sandinistas won the presidency in Nicaragua, years after being voted out of power amid a United States–backed Contra insurgency. In Uruguay, Tabaré Vázquez, a socialist of the center-left Broad Front coalition, took office in March 2005 with the support of former Tupamaro guerrillas. In neighboring Argentina, President Néstor Kirchner had successfully steered the country toward rapid recovery and growth in the wake of its devastating 2001–2002 economic crisis; his success came in large part as he scorned the policy mandates of Washington-based international financial institutions like the International Monetary Fund.

Chávez, by far the most radical of the lot and with the largest domestic base of support, was expected to win a new six-year term in office and would surely continue using his influence and seemingly endless petrodollars to create political space for other governments in the region. Rafael Correa had just won the Ecuadoran presidency on an anti-neoliberal platform and had previously negotiated a joint bond offering with the Chávez government during a brief stint as minister of finance in Ecuador. Bolivia's first-ever indigenous president, Evo Morales, who openly cultivated relationships with Chávez and Fidel Castro, despite grumblings from the U.S. State Department, had taken office in January 2006. A new Latin America based on democratic elections and popular movements was emerging in response to the authoritarian and military-backed regimes once supported by the United States.

On the eve of Venezuela's 2006 presidential election, it was too early to predict what the new Latin America would look like, how cooperative with each other its radical leaders would be or how successfully their efforts to forge a new model of government would prove. To some extent it still is. Certainly there are vast differences between the new regimes in different countries. Lula and Bachelet, for example, seem committed to maintaining strong relations with the United States and to representing the economic status quo, while Morales and Correa appear more willing to defy the United States and take local elites head-on. Nicaragua is a desperately poor country that could quickly become dependent on aid and investment from its allies, while Venezuela is the planet's fifth largest exporter of oil and has a hard time spending its wealth effectively, despite widespread domestic poverty. Finally, while the left has made impressive electoral gains in Latin America since Chávez first took office in January 1999, there are still more countries, like Colombia and El Salvador, that remain strongholds of United States influence and conservatism.

Around 10 P.M., a few minutes after the news of Pinochet's heart attack, all the local channels cut to the president of the National Electoral Council. With 78 percent of the votes counted, she announced, Chávez had won more than 60 percent—the final results gave Chávez 63 percent to Rosales's 37 percent. Outside we heard fireworks, and even in the quiet, middle-class neighborhood we were in, the occasional shouts of *"Viva Chávez"* rang out. I got word from a journalist friend covering the opposition headquarters that radicals among them were pushing Rosales not to recognize the results and there were calls to take to the streets in protest. The high heels and three-piece suits that were the dress code at the Rosales campaign headquarters would have made for a hilarious street protest, but it was not to be. Rosales did the honorable thing and recognized the trouncing he had received for what it was.

Fighting off sleep, Pablo, Liza, and I donned our pro-Chávez red paraphernalia and raced out to join the inevitable celebrations. There wasn't a taxi to be found so we walked to the metro through empty streets of a neighborhood that had largely been silenced by defeat. The subway car we got in was the venue for a party that grew larger and noisier at every stop. Chavistas on their way to the big celebration at the palace embraced any and all strangers as they boarded the train.

Twenty minutes later we joined the thousands who were charging up the hill toward the palace in the pouring rain. Trucks and cars ferried ever more people in, horns blaring, and music blasting. The streets around Miraflores were a sea of red. Fireworks lit up the sky and street vendors brought out coolers of beer. Around 2 A.M., drenched and weary from having been awake for twenty-four hours straight, I set off through the empty center of the city on the long, wet journey home. It was a walk that would have been out of the question on any other night of the year, a sure way to get mugged or worse. But tonight the sole intention of the few people I encountered was to celebrate the Chávez victory.

Arriving back at the run-down cement block I called home, I couldn't help but feel I had just witnessed a historic event. For all the problems facing the Chávez government, it clearly had a democratic mandate to run the country. Since leaving my apartment in the early hours of the morning I had observed an eruption of democracy the likes of which I had never seen before. In Venezuela, voting and political engagement is not a chore, but a national fiesta. Until the country's political opposition learns to recognize that in Venezuela, as across the planet, the rich are a small minority, they won't even begin to have a chance to win a national election. Chávez was taking big risks but, by aligning himself with the poor in a country where the popular vote decides who rules, he had made a safe bet.

Pilgrimage of the Displaced

wo months after my stint as the fixer for the news crew in Caracas, I headed off to Medellín, Colombia, to meet my mom, Bernardine. Nestled in the Andes, Medellín is the hometown of both the infamous drug lord Pablo Escobar and the current president of Colombia, Alvaro Uribe. Though it was my first time in the city, my mom had been there on several occasions previously. All her trips to Colombia, like this one, had been on human rights missions at the invitation of a Colombian colleague, a Franciscan nun named Sister Carolina Pardo.

Sister Carolina, a smiling, energetic woman in her late thirties with a thin, boyish frame, is highly regarded in Colombia's human rights community; her office has received numerous threats from paramilitary groups because of its work defending peasant communities. Deceptively quiet, her strategic thinking and natural social tact make her profoundly charismatic even though she doesn't take up much space in a group. She comes from a comfortable background but has chosen to cast her lot with the country's most dispossessed. It was a decision that must have been cause for some tension in her family and religious community, not least because of the great personal risks it involved. Sister Carolina speaks nearly perfect English, thanks, in part, to time she spent in a sort of exile at a master's program in clinical social work at Loyola University in Chicago from 2004 to 2006 when the threats against her in Colombia were at a peak. It was during that period she and my mom developed a close friendship and working relationship. Both in Chicago and on her return to Colombia, Sister

Carolina worked at centers for victims of torture. On her second trip
to the Andean country, my mom traveled with Sister Carolina into the
Chocó region in northwest Colombia, on the border with Panama.
Now, years after their first trip, I was joining them to go back.

Human rights come into constant, direct conflict with global economic growth and wealth accumulation in the Chocó region on the
Panama-Colombia border. The narrow isthmus is the target site for
development projects including the completion of the Pan-American
Highway, a pipeline to carry Venezuelan oil to Pacific ports, and an
alternative shipping channel to the Panama Canal. In 1996, the price
of land there doubled following then President Ernesto Samper's
announcement of a plan for a new interoceanic highway link, connecting the Pacific and Atlantic. The Chocó has also attracted agriculture, timber, coal, and mining interests from Colombia and abroad.

The sparsely populated area is home to small subsistence agricultural communities, of which about 20 percent are indigenous and 70
percent are made up from the descendants of Africans brought to the
colonies as slaves. For generations there have been virtually no government services or support in these jungle backwater communities.
Between fishing and collective, low-intensity agricultural projects,
most families in the Chocó earn around $1,000 a year. In a region
almost entirely outside the cash economy, that level of income allows
for a decent, if humble and precarious, existence. In the winter, the
rain turns everything to mud and swamps. In the summer, the sun
and humidity are relentless. Most families grow rice, yucca, plantain,
and collect fruit from the jungle and fish from the rivers and streams.
Coconut-flavored rice with fried river fish is a local specialty.

In 1997, shortly after the release of President Samper's road plan
boosted land values, the Colombian government decided it was time to
increase its presence in the area. Colombia is in the midst of a several-
decades-long armed conflict pitting the government military against
historically left-wing guerrilla groups, the largest of which is called the

Revolutionary Armed Forces of Colombia, or FARC-EP, and nonstate right-wing paramilitary groups generally allied with large landowners and often working in concert with the state-controlled military against the guerrillas.

In 1997, paramilitary groups began targeting the communities in the region. Boats carrying food in were blocked; men traveling to town were assassinated; local leaders were threatened. It was in this context that the Colombian government decided to make its presence felt in the Chocó. Rather than building roads, or sending tax collectors, doctors, and teachers, the anti-guerrilla 17th Brigade of the Colombian army moved into the jungle with heavy air support for an offensive against the FARC-EP guerrillas who were supposedly in control of the region. Although guerrillas traveled the area's extensive waterways, estuaries, and mangrove swamps, according to locals, they didn't set up bases or settlements. On February 24, 1997, under the leadership of General Rito Alejo del Río, the army initiated Operation Genesis. Early that morning, planes and helicopter gunships opened fire on seven hamlets. For several weeks previously, paramilitary troops had been harassing local communities, killing livestock, stealing food, damaging tools, threatening farmers, and raping women. All in all, approximately eighty locals were killed in the joint military-paramilitary operation.

Three days after Operation Genesis started, a young local farmer named Marino López was heading out to his daily work in his family's rice and yucca fields. As he walked along the Cacarica River near his village, a group of paramilitaries called him over and ordered him to climb a tree to get a few coconuts for them. When he got down with the coconuts they accused him of being a guerrilla and proceeded to insult and beat him. One of the uniformed paramilitaries grabbed a machete and began hacking away at the unarmed farmer's limbs. When they had finished their work, Marino no longer had his arms, his legs, his testicles, or his head. The paramilitaries then forced Marino's family and community to watch while they used his severed head for a ball in a gruesome soccer match. Word quickly spread through the communities in the area that the same fate awaited anyone who didn't leave. In the days that followed 3,500 peasant farmers abandoned their land, their villages, their way of life.

Ten years on, just two months after Chávez's landslide reelection in Venezuela, my mom and Sister Carolina met me with smiles and hugs at the airport in Medellín. We were there as part of a one-hundred-strong delegation of international human rights activists and journalists from fifteen different countries who wanted to learn about and support the local communities. We were to join a larger group of Colombians, many themselves displaced from other regions around the country, on what they called a "pilgrimage." The plan was to visit several different communities that had been displaced by government or paramilitary violence. The pilgrimage part of the trip involved a weeklong retracing of the routes taken through swamps and jungles when the local communities fled their lands in the wake of Marino López's murder and Operation Genesis. For many members of the community the pilgrimage had a spiritual significance, but practically, it would also enable them to visit parts of their land outside the small villages to reexert ownership of their ancestral territory.

Sister Carolina worked with a Colombian NGO, Justicia y Paz (Justice and Peace), that had helped organize international support for the event. I had been invited along to act as an interpreter for my mom and to help carry our heavy camping gear over the difficult terrain. As outsiders, especially as the only two white *estadounidenses,* the simple presence of my mom and me in the region provided the local people with a modicum of protection from paramilitary attacks. However, as is often the case with this sort of international solidarity work, our participation was likely of greater benefit to us than to those we were visiting.

Heading out from Medellín's urban sprawl to meet up with the rest of the delegation, my mom, Sister Carolina, and I caught a series of buses, *colectivos* (shared taxis), and jeeps for the long journey into the backcountry. As is common in much of Latin America, busy markets had sprung up around the bus stations. Find a traffic jam, bus terminal, or border crossing pretty well anywhere on the subcontinent and there is sure to be a group of entrepreneurs selling plantain chips, boiled maize, rapidly melting ice cream, bottles of Coca-Cola, and assorted Chinese imports.

As the towns we passed through got ever smaller, the military presence, including brand-new tanks and armored personnel vehicles, paid for with the help of United States tax dollars, grew more intense. After a while the tiny towns and villages started to look the same: they were all dusty and unremarkable, named after a saint or a nearby water source. Garbage piles of plastic bottles, cardboard boxes, banana peels, and other unidentifiable refuse piled up around the stations and drew crowds of emaciated dogs. Blackish gray water crept through the dirt, attracting flies and exuding a putrid smell. A young girl carried her infant sibling on her back. The faded pink Coca-Cola sign, the squawking chickens, the old men in the shade playing cards, the idle taxi drivers, and the broken-down trucks became familiar sights.

After the early morning flight, I tried to rest but the bumpy, unpaved street and the dusty heat made real sleep impossible. Eventually we left the main road and turned onto a dirt track only passable by 4x4s like the one we were in. Half awake, half dozing I stared out at an unrelenting landscape of African oil palms extending into the distance as far as the eye could see.

After several hours on the road we came to a halt in Curvarado. A large group of people, mostly Afro-Colombian, surrounded our jeep. On one side of the road was a pile of Del Monte banana boxes waiting to be picked up and shipped to port. On the other was a sign reading: "Biodiversity Humanitarian Zone, Curvarado Community, We all defend our land." We unloaded our bags and supplies with the help of the kids milling about, and one of the community matriarchs invited us to crawl under a barbed wire fence that surrounded the humanitarian zone. This community, and several others in the Chocó, had returned from years of forced displacement to find their land occupied, their villages razed, and their crops replaced with endless acres of oil palms and bananas. At great personal risk and with the support of national and international NGOs they had moved back onto their old land. They called their resettlements humanitarian zones because they wouldn't tolerate the presence of any weapons or armed groups, including the army, the paramilitaries, or the guerrillas, within the areas marked with signs and barbed wire fences.

The resettlement town was a work in progress, just a handful of wooden shacks with hammocks strung up in the common areas, and a couple of large cisterns for collecting rain or depositing water hauled from the river. We had arrived just in time to join the community and the rest of the peace brigade for a lunch, more nutritious than mouthwatering, of soy cooked with onions and tomato, and a gigantic pot of boiled yucca and green plantain. Lemon-flavored water sweetened with raw brown sugar was served from a five-gallon plastic jug. After setting up our tent on the hard-packed dirt next to those of the rest of the brigade, I decided to cool off with a "bath" in the muddy river nearby. The silt-laden water was the only available way of washing.

In the afternoon a group joined one of the recently returned farmers on a hike out of the fence surrounding their resettlement to the land he farmed before the displacement. Enrique Echeverría had a weather-beaten complexion and soft, dark eyes. His hands, clearly those of a man who has worked every day of his life, carried a machete, which he kept in a leather scabbard on his belt. It took us more than an hour of hard walking to get past the African palm plantation that now covered his land. As we walked, Enrique pointed out the dried streambeds that had previously provided his family with fish but that the intensive monoculture of the African palms had drained dry. He explained why the financiers, backing the paramilitaries who had forced them off the land, created palm plantations and brought in outside labor to run them. "Palm plantations are a lot of work to set up, especially in the first few years when they need to be planted, tended, and irrigated," he told us. "Our community has always preferred a diversity of crops that we use to feed our families and keep our land healthy and balanced. So once we were forced out, they had to bring in *pobladores,* outsiders to help the paramilitaries with the backbreaking work. After the first five years, when the plantation is up and running and the trees start yielding fruit, it is a profitable cash crop."

I had never before heard of African palm but I now learned that they grow as high as sixty feet and can produce up to one hundred pounds of fruit per harvest. Once mature, the trees are harvested every five months or so, and the fruit's seeds produce an oil that can be used for everything from cooking to ethanol. The palm nut meal serves as livestock feed. Just one acre of palms can produce over five hundred gallons of ethanol a year, or more of lower grade oils, making for a lucrative investment. Cash crops like banana and African palm are excellent for laundering drug money or other illicit funds—something Colombian paramilitaries constantly need. For example, a paramilitary group generates millions of dollars in illegal cash profits from drug trafficking. The cash is then used to buy tools, seeds, fertilizers, and to pay laborers to plant, tend, harvest, process, and ship African palm. When the palm products are sold, the money generated is "clean." This type of cultivation of African palm leads to desertification of the soil, so, after a few years of palm oil harvests, it is not possible to reforest the lands or to go back to sustenance multi-crop farming. Enrique was dismayed that a crop being promoted as a so-called green alternative to oil was the cause of so much bloodshed, violence, and environmental damage in his community.

We walked on and eventually the palms thinned out, replaced by thick jungle undergrowth. A little farther on we came to a clearing where Enrique, after his return from displacement, had started his new farm. To work his fields every day, Enrique had to make the same hour-long, three-mile journey we had just completed, sometimes in the company of his two sons but often alone. Though today we international observers provided him a little protection, the risk of running into hostile paramilitaries was real. We helped him put up a big hand-painted metal sign declaring that he had returned and that the land he was farming was titled property of his community and family. We then harvested a sack of *maíz* for dinner that night and, using palm branches as improvised umbrellas against a driving, heavy rain, started the long trek back to the humanitarian zone. Some of our group slowed down in the mud, but I had knee-high rubber boots, Colombian-style, and by pushing myself was just able to keep up with the farmers. I overheard Enrique talking with one of the other Colombians accompanying us: "I finally got the government to recognize my legal claim to the land and issue the paperwork and everything, so I don't think the paras will kill me for coming back. I hope not anyway." He sounded as though he was trying to convince himself as much as his companion.

The next morning, we said good-bye to Enrique and the peace settlement and boarded an old school bus refitted to carry passengers, livestock, and cargo. Our next stop, after a long and bumpy bus ride, was a coastal city called Turbo, where we ate dinner in a restaurant set up by widows from another displaced community, Cacarica. While we were taking turns eating plantain and fish soup in the tiny restaurant called Clamores, or clamors, small groups of soldiers in uniform and carrying automatic weapons started drifting by. At first it was just two or three of them. Then three more passed. Eventually, some twenty soldiers were gathered at the corners on either side of the open-air restaurant. It wasn't clear what their purpose was but if it was to intimidate us, they succeeded. The military had no reason to be hostile but in Colombia's brutal armed conflict no one is ever eager for the scrutiny that groups of internationals with cameras bring. Our group leaders from Justicia y Paz spoke with the restaurant staff and then with the soldiers and decided that we should finish our meals quickly and continue on our way.

We checked into hotels for the night, a three-floor walk-up with worn-down rooms and dirty throw rugs at the door. The beds, cheap to begin with, showed their age with a clear depression in the middle of the mattress and stained sheets. Television, air-conditioning, room service, and free toiletries were luxuries not even contemplated by management. The shared bathrooms at the end of the hall were dank with puddles of water on the broken tile floor serving as a breeding ground for mosquitoes. Fortunately the poor overhead lighting made it impossible to judge when the place had last been mopped down, if ever.

Once we were settled in our temporary homes, dozens of displaced Afro-Colombians joined us for a long evening walk out to the *coliseo,* or sports stadium, on the edge of the city for a candlelight vigil. Outside the small stadium, we saw a monument to the nearly eighty people who had disappeared, presumably killed. As night fell, one of the matriarchs from Cacarica, a striking Afro-Colombian abuela (grandmother) with silver-gray hair, told us the story of her community and sang a song about the violence in the Chocó region. Her high singing voice sounded, to my unfamiliar ear at least, off-key. But the power of her story against the silent backdrop of the night sky was more than enough to command the attention of everyone in attendance.

She told us how, in February 1997, hundreds of families, thousands of people, over half of them kids, grabbed what little they could carry and fled on foot and canoe the land on which they had been raised. The joint paramilitary-military action had left them with no choice but to evacuate. Far from being punished for these crimes, General Rito Alejo del Río, the army commander in charge of Operation Genesis, was rewarded. The then governor of the nearby state of Antioquia, Alvaro Uribe, now in his second term as Colombia's president, hosted a banquet at which he honored the general with the title "Pacifier of Urabá."

President Uribe, a darling of the U.S. State Department, has a sordid history. His popularity in Washington as a conservative, pro–United States, neoliberal politician notwithstanding, as early as 1991 a U.S. Defense Intelligence Agency document described him as a "close personal friend of Pablo Escobar," the late drug lord from Medellín. Uribe served as mayor of the city and later regional governor. As governor, Uribe was instrumental in establishing a civilian vigilante organization, CONVIVIR, that quickly became a right-wing armed paramilitary network fighting a vicious war against the country's leftist guerrillas and their sympathizers. Uribe's own father was killed by the FARC-EP in a botched kidnapping attempt. The paramilitaries that grew out of Uribe's CONVIVIR are widely believed to be responsible for the majority of civilian deaths and human rights abuses in the ongoing conflict. Like the FARC-EP and sectors of the state military apparatus, the paramilitaries became involved in drug trafficking and used cocaine profits to fund their arms purchases and operations. While the FARC-EP mostly tax growers in the regions they control, the paramilitaries and military are reportedly actively involved in the more lucrative trafficking as well.

Uribe's presidency brought improvements in security for much of the country, but he was widely seen as a puppet of the United States government and an ally of the paramilitaries. Successive Colombian governments had pursued an aggressive privatization plan including the selling off of education and health care systems, and natural resources like oil. Uribe had sought out multibillion-dollar aid packages from the United States and international financial institutions. For example, in 2003, in exchange for a $2.1 billion line of standby credit from the IMF, the Uribe government moved forward with privatization plans for a major Colombian bank, fired tens of thousands of state workers, reformed tax, labor, and pension laws in line with IMF guidelines, raised the value added tax, which disproportionately burdens the poor, and invested heavily in a military solution to the national conflict.

A lone flickering candle illuminated the grandmother from Cacarica as she explained in a steady voice how the displaced communities had fled chaotically in various directions in search of a safe haven. One big group hiked for two days, over difficult terrain through Los Katios National Park, to reach Panama's Darién region in search of refuge across the international border. Others headed south to the nearby port city of Turbo, where our candlelight vigil was taking place. Although Turbo was a paramilitary stronghold, it was the major settlement nearest to the Cacarica river basin and became home to these displaced farmers and families for the next six years. Two thousand people began living in improvised settlements in Turbo's suburbs and in the sports stadium where our group had now gathered for the vigil.

A quick glance over my shoulder revealed the cramped space that so many people had called home during the years of their displacement, the cement floor where they had slept, and the leaky roof that had made keeping dry in the rainy season impossible.

The grandmother's voice grew quiet, forcing me to lean in so as to be able to hear well enough to interpret for my mom, who spoke no Spanish. Luckily for me, Colombians speak clear, steady, and well-enunciated Spanish. Of course there were expressions that I had never heard before, *colombianismos,* as they're called, which were difficult to understand and translate. For example, the grandmother spoke of "being in the pot" (*estar en la olla*), which I eventually understood to mean being in a difficult situation economically. As she talked, her voice betrayed the shame she felt when, upon their arrival after being displaced, they filled the Turbo stadium with sacks, awnings, ropes, hammocks, and mattresses. At night, coughing and the crying of babies echoed through the building; there was no privacy, no personal space. During the rainy season water constantly leaked through the makeshift roof and soaked people's belongings. Babies born in the stadium knew no other way of life. Desperate poverty made the young men easy targets for paramilitary recruiters, and more than a few of the young women turned to prostitution to support their families.

Recovering her composure, her voice gathering strength, the gray-haired grandmother denounced the economic interests behind her community's displacement. Hot wax from the candle I was holding dripped over my fingers but couldn't distract me from her riveting tale. During the three years that the people from Cacarica were displaced, paramilitaries and multinational corporations financed the so-called development of large tracts of their land. For many Colombians, Cacarica is proof that the frequent expulsion of communities across the country stems not primarily from conflict between guerrillas and paramilitaries but rather from financial and political interests associated with multinational corporations and, often, the Uribe administration, that want to start profitable agribusinesses on lands that do not belong to them.

Though they had fled their land without a fight in 1996 after the brutal murder of Marino López, the people of Cacarica were not pre-pared to simply give it up. They quickly became aware that if they were to get it back they would first need to obtain legal title from the state, something they lacked because many of their ancestors had set-tled the Chocó well before the arrival of the Spanish colonizers, and because they lived communally. Law 70, passed in 1993, recognized collective territorial rights of communities such as those in Cacarica, but it required various legal and bureaucratic steps before an actual title could be granted. So the community leaders, with the help of a few NGOs like Sister Carolina's Justicia y Paz, set about lobbying the government in Bogotá.

Colombia has more internally displaced people than any country on earth, except for Iraq and Sudan. But the people of Cacarica stood out by dint of their determination not to give up in the battle for their land. In October 1999, the government finally granted a collective legal title to the twenty-three villages of the Cacarica basin for 250,000 acres of land and, the following February, after three years of living in the stadium, more than 85 percent of the community prepared to return. Over the next year, the community began rebuilding their homes and villages, reclaiming small plots of land for farms, and slowly trans-porting elderly and infirm members of the community upriver once plots of land had been sown and simple homes constructed.

In June 2001, when the return from displacement was finally com-plete, the military harassment began once again. Community mem-bers, including children, were held captive for several days, and the threats and abuse became constant. Soldiers of the army's 17th Bri-gade, the same one responsible for Operation Genesis, which initially drove them from their land, tried to bribe them to begin growing coca or African palm, rather than their traditional subsistence crops. The communities were also pressured to allow major companies to con-tinue working their land illegally. This time, however, the community was prepared. With the help of Justicia y Paz, and Peace Brigades International, another international NGO active in the region and on our trip, they were able to document every military and paramilitary violation. The NGOs helped leverage international pressure and support to prevent another mass forced displacement. The harassment did take a toll, however, and by 2007 just eight hundred of the 2,500 returnees were still left on their collective land.

Those who stayed came up with the strategy of forming humanitarian zones, which were well marked with signs and barbed wire fences. Several of the newly founded hamlets such as Esperanza en Dios (Hope in God) and Nueva Vida (New Life) joined together to form a community organization called CAVIDA (Community of Self-determination, Life, and Dignity). CAVIDA was the community organization that invited us and offered to host our delegation to commemorate the ten-year anniversary of their displacement.

When the grandmother finished her tale, we began a ceremony in which displaced people from the Chocó and representatives of displaced communities from other parts of Colombia, who had come along with the delegation, shared their stories about disappearances and murders of loved ones: husbands, brothers, and fathers. Then the internationals in the group began. An Argentine mother of the Plaza de Mayo lit a candle for her daughter who had disappeared more than thirty years ago in that country's Dirty War against the left. A Chilean ex–political prisoner under Pinochet lit a candle for his companions who never made it out of the torture camps. A Brazilian woman representing the MST, the Landless Workers Movement, lit a candle for peasants recently killed in Brazil while fighting for a small plot of land to plant.

Though I tried to concentrate on interpreting for my mom, there were several moments in the proceedings where I could not stop myself from choking up. I couldn't help but think about my own biological parents' decades in prison, my father's continuing incarceration, and the three men who were killed during the crime my parents participated in. I considered lighting a candle and sharing their plight with the group, but then decided against it. Perhaps it was too hard to break out of my role as interpreter and take on the role of participant, or maybe I didn't feel up to the task of trying to explain my parents' use of violence to these people who themselves had suffered so much. Certainly I was self-conscious of our position as the only two representatives from the United States, a country that, directly or indirectly, had fueled the violence in all of the Latin American countries represented in our solemn gathering.

The next morning at six we all boarded high-speed motorboats, or *pangas,* that Peace Brigades International had provided and crossed the Gulf of Urabá into the Atrato River system. The plan was to go all the way to the Cacarica River humanitarian zones by nightfall, with a stop en route at La Balsa, an area that was still under the control of paramilitaries and where more than a few community members had been tortured, killed, and buried in unmarked graves. For the previous couple of years, President Uribe had been leading a so-called demobilization of the paramilitary forces, essentially offering amnesty in exchange for guns. The program was widely criticized as too lenient on the groups most responsible for gross human rights abuses in the country's ongoing violence. We wanted to investigate what was actually happening on the ground. Several members of the CAVIDA community accompanied us, including a mestizo man named Cristian Cabezas who had a bushy black mustache and sported a fringed leather sombrero. He had farmed the area around La Balsa before being driven off his land ten years earlier by the paramilitaries.

Our boats were forced to stop at an artificial dead end, an improvised dirt dam across the river that a huge CAT land mover, and a couple teams of men were still working on. Cristian seemed alarmed. In the confusion that followed no one seemed to know what was going on. An army officer, visibly surprised at our presence, approached the representatives from Justicia y Paz and asked what we were doing there. They explained that we were accompanying the legal tenants of the land to visit their property. After talking among ourselves we decided that we would walk the rest of the way to Cristian Cabezas's land at La Balsa. As our hodgepodge crew unloaded from the *pangas*, a number of people in the delegation took out cameras and begin filming, to the evident discomfort of the men working on the dam. They did not, however, move to stop us. Sister Carolina, quickly reading the situation, explained to us that the dam they were building would direct river water for their cattle, timber, African palm, and banana operations. Sure enough, as we walked we passed massive piles of timber harvested illegally and cattle being driven along the river.

Farther down the baked mud path and out of earshot, Cristian explained that the workers on the dam were *pobladores*, colonizers the paramilitaries had brought in to work their plantations after forcing the original inhabitants, like him, out. The *pobladores* and paramilitaries wouldn't have let Cristian pass onto his own land but for the team of internationals and NGO representatives with cameras right behind him. Our role there made me think of a Zapatista saying I had learned while exploring Chiapas years earlier: "If you have come to help us, please go home; if you have come to join us, welcome. Pick up a shovel or a machete and get busy." In Colombia with Cristian and the other displaced my digital camera would be more useful than a machete: the solidarity we showed by joining the community and documenting the paramilitary activity were key steps in their strategy to reclaim control of their land.

There was no shade from the midday sun on the three-mile walk— which we had planned on boating—and so when our group, dehydrated from the unanticipated hike, came upon a couple of wild guava trees, we fell on the fruit like vultures. Eventually we rounded a bend and entering through a gate came upon a massive banana processing plant. The capital-intensive project boasted heavy machinery, imported fertilizers and insecticides, several large houses and barns for processing, and endless Del Monte cardboard boxes. In between the barns was a red farmhouse with screen doors and windows. It appeared to shelter workers and provide office space for the managers. The road ran right in front of the house and barn. All around the work site the grass had been tightly cropped by grazing horses.

Behind the barns a green banana grove stretched into the distance as far as I could see. This was the first time since his displacement that Cristian had been able to go back to where his family farm had been, and what he found dismayed him.

Our group explored the vast complex and the edges of the several hundred acres of banana plantings. A company called Multifruit ran the operation, selling the bananas directly to Del Monte for export. We saw one of the local paramilitary leaders consorting openly with an ex-community leader who, we were told, had improperly signed over the land to Multifruit several years earlier. The community has a collective title to the land, which means no individual member should have had the authority to sell or subdivide the holding. But Multifruit hadn't been worried about the details—convincing a local leader to sign their title was a trick going back hundreds of years. It gave them a legal pretense to continue controlling the disputed land in Colombia's frontier for years, especially when the illegitimate deed was backed by well-armed paramilitaries. When Mario saw us taking pictures he called in his own crew of cameramen to take photos of our group. Although those of us from abroad weren't worried about our own safety, we were concerned about the possible long-term repercussions for Cristian and the other locals whose images were recorded. We decided we'd seen enough and began the long, hot walk back to our *pangas*.

Our afternoon *panga* ride to the Cacarica River communities took us along some of the most pristine and ecologically diverse freshwater systems on earth. The region is home to nearly one hundred different species of reptiles and six hundred of birds, including several, such as the plumbeous forest-falcon and the banded ground-cuckoo, that are endangered. Eventually the river became too narrow for the *pangas* to navigate and we had to offload all our equipment and begin a several hour hike with heavy packs and tents to get to our destination village. Night fell before we were halfway there. It was pitch black and the air was full of mosquitoes but we struggled on. Rarely have I been so pleased to arrive at a place with no running water, no electricity, and no bed.

That night I shared a tent with my mom and Sister Carolina, who managed to go to bed and wake up with a smile despite the fatigue of the previous day's activity. Emerging the next morning, I found myself in the orderly town of New Life, home to about 150 families, each with their own house built on stilts to keep above the mudflows during the rainy season. Small kids were everywhere, generally unsupervised by adults. There were a few big community platforms—simple wood constructions elevated off the ground for protection from floods and shaded from the hot sun with dried palm fronds overhead—where we would later eat our meals and hold meetings. A big outhouse with eight seats above the same not-quite-big-enough hole dominated the center of the town. Sister Carolina, her other responsibilities notwithstanding, made time and energy to show me around the settlement while the women in the village set about cooking our group a massive meal of rice and canned tuna over an outdoor wood fire. Near the entrance to the settlement the community had built a monument honoring their fallen comrades with a small white cross for each of the dead and cement casts of hundreds of hands coming out of a wall behind the crosses. On one edge of town, clearly visible between a row of wooden houses and the perimeter fence, there was a massive portrait of an Afro-Colombian man's face on a bolt of white cloth attached to tall bamboo poles that rippled in the breeze. Sister Carolina told me solemnly that this was Marino López, the young farmer whose agonizing death had prompted his community to flee.

Early the following morning my mom, Sister Carolina, and I left New Life on the next stage of our journey. An arduous hike of twelve miles through the Chocó-Darién border region took us to an indigenous village called Join Poboor populated by the Wounaan tribe, not far from the Panamanian border but still inside Colombia. The inhabitants of Join Poboor were among those who had been forcibly displaced, removed from their ancestral land by the government, which insisted that the territory was a Colombian national park and needed to be protected. This same government was simultaneously promoting a plan to build a major highway through the area, intending to fill the sixty-mile gap in the Pan-American Highway that otherwise runs continuously from Alaska all the way down to Patagonia. The break in the road, the so-called Darién Gap, represents a significant obstacle to economic plans for integrating the Americas and increasing regional trade. But the road construction necessary to close it would mean the destruction of one of the most ecologically unique and sensitive ecosystems on earth.

The Chocó-Darién has one of the highest rainfalls on the planet, as much as fifty feet per year in places and, as result of its isolation, some of the planet's most diverse flora and fauna. The forests we were hiking through are home to jaguars, tamarins, tapirs, giant anteaters, pumas, ocelots, and any number of species of monkey. An estimated nine thousand species of vascular plants thrive there. The area is primarily made up of lowland riverine forests bordered by isolated mountain ranges, reaching over a mile high covered in wet cloud forests with dense layers of moss and tangles of vines and orchids. The rivers we navigated flow out into the ocean through large, complex estuaries and extensive mangroves. Luckily for us it was the summer so much of the swamp land we crossed was dry enough to walk through with only the occasional need for river fording or improvised bridges.

We followed the route that the displaced families from CAV-IDA had taken on their way north to Panama ten years earlier. I maintained a brisk pace, forcing myself to keep up with the Afro-Colombian leaders and guides, which was no easy feat since I was carrying my mom's gear as well as my own. She was following behind with Sister Carolina, who, with her usual sensitivity, realized that I would be eager to go ahead and my mom would want someone with her who spoke English. The guides and I arrived at Join Poboor around midday and stopped for lunch and a rest. I threw off my heavy backpack and stretched my aching legs before fully taking in the surroundings. The dozen or so houses were simple affairs: tree trunks served as beams to support elevated platforms on which stood huts that were open on all sides and roofed with thatch. The river, clear and slow-moving, drifted by on the north side of the settlement. The men of the village wore high black rubber boots, and threadbare

T-shirts and shorts. The women mostly walked around barefoot and topless with bead necklaces and simple cloth skirts. Shy, naked kids were everywhere. One of the local guides offered me a glass of viscous yellow mush—sweet plantain *chicha*, a traditional fermented beverage that is energy-rich and refreshing.

As I drank my *chicha* and took in the sights and sounds of the indigenous village, I tried to reconcile what I learned in school classes on development with the reality of the communities that had invited us into their virgin, "underdeveloped," territory. Liberal development theorists advocate the inclusion of regions like the Chocó-Darién in the global economy, and argue that what poor people there, and across the planet, need is to get their feet on "the first rung of the development ladder," that "a rising tide lifts all boats." But the reality is that the so-called development ladder is anathema to communities like CAVIDA and Join Poboor. Of course they have real human and material needs that, if met, would increase their life expectancy and quality of life. But they also recognize that development and global economic growth entail a high human and environmental cost, especially when imposed from above. Oil pipelines, highways, and canals may offer short-term employment and an influx of cash for these communities, but they are inevitably accompanied by massive environmental damage and the destruction of local culture and traditions. If poor local communities are not empowered to direct the development of their lands themselves, then modernity won't alleviate their poverty in any durable, meaningful way. The development game has winners and losers; poor Colombians in the Chocó know from experience that they are likely to be the latter.

We'd stopped in the village for an hour or so when it occurred to me that there was no sign of my mom. The possible presence of armed groups and smugglers in the area did nothing to quell the rising sense of anxiety I felt about her continuing absence. Where could she be? The rest of the internationals had by now trickled into the village and were lounging around looking somewhat incongruous with their dreadlocks and Che Guevara T-shirts. I started asking around with increasing urgency if anyone had seen her and Sister Carolina and soon realized that everyone apart from them had arrived. After I'd told some of the local guides about their failure to show up, the Wounaan began to organize a search party. I was putting my boots on to join in when I saw one of them chuckling and saying something in their language that I couldn't understand. One of the Afro-Colombians explained that they didn't want me going with them—I would only slow them down and be a liability.

It was hard to eat lunch knowing my mom was lost somewhere in one of the most remote regions on earth, but I made an effort to fill up on the tinned tuna and plantains. There was still no sign of my mom as our group began preparations to leave on the last push to the border. I was weighing whether I should stay on my own in the village or leave with the rest of the party when we spotted a small dugout canoe coming around the bend of the river. As it approached I could make out that my mom and Sister Carolina were among those smiling onboard. Relief washed over me and I raced down the bank to help them ashore.

It turned out that my mom had fallen and injured her knee. By the time she had rested enough to continue, the others had gone on ahead and she and Sister Carolina had lost the trail. Fortunately for them, a local Afro-Colombian leader of the Cacarica community had been fishing in the river nearby. Sister Carolina stumbled upon him and he brought them downriver on his canoe. With my mom's knee still painful and strapped up it was decided that the best thing was for her to remain behind in the village. I would have to pass through the village on my way back from the border so it would be easy to find her and the day and a half of rest would do her good. She seemed okay; we had no way of knowing at the time that the accident would subsequently lead to a life-threatening staph infection requiring four surgeries and months of antibiotics and physical therapy. Sister Carolina happily agreed to stay with her and not finish the pilgrimage she had helped plan. I hugged them good-bye and crossed the river in a canoe filled with supplies.

∽∽∽

As we set off for the last leg of the journey, we split into smaller groups. An advance party of locals, carrying the heaviest loads, headed off at full speed to get to the campsite in time to set up tents, get a fire going, and scout out the area. It was essential for them to have a number of internationals with them for protection in the event that they ran into military patrols or paramilitary groups. I eagerly volunteered. The terrain got hillier and the jungle more dense as we neared the Panama border, the heart of the Darién Gap. The accumulated exhaustion from days of hiking began to take its toll and within thirty minutes of leaving more than half a dozen of the internationals gave up and returned to the indigenous village where my mom and Sister Carolina had stayed. My back was cramped from the weight of my bag, now filled with kilos of rice, plantains, and canned tuna, and my legs began to struggle with each step. I had no choice but to stop to rest and wait for the next group behind our lead party. It turned out that not a single international could keep up with the advance group of locals. The physical fitness of these men and women and their knowledge of the terrain were spectacular. Most of the young men had bodies that rippled with muscle and the women were clearly accustomed to more than their share of physical labor. Some managed to practically run the trail barefoot or in flip-flops while others had the knee-high waterproof boots that are great for the swampy terrain but provide no ankle support.

Once I'd joined the slower group I was able to keep trudging forward. At one of our frequent breaks, somebody opened a banana leaf they had been carrying to reveal a kilo of raw cane sugar. It gave us the energy we needed to keep pushing on to that night's campsite on the Colombia-Panama border. The point of the mission had been to retrace one of the routes taken ten years earlier when the community fled their homes in the face of Operation Genesis and the murder of Marino López. That night's campsite was within striking distance of the border itself: at this jungle outpost the border was marked by a simple stone engraving on a hill. In 1997, when the refugees crossed into Panamanian territory, they met a hostile welcome. The Panamanian authorities, in violation of their international treaty obligations under the 1951 Refugee Convention, denied them refugee status and forcibly returned them to Colombian territory. They had no choice but to march dozens of miles back through the Chocó region, risking their lives at the hands of hostile paramilitaries and army brigades, and exposing themselves to the extremes of their untamed territory. Once our group made it to the border I turned around and headed for home—stopping to pick up my mom, Sister Carolina, and the other stragglers. Unlike the forced march ten years earlier, we knew that we would have a safe place to sleep each night of our journey out of the Chocó.

I'll never forget the experience of those days in the Chocó-Darién Gap. It is a region on the front lines of a global battle between human rights and corporate greed, between self-determination and outside domination. It is a place where one can walk for fifty feet, turn around, and have no idea where one came from, where one can feel living creatures all around but rarely see anything other than dense jungle. It is a place where the people are impossibly tough and physically resilient, yet human survival is visibly frail, never far from the edge of extinction.

Of Indians and Oil

I n a way, it started with Elizabeth. She has been one of my best friends since I put ice down her shirt at an eleventh birthday party back in 1991. She wore a pretty summer dress and had neatly brushed brown hair framing her face. At that point, I had a greasy mullet, a cutoff T-shirt, and cowboy boots under jeans with big holes at the knees. The ice down the shirt was my feeble attempt to flirt. I managed only to land myself a friend for life.

After college Elizabeth moved to Ecuador. As a charming gringa with a thick accent in Latin America, it was just a matter of time before she learned to appreciate the benefits of the gringo wild card. Occasionally, on weekends, she would walk into the luxurious Swiss Hotel like she owned the place and spend the day sunning by the pool and relaxing in the Jacuzzi. She looked like a guest and so nobody challenged her. As months passed, she learned to speak Spanish with a typical Quito twang: slow and clear with a bouncy rhythm that sounded almost exaggerated even when spoken by native quiteños.

She found a job working for an indigenous organization called Fundación para la Sobrevivencia del Pueblo Cofán, Foundation for the Survival of the Cofán People. I had been to Ecuador's Amazon region before but I never heard of the tiny Cofán tribe—fewer than a thousand remaining in a country where nearly 40 percent of the population, five million people, are indigenous. While I was living in Venezuela, in 2005, she called excited to tell me about them. "Starting in 1972," she explained, "Texaco set up drilling rigs all over the traditional Cofán hunting grounds, and back then the Cofán were a much

171

larger tribe." The oil companies built roads, pipelines, and helipads throughout Cofán territory. Oil operations dumped nearly 18 million gallons of crude oil and toxic waste into nearby rivers, totally destroying their environment and way of life. Today, the Cofán are part of a precedent-setting class action lawsuit against ChevronTexaco but the case has dragged on for years. With no resolution in sight, jurisdiction was transferred from the United States to Ecuador. Elizabeth explained how a group of Cofán migrated farther into the Amazon, away from the oil contamination, and founded a new village called Zábalo. Then Petro-Ecuador, the state oil company, found oil near the new village too. The Cofán organized a successful resistance movement, including burning drill platforms and holding oil workers captive until their higher-ups agreed to recognize the integrity of Cofán territory. According to Elizabeth, Zábalo and other settlements with a high degree of isolation from recent colonizers practiced a more traditional way of life, while Dureno and the other villages close to the oil activity had been culturally overwhelmed.

Today, other small Amazon tribes face the threat of oil in an all-new national political context. I made plans to go back to Ecuador not only because I owed Elizabeth a visit, but also because I wanted to see what the real impact of oil development was on the Cofán culture and how a more progressive government would approach the problem of Indians and oil. Rafael Correa's 2006 election to the presidency of Ecuador had been widely hailed as part of Latin America's shift to the left. Correa is tall with light eyes, dark hair, and a politician's broad smile. He is the first ever Ecuadoran president to speak an indigenous language, Quichua, and he combines linguistic facility with a Ph.D. in economics from the University of Illinois. His charisma and political savvy no doubt helped him get elected. But Ecuador's indigenous movement, arguably the most powerful in the Americas in terms of stand-alone political influence, was largely responsible for the political context in which he rose to power—no small accomplishment in a country where many indigenous people were barred from voting as recently as 1979.

Over the last thirty years, Ecuador's indigenous movement transformed rural organizing and shaped state policy on multicultural education, agrarian reform, and territorial autonomy. Most of Ecuador's indigenous peoples have their own tribal structure, but are also organized regionally with one group for all of the peoples of the Amazon, one for the coastal peoples, and another for the Andes—where the country's indigenous peoples are concentrated. These regional groups joined to form CONAIE (Confederación de Nacionalidades Indígenas del Ecuador, Confederation of Ecuadoran Indigenous Nations) in the 1980s. Although the confederation includes most of Ecuador's indigenous groups, the highland Quichua are by far the most influential. CONAIE took on a major national role following a countrywide strike in 1990, and in 1995 it led a national coalition in founding a political-electoral wing of the indigenous movement known as Movimiento de Unidad Plurinacional Pachakutik Nuevo País, or simply Pachakutik. In the 1996 elections, Pachakutik won significant legislative representation: more than seventy electoral victories out of roughly one hundred candidacies.

Then, in 2000, CONAIE formed an unlikely alliance with midranking military officials, who were subsequently jailed after overthrowing President Jamil Mahuad. Mahuad was a complicated character: a fiscal conservative, he had abandoned Ecuador's own currency in favor of a fully dollarized economy and orchestrated a bank "bailout" widely perceived as benefiting a major contributor to his campaign, but he also signed a peace agreement with Peru ending a bloody border dispute. Ecuador's former currency, the sucre, disappeared from circulation and now only United States dollars are accepted for commercial transactions. Other Latin American countries such as Panama and El Salvador have also scuttled their currency in favor of the greenback. After Ecuador's dollarization in 2002, CONAIE backed the election of President Lucio Gutiérrez. Gutiérrez had supported the overthrow of Mahuad from a key position within the military and run on a campaign of fighting corruption and reversing neoliberal economic reforms. After taking office, Gutiérrez repaid CONAIE by appointing two indigenous leaders to cabinet positions but then continued pushing the same policies as his predecessors, including supporting the Free Trade Area of the Americas. When that regional trade agreement fell apart, Gutiérrez pushed an unpopular bilateral trade agreement with the United States. In 2005 middle-class quiteños took to the streets and spearheaded a movement joined by the left, including the indigenous movement, to drive the president from office. His vice president, Alfredo Palacio, replaced him and finished the term.

As president, Palacio named a new minister of economy and finance: Rafael Correa, an outspoken critic of Mahuad. But Correa was forced to resign after just four months as minister—time enough to defy the advice of the IMF, to oppose Ecuador's entry into free trade deals with the United States, and to negotiate a bond offering with the Chávez government in Venezuela. Correa went on to found a new political party and launch a presidential campaign based on a nationalist, anti-neoliberal, social justice platform. Correa's toughest competition came from Alvaro Noboa, a banana magnate and the country's richest man with a personal fortune of more than $1 billion. Noboa represented the economic status quo and market-friendly pro–United States, conservative policies. Correa won, but only in the hotly contested second round. Elizabeth and her progressive Ecuadoran friends supported Correa because they saw him as allied with the country's poor majority. While undoing dollarization was never on the agenda, Correa called for renegotiation of the country's massive debt, publicly denounced the Washington Consensus, and expelled the World Bank representative to Ecuador. Still, the far left in Ecuador has been openly critical of Correa's economic policy thus far.

In May 2007, I flew into Quito, Ecuador's capital city, on my third visit to the country. Elizabeth met me at the airport and I stayed in her small guest room, cozy in its clutter. Elizabeth had to leave Ecuador a few days after I arrived, but before her departure she introduced me to an impressive group of friends—mostly Ecuadoran but also Spanish, Swiss, *estadounidense,* and French. Her *panas*—Ecuadoran for amigos—and I were kept busy with invitations and activities day and night—one friend invited me to visit the women's prison where she worked, another brought me along to a poor neighborhood where he organized weekly cultural activities, a third took me to a community meeting about women's rights in the upcoming constitutional reform process. Then, one day, Ana, a bespectacled Ecuadoran woman who worked researching gender and indigenous rights for an international academic institution, invited me to join her for a trip to interview an indigenous community. We met in an early morning rainstorm and sleepily boarded an overcrowded, intricately painted bus. The jostling for seats, the children on laps, the colorful indigenous garb, the brightly colored bus interior, the roar of the engine were by now very familiar to me; it felt like a kind of home. The two-hour drive north along Andean mountain roads carried us a world away from Quito's urban bustle through ancient Andean agricultural valleys to a town called Cayambe. Our destination was on a dirt track surrounded by rolling green hills and farms. The offices of the Federation of Popular Organizations of Ayora-Cayambe, a local CONAIE affiliate that represents fifteen indigenous communities, was housed in an adobe building with ceramic shingles on the roof.

The altitude left me out of breath and the building we entered was unheated. We were invited to sit down in the director's office, a plain room with a thatched ceiling and two bare lightbulbs. Ana and I were there to interview the head of the organization's women's group, Magdalena. I deferred to Ana for the first part of the interview and took stock of my surroundings.

The office had a couple of simple desks, file cabinets, and an old computer that looked as though it received less attention than the manual typewriter nearby. Apart from some framed certificates, the only decoration on the walls was provided by a plastic-framed picture of Jesus and a promotional calendar with a color photo of a buxom blonde wearing nothing but a bikini bottom and high heels. The irony of discussing gender rights and indigenous movements in a room watched over by an aspiring Playmate of the Year seemed lost on everyone but me. After all, it was our conversation that was unusual, not the picture on the promotional calendar. All across Latin America, tiendas, bars, and small businesses of every kind display advertisements featuring women with silicone-pumped bodies and bleached blond hair.

Magdalena, the Latina talking to Ana and me, wore a colorful multipleated skirt and a heavy sweater over several thin layers, mostly wool. She sported a traditional felt bowler hat with a ribbon around the outside, and loafers, dirty from walking on country roads. Her hair was long, dark, and neatly braided. Gold-colored necklaces contrasted agreeably with her dark brown skin; her cheeks had a reddish tinge from childhood exposure to the elements at high altitude, common among indigenous peoples in the Andes. In answer to Ana's questions, Magdalena explained the difficulties women faced in their impoverished communities: "Girls and women have many household chores, child care responsibilities, and work around the farm. Those responsibilities come first for the girls while the boys are in school."

According to Magdalena, United States–oriented economic policies, particularly the dollarization of the economy, had totally undermined the area's traditional sustenance farming economy. "Our costs went up tremendously because everything was priced in dollars. Our markets were flooded with products from Colombia, Chile, and Peru, and we couldn't compete. At the same time our purchasing power and quality of life fell because of rampant inflation and devaluation of our currency in the months before dollarization." Once the economy was in dollars, the government lost all control over monetary policy, officially delegating it to Washington. Credit in dollars was too expensive for most indigenous farmers but not for multinational export-oriented producers, contributing to a shift away from production for the local markets. "Many of us had to sell or abandon our land in favor of work in the informal sector or in flower export companies," Magdalena continued. "Our ancestors have been farming the mountains for thousands of years but these days you've got to have faith to farm."

Women had little or no chance of attaining economic independence without the support of a man, she told us. Two fields of work were available to women in the area and both paid well below the official minimum wage of $180 per month. There was employment as a domestic servant for $100 per month, or work for one of the local cut flower export businesses for $150 per month, with much of the wage coming in the form of credit at the expensive company store. People got sick from the chemicals at the flower greenhouses, sexual harassment was widespread, and the harvest season required eighteen-hour days and seven-day weeks with no overtime pay—impossible for women with family obligations. Despite these and other obstacles, Magdalena argued that it was women who led most of the organizing efforts in the area around issues including land tenure, bilingual education, and literacy. As she talked about the miseries of work in the flower industry and the perseverance of women organizers in the community, I thought with shame and guilt about the bouquets I had bought over the years: these women in Ecuador sacrificed all so that I could find a dozen roses at the corner store for $29.99 even in the middle of a long Chicago winter.

When I asked about her perspective on national politics and on President Correa and his new government, Magdalena seemed hesitant to answer. Ana later explained that most indigenous organizing is based on local not national issues, that Pachakutik has been most successful in winning local offices in elections with much more limited success nationally. She also told me that Pachakutik wasn't overly optimistic about or supportive of Correa because of its recent experience pushing Gutiérrez to the presidency and then having him betray the indigenous movement.

Back in Quito, I met another one of Elizabeth's friends at a party. Inéz, a highly energetic Spanish woman with a thick Catalan accent, was living in Quito studying environmental policy. She wanted to know if I was going to see Alberto Acosta's presentation on the ITT the next day. I had no idea what she was talking about. "Ishpingo-Tambococha-Tiputini is in Yasuní National Park," she continued to her still mystified conversant. "They are deciding how to develop a

massive oilfield." It occurred to me that the last thing I wanted was
to spend one of my precious days in Quito listening to an academic
go on for hours because he thinks he gets paid by the word. I told
her I would try to make it and headed for the kitchen to top up my
glass of Gato Negro, a Chilean wine.

The next day, against my better judgment, I decided I might as
well go to hear what Acosta had to say. I arrived a bit late but Inéz
had graciously saved me a seat in the lecture hall packed with media,
activists, government officials, and academics. Acosta, I soon learned,
was the minister of energy and mines in Ecuador. A few minutes after
I squeezed down the aisle to my seat he began a PowerPoint presentation on the Correa government's radical proposal for the ITT oil
block.

He started by explaining that the ITT block is inside Yasuní
National Park, a 2.5 million acre tropical forest preserve classified by
UNESCO as a World Biosphere Reserve in 1989. It is, he said, one of
the most biodiverse regions on earth: in two and a half acres of Yasuní
there are as many species of native trees as in all of North America.
His presentation included nature shots of muddy rivers, green pan-
oramas, and turtles on a log, the kind of thing one might find in a
Sierra Club magazine. The park is home to nearly half of all the species of birds and mammals in the entire Amazon basin. The region is
also the ancestral land of the Waorani peoples and at least two other
tribes, the Tagaeri and Taromenani, living in deliberate, voluntary
isolation from Western civilization. On my previous trips to Ecuador I
had spent time in the forest near the ITT block, in frontier settlements
and biological research stations along the Napo River. Acosta's slides
brought back vivid memories.

The men sitting around me in the auditorium were dressed in suits
and ties; the women were made up and wearing dresses and heels.
Many wore badges identifying them as employees of the Ministry of
Energy and Mines, the Ministry of Tourism, or the Ministry of Planning. I felt distinctly underdressed in my bright yellow T-shirt with a
picture of two Mapuche Indians from Chile. I reassured myself that
at least the slogan on the shirt was politically appropriate: "When the

last tree has been cut, when the last fish has been caught, when the last river has been poisoned, then they will realize that you cannot eat money."

Acosta showed the inroads oil exploration activity in Yasuní National Park had already made, opening three highways that made it possible for nonindigenous settlers to enter pristine wilderness areas and illegally harvest wood or clear land for farms. The roads certainly made travel easier but they also brought illnesses, noise pollution that scared off wildlife, abundant low-priced alcohol, and easy exit routes for young people to the cities.

Beginning oil production in the ITT block would surely bring more roads, more colonization, and more environmental and cultural destruction. When Acosta began talking about the grave environmental damage from oil extraction, spills, refining, and consumption, the slides on the screen showed horrifying images of oil-streaked rivers. Burning fossil fuel, he reminded the audience, is the number one source of CO_2, a primary greenhouse gas. Showing his calculations on the screen, he assured us that the ITT oil could release over 108 million tons of carbon into the atmosphere—not including all the carbon released when roads built for oil extraction allow for slash-and-burn agriculture to clear thousands of acres of forest a year. The extensive reserves in the ITT block were low-quality, heavy crude oil that would require onsite processing before being transported via pipeline. That meant billions of dollars of investment—likely to come from a partnership with a global oil conglomerate that would take a huge cut of the profit. He pointed out that four barrels of oily water would need to be reinjected into the ground for every barrel of oil extracted in order to maintain pressure in the wells and to dispose of waste.

The field has nearly one billion barrels of reserves of crude oil, or 20 percent of Ecuador's total oil reserves. The minister estimated that the ITT block could yield profits from the sale of crude, without considering profits from refining, shipping, or processing, of $720 million per year for twenty-five years. That is serious money in a country like Ecuador where more than 40 percent of the country's nearly 14 million people live in poverty, and 38 percent of the 2006 annual budget was dedicated to servicing debt.

But the minister wasn't there to boast or beg; he was there to present the Correa government's radical proposal: keep the ITT block oil in the ground. Ecuador, he told us in careful, emphatic words, would protect the environment and its indigenous people by not harvesting the oil. In exchange, it would ask rich countries concerned about climate change and preserving the Amazon to compensate the country with 50 percent of the sacrificed income. Showing the numbers, the risk factors, and the discounts on the screen, the minister said the international community would have to come up with $1.75 billion in compensation to make it viable to keep the oil in the ground.* The money would go to a fund that might be co-administered with international partners, and that would pay for alternative energy sources, and environmental and social development programs. The compensation could come in various forms: government-to-government grants, debt forgiveness, voluntary donations from society or NGOs, and the sale of international credits for nonexploitation of crude oil, based on the carbon credit market model. The minister was unequivocal: Ecuador was not asking for charity; it was asking the international community to share the burden of protecting the earth's environment and biodiversity.

As Acosta outlined this innovative scheme, I became increasingly excited. This, it seemed to me, was what governments willing to think outside the Washington Consensus box could come up with. It was about time that the cost side of the cost-benefit analysis of resource extraction included environmental damage, species extinction, losses from the destruction of the ecotourism industry, and the annihilation of indigenous peoples. Why should Ecuador keep pumping oil when most of the money went to foreign companies and what was left for Ecuador didn't even come close to covering its debt payments to Washington-based financial institutions or its own energy import needs?

---

*The amount was later revised upward to $350 million per year for at least ten years.

The presentation ended when Acosta showed us a picture of three beautiful indigenous girls finishing a swim in a clean river. He told us that the future of Yasuní depended on us: the girls had years and years ahead of them if we protected their home, but all the oil in the ITT block would provide the planet with just twelve days' worth of oil. Were we ready for a post-petro era?

In hindsight I've come to realize that Acosta's proposal wasn't all altruism, ecology, and human rights. If Ecuador produces less oil it will help drive prices higher for the oil it does produce. But his presentation made me even more anxious to visit a Cofán community and see for myself the impact of oil extraction. Before she left Ecuador and her job with the Cofán, Elizabeth arranged for me to spend a few days in their biggest town, Dureno. I was supposed to accompany a joint group of Cofán and Chicago Field Museum scientists on a rapid biological inventory to document the diversity of fauna in the area and go with Cofán leaders to negotiations with neighboring communities in the river's headwaters. My only contact in town was a tribal leader named Gonzalo with whom Elizabeth had worked closely. Before she left she told him about me and he generously offered to host me and let me join him for a few days of work in the jungle.

Getting to Dureno from Quito required crossing over the Andes into the Amazon basin: either a bone-rattling overnight bus ride or a short hour-long flight to Lago Agrio. Uncharacteristically, I decided to fly. The small city, just miles from the Colombian border, was originally set up as a base camp for Texaco oil workers in the 1960s but quickly grew into the regional capital and transportation hub for the surrounding rain forest. Over the years it became a destination for refugees displaced by Colombia's violence, as well as armed groups involved in the ongoing fighting there. It is no coincidence that the city has one of the highest per capita murder rates in all of Ecuador. Suffice to say it is not the kind of place to dally. From Lago Agrio airport I caught a bus along paved roads that headed out of town following an oil pipeline beside the Aguarico River. About two hours later I got off at a nondescript crossroads and hired a canoe to take me through a complex series of river channels.

I was dripping with sweat in the hot, humid air when I got out of the canoe on the opposite shore of the Aguarico. The water was too polluted from oil operations for me to even consider cooling off with a swim. The town wasn't located right on the river shore, but a half mile into the jungle along a rough dirt track through thick undergrowth.

When I finally walked into the Cofán town of Dureno, it was overrun with small children and emaciated dogs. Unlike more isolated indigenous communities I had visited, Dureno had irregular electricity allowing for television, radio, and even patchy cell phone coverage. The houses in the village, maybe fifty in all, were open-air, wood-framed, and elevated as much as fifteen feet on stilts to avoid flooding during the rainy season. Their open faces made them look as though an entire wall had been sliced off. There were no paved roads or automobiles to be seen and most people dressed in the kinds of casual, threadbare clothes my family donated to the Salvation Army ten years ago. The older women wore *ondiccuje*—simple but colorful handmade cloth tunics with matching knee-length skirts. Aside from the tunics and the Cofán language, A'ingae, spoken as a first and primary language throughout the town, there wasn't much to suggest that this was an indigenous community at all. Rather, Dureno had the air of a desperately poor rural settlement on the fringe of modern civilization.

I found a shady spot to wait for Gonzalo under his well-built house. His wife, Lucy, saw me waiting with my backpack and invited me inside until Gonzalo came back from the jungle. It turned out they had begun the survey of fauna several days before I got there. Eventually a group of children showed up and began practicing a dance to blaring Andean music on a sound box. It was fun to watch but a sure sign of a people whose culture was being infiltrated: the Cofán, a lowland forest people, were practicing Andean dance from the highlands, where the majority of Ecuador's indigenous people, especially Quichua, live.

That night in Dureno there was a town gathering to celebrate

Mother's Day in front of the one-room schoolhouse. Almost everyone turned out for the event. After a series of Western and Quichua dance performances, kids were called up one at a time to read poems or declarations of love for their mothers. I was able to follow the event because they were all reading in Spanish, a language few of the kids or their mothers spoke with any fluency. It was touching but uninspired; it might have been a school event anywhere.

The next morning Lucy's oldest son, Oscar, woke me by falling hard on the wooden floor outside my room. He was a young fifteen but was already, at 10 A.M., in a drunken stupor and could barely walk on his own. Lucy was visibly distraught, as was her mother-in-law, Elena. I jumped up to help carry Oscar down the steep stairs to the safety of the ground below. Grandma Elena chided and scolded loudly while Oscar fell asleep in the dirt.

Most of the men and adolescent boys I had run into around town that day were either busy drinking in groups or already in a drunken stupor. A few guys were passed out in the schoolhouse sleeping on tiny wooden desks. The women were occupied taking care of their men and the dozens of young children, or doing housework. Two young men staggered across the middle of town and beckoned me over to a nearby house. Not being a big drinker, and already appalled by the rampant alcoholism in the small village, I was hesitant to join them. But after days sitting around the village having nothing to do but wait, read, sleep, play with kids with whom I shared no language, I decided to try something different.

The men led me to a house, a dilapidated wooden structure. Inside, a wrinkled grandmother was making bracelets and necklaces from local plants, seeds, and beetle shells—like many of the old women in town she made *artesanía* to sell in the nearby city of Lago Agrio. With a big smile she gave me a bowl of slightly alcoholic *chicha* made from fermented yucca, and then the guys brought out a bottle of grain alcohol and a box of sickly sweet peach wine. My plan was to slowly nurse my glass so as to drink as little as possible, but there was only one little plastic cup and their style was to pass it around for shots in rapid succession. I still figured I would be all right because they were both drunk when we started and there was only the one box and the one bottle visible. But once we emptied those, more appeared as if by magic—an endless supply that eventually did me in. I have little memory of anything we talked about except that one of the guys, named Clavijo, kept asking me if I could get him a job in the United States and I told him I'd love to help but the problem was getting a visa.

Sometime later that afternoon, the dark, sandy Amazonian soil clung to my hands and clothes while I retched again and again. A nasty mix of fermented yucca, peach wine, and grain alcohol spewed out of my stomach, and I rolled over in the dirt to try to catch my breath. As I lay there, pathetically spread-eagle, I looked up, past a big, blurry papaya tree, to the white clouds and blue sky overhead. But they wouldn't stay still, the whole sky seemed to be rolling around, and looking at it made me sick again. A few of the local kids came over to stare at the spectacle. I was in a vulnerable and embarrassing position.

When I finally got up from the ground covered in dirt and with wine stains on my shirt, I staggered to the house where I was staying and nearly fell off the stairs to the hard foundation far below. I had to crawl on all fours as the earth appeared to be rolling around me. I struggled to get to the bed under a mosquito net to sleep. It was mid-afternoon and the sun still shone bright and hot above.

After my hangover wore off, I decided not to touch alcohol for the rest of my time in town and, instead, to try to do something useful and help out around the house. During the week, Lucy worked a couple hours away in Lago Agrio, and Elena, the grandmother, was in charge of the kids and the household chores. I helped her harvest bananas, wash dishes, and repair her house after I fell through one of the rotten wooden steps. I also watched her make jewelry that she then proceeded to try to sell to me, not entirely unsuccessfully.

As she sat on the floor weaving jungle seeds into plant fiber brace-lets, Elena, with her graying hair, wrinkled skin, and missing teeth, appeared older than her fifty-three years—but not the least bit feeble. Despite a pronounced limp she was tough and strong from a lifetime of manual labor in the jungle. She didn't speak much Spanish, but her eyes and head were full of wisdom acquired from a lifetime in the jungle, knowledge best, or perhaps only, communicable in her native A'ingae. A Cofán woman who lives long enough to raise her grand-children to adulthood has lived long enough to know it all. When her husband ran off to Colombia and left her with young children she learned about shame and betrayal. When one of her children died in birth she learned about sorrow and loss. When her son became an expert hunter she learned about wealth and pride. She had seen the rivers flood and wash away entire villages so she knew what despair was, and she had witnessed the community survive epidemics so she knew what gratitude meant. She had seen the benefits of steel machetes, zinc roofs, and concrete foundations so she knew the gift of technology; but she had also seen the devastation of a poisoned river, superhighways, and inexpensive pure alcohol so she knew that technology came at a cost.

We became friends of sorts during the days I spent in her family's house. As she wove strings together to form a bracelet, she expressed her frustration with the alcoholism in the community. She told me how much better things used to be, before the oil developments, before Lago Agrio sprang up in the middle of their hunting grounds. I shared my plantain chips with her, which she eagerly accepted, though with-out teeth she struggled to soften them enough to swallow. She might have been a grandmother anywhere on earth reminiscing about the good old days, but her way of life hadn't just changed with the times; it was on the verge of extinction.

One night the whole family gathered to watch the Miss Universe 2007 Pageant on their grainy fifteen-inch television. I still wonder what thoughts floated across Elena's mind, watching her young grandchil-

dren eat freshly shot jungle bird soup in front of a formal wear competition. Cultures were clashing every day in this little patch of jungle
and it was painfully obvious who was losing. The Cofán in Dureno
were too few to resist the onslaught of the West as it arrived across the
airwaves and highways. They didn't record traditional Cofán music
and so their sound systems inevitably blasted nontraditional rhythms.
Their kids preferred to watch television than explore the jungle. Their
environment had been destroyed and so they earned their meager liv-
ings in Lago Agrio, which required constant contact with non-Cofán
people. I began to understand why the Cofán had founded a new village deeper in the Amazon.

Late in the evening of my last night in Dureno, about a week after
I arrived, Gonzalo came home. He was more heavyset than most men
in town, with a round face that framed a big smile. After laboring
up to the raised platform of his house, he bear-hugged his younger
boys. He gave Lucy a kiss and they talked briefly in A'ingae before
she went back to the kitchen to finish preparing dinner of white rice
with greasy scrambled eggs. "You must be Elizabeth's friend," he said
to me. "Sorry I got caught up in the headwaters these past few days.
Nice to meet you."

Initially, though I kept it to myself, I couldn't help feeling a little
annoyed: I had traveled from the United States to Quito, from Quito
to Lago Agrio, from Lago Agrio to Dureno, just to spend time with
him and other tribal leaders. I had given plenty of advance notice of
my arrival. Now, after five days in the town and just as I had to head
back to Quito, he finally showed up. I soon realized, of course, that
he had more pressing matters to deal with than meeting me. In any
case, we were in the Amazon, on jungle time where a few days here
or there rarely make a difference. It was, after all, my fault for flying
in with my city schedule. In the United States, and even in big cities in
Latin America, people live as slaves to time, driven by the rotation of
the hour hand, totally dependent on the ticking of the minute hand.
But here time has a more elastic meaning and it is people who drive
time, not the other way around. Human actions fill the days and give
meaning to the passing of the hours. Thus, in practice, expecting any-

thing to happen "on time" in Latin America's nether regions is at best naive. It behooves the traveler to learn to enjoy, or at least to tolerate, the endless waiting, because here people often spend their whole lives waiting for something or other.

I questioned Gonzalo about what was going on up in the headwaters. Upriver from Dureno on the Río Cofanes, he told me, were several settlements of nonindigenous people that had sprung up as part of a gold rush. The Cofán were trying to negotiate an alliance with them to help limit the environmental damage to the area and maximize their voice in resisting corporate or federal government intrusions. They were hoping to team up and lobby the Correa government to give them a collective legal title to the land. "Too bad I couldn't join you," I said. "I would have loved to see your work in action."

"Well, you're welcome to stay as long as you like," he answered with apparent warmth. But though the smile seemed genuine it reminded me of the way I had offered Clavijo, my drinking companion, help if he made it to the United States, knowing full well that he would not be able to take me up on my generous offer. "What do you think of Dureno anyway?" Gonzalo asked.

It was an apparently straightforward question but the more I thought about it the more difficult I found it to answer. It raised myriad other issues for me that suddenly seemed complex, intractable even: What was my role as an outsider in the town? What had I expected to accomplish in a few short days there? The traditional culture of the Cofán seemed to be eroding in front of my eyes in a way that they had little control over. But how much freedom did I have in choosing the way I lived? I could opt not to own or watch a television but I couldn't simply decide not to live in a society shaped by mass media transmitted via radiowave and satellite. I could choose to live in Latin America but I couldn't change the fact that I would always be a gringo.

The Cofán foundation that Elizabeth worked for sought to acquire control of vast tracts of Amazon forest precisely so that Cofán children and grandchildren would have the freedom to determine for themselves how to live. Cofán culture, like so many traditional ways of life, is inherently tied to the land. Without it the people have no option but to assimilate. With land, they have choices, at least, about whether, and how much, to resist outside society. Though I didn't come from an indigenous culture, I too had sought ways to resist and rebel. My travel was, in part, a way to avoid falling into the social pressures and norms my peers in the United States faced, and perhaps of avoiding the complications of defining a life divided between elite academic institutions and weekend prison visits to my mom and dad. What implications did such a peripatetic life have for my ability to maintain a sense of self or to relate to a community?

I'd come to recognize a contradiction at the heart of my traveling around Latin America and the rest of the globe: the airplanes and buses I take consume far more than my share of the planet's nonrenewable resources, especially oil. Yet, at the same time, I seek to live in solidarity with groups like the Cofán in their struggle for survival and autonomy. On balance, my journeying probably does the earth more harm than good. I have benefited enormously from my Latin American hosts' generosity and willingness to teach me about their lives and their struggles, but all too often I have little to offer in return. Ever since my first trip to Guatemala eight years earlier, I had been repeatedly impressed with the generosity of the people I met throughout Latin America. Their willingness to give does not flow from a feeling of security or privilege, like my own, but is born out of a culture of necessity and interdependence. The munificence that I encounter in my travels often makes the rugged individualism of my own culture feel more like a prison.

All these issues were raised for me by Gonzalo's apparently straightforward inquiry. But I could not even begin to explain to him the complexities and doubts of my own feelings. Instead I mustered a vague, noncommittal summary of my time in Dureno, describing how kind his family had been, how much I had enjoyed the company of his mother and children, but also how enormous the problem of alcohol seemed. At this latter point he nodded, in what seemed a knowing way, making me wonder if he'd heard from others in town about my low tolerance for drink. Then, deftly handling his machete, he scratched a rough map of the area into the caked dirt on the stairs of his platform. "The town where we are, Dureno, is here," he said, marking a little X along the winding line that represented the river. "But the oil developments, roads, and colonization by nonindigenous settlers have destroyed the environment on all sides." Dureno is an isolated island of forest in the midst of an ever-expanding sea, a sea of development. The Cofán, Gonzalo told me, had the great misfortune to live on top of an oilfield during the petrol era.

A few months after I said my good-byes to Gonzalo and his family, I received an e-mail from Elizabeth with the title COFAN VICTORY. The e-mail said simply, "See attached. xo." The attached document was a long description of a trip a group of sixty Cofán took to Quito to meet with President Correa and his cabinet. The meeting had been set up so the government could sign over legal title of 75,000 acres in the headwaters along the Río Cofanes, bringing the total land under tribal control to roughly a million acres. President Correa himself signed the document as an official witness, along with the ministers of environment and of indigenous groups and social movements. In exchange for legal title the Cofán assumed responsibility for protecting the land's biodiversity. Their millennia in the Amazon basin had, no doubt, left them well prepared for the challenge.

Bolivian Hearts and Mines

At more than thirteen thousand feet, the windswept altiplano airport in El Alto is one of the highest on earth. I arrived well after midnight in June 2007. It was my fourth trip to the landlocked Andean republic of Bolivia. I had returned, this time, to see how Bolivia was progressing under President Evo Morales. I had followed with interest the political currents and elections that brought a wave of progressive, nationalist governments to power across the region since I first traveled to Guatemala in 1999. Now I was curious to see how Morales's government, the latest manifestation of this trend, was confronting Bolivia's tortured past.

Referred to simply as Evo, Morales has been widely hailed as the country's first ever indigenous president since the Spanish conquest 470 years ago. Evo is an extraordinarily charismatic nationalist and was elected thanks, in part, to his vocal criticism of United States government efforts to eradicate Bolivia's coca crops, his opposition to the neoliberal economic model, and his willingness to publicly embrace his indigenous roots. As he sought election to the presidency he benefited from the experience of President Chávez and the Venezuelan revolutionary process. With declarations like, "If the nineteenth century belonged to Europe and the twentieth century to the United States, the twenty-first century will belong to America, Latin America," Evo inspired millions.

It was late at night when I left the terminal building and buses were no longer running. I caught a cab to the exclusive south side of the city where I planned on staying at the house of Patricia, a Bolivian friend I first met year earlier while she was on vacation in the United States. I was looking forward to seeing her. She lived in a new house that was tastefully designed and spacious. My guest bedroom had a full wall of windows looking out onto the mountains, a king-sized bed, a walk-in closet, and a private bathroom with a Jacuzzi. It was just days since I had left the Cofán in Dureno, but I was in an entirely different world. Maids washed my clothes, made me a big breakfast every morning, and called taxis for me when I was going out. After nearly four years of traipsing around from place to place, and not having my own room—unless it was in a seedy hotel—I was happy to have found a clean place to unpack my bag. In exchange for a few days of comfort and companionship I was prepared to overlook the incongruity of staying in such luxurious surroundings while doing my research.

While Patricia was at work, I planned on meeting with political contacts in the dirty centro or up in La Paz's sprawling impoverished sister city, El Alto. So many little things about the country were exactly as I remembered from previous trips: the literally breathtaking altitude and the views of the snowcapped Illimani mountain peak; indigenous women with long dark braids, felt bowler hats, and brightly colored woven tapestries; the omnipresent shoe-shine boys with ski masks to hide their shame; or the sweet, juicy chicken *salteñas* baked hot for breakfast.

But when I looked deeper, the country was in the midst of a peaceful revolution like nothing I had ever seen before except, perhaps, in Venezuela. Evo's government and the Bolivian people were simultaneously immersed in dozens of major political debates: a so-called nationalization of the nation's gas reserves, actually just a renegotiation of contracts with companies harvesting the extensive natural gas fields; tumult in the coca industry over efforts to enforce production limits in certain regions even though Evo was himself president of the coca growers union; several eastern provinces centered around the city of Santa Cruz trying to secede from the Andean highlands; tax hikes on the mining sector as the government expanded its own mining operations in a renationalization of sorts; and fierce deliberations in the Constitutional Assembly where progress toward drafting a new constitution had been slow to nil.

The idea of refounding the political system, attempting to do away with the bourgeois state through writing a new constitution, wasn't limited to Bolivia. Around the region, radical populist candidates including Morales in Bolivia, Correa in Ecuador, and Chávez in Venezuela ran successful political campaigns based, in part, on condemning neoliberalism and promising to convoke constitutional assemblies to rewrite the rules of the game. In Venezuela, in 1999, thanks to an opposition boycott, Chávez's coalition was able to quickly and democratically put in place a new constitution that dramatically increased social and economic guarantees such as social security, health care, education, respect for women's and indigenous rights, and also strengthened the executive branch. Constitutional transformation appeared to be a promising way to entrench a democratic and peaceful revolution. Equally significant, the process politicized the masses, gave them a feeling of ownership over the new document, and reinforced and legitimized the new government's call for radical change.

But there were problems with this strategy too: in Ecuador and Bolivia the political opposition was putting up a real fight, making attempts to reconstruct the legal basis of the state time-consuming and costly. That raised the question as to how much political capital newly elected governments should spend on drafting an alternative legal framework in countries that had only a limited ability to enforce the rule of law. There was also a danger that constant revision of a constitution devalues its otherwise timeless, above-politics quality. As soon as he won reelection in 2006, Chávez called for a series of amendments to the constitution he had put in place in 2000. If every presidential election were to be followed by an overhauling of the constitution, then the state would spend most of its time redrafting progressively weakened legal codes rather than expanding services or enforcing existing rights.

The secession movement in the opposition-dominated region around Santa Cruz wasn't just about politics; it also involved profound cultural difference. While the population on the Andean side of Bolivia was largely indigenous people, the lowlands exuded a more Western, consumer-oriented way of life. La Paz had a strong intellectual and arts base; Santa Cruz, plastic surgeons and shopping malls. The effort to secede is as much about the country's cultural divide as it is about control of natural gas revenues.

On my first day in La Paz, I piled into a public minibus headed up the windy highway to El Alto—I was the fourteenth person in the small vehicle. I might have just taken a taxi, but at 25 cents the price was right for public transportation. It took twenty minutes to climb out of the basin in which La Paz is nestled and reach the plateau above, where, over the last thirty years, the twin city of El Alto has sprung up with little planning and much poverty. I was unsure where to get off for a meeting arranged at the last minute and felt acutely self-conscious about being, by a long stretch, the tallest and whitest person in the vehicle. The Aymara woman next to me wearing a felt bowler hat, and a brightly colored, multilayered petticoat into which her young son had all but disappeared from view, fit in perfectly. While seeking to avoid becoming the center of attention in the overcrowded space, I tried unsuccessfully to get the driver's attention to ask where my stop was. The woman next to me took pity, chuckling softly as she told me to get off at the next intersection. I thanked her and asked how to get from the stop to my meeting point, did I just *"seguir al recto hasta llego?"* To my intense embarrassment everyone in the minibus started laughing. It wasn't until I was out in the street that I realized my mistake: instead of asking if I just continued straight—*seguir recto*—I had asked if I continued to the rectum until I arrived. Worse still, the verb I had chosen for arrive, *llegar,* has a double meaning in Spanish with an explicitly sexual connotation.

I met Julio Mamani, a journalist and organizer, in front of a union office where he had just finished a meeting. The streets were swarming with people, packed with minibuses and trucks. It seemed as if no matter where I stood I was in someone's way. "Let's sit down and drink some mate while we talk," Julio offered. Seated in one of the hundreds of hole-in-the-wall snack shops on the bustling streets of El Alto, I told Julio that I wanted to learn about Evo's rise to power, his first years in office, and his government's relationship to the grass-roots organizations that elected him. The reemergence of the Latin American left today is unlike previous reformist movements in the region that derived political power from vertical relationships to unions, peasant associations, and party hierarchies. Today's progressive political movements in the region tend to have more horizontal power structures and to rely on a diverse array of social movements. These kinds of groups make up the radical left in the United States today too, but with seemingly no impact on electoral results.

Julio, dressed casually and in somber colors, was slow to talk. I couldn't tell if he was shy, which seemed unlikely given his work as a journalist and organizer, or if he was skeptical of me and my pretenses. The latter seemed a distinct possibility. I had introduced myself as a freelance writer with a radical family background and it occurred to me, as on many occasions previously, that I might appear as just another rich kid without a proper job looking to make a name for himself off of Latin America. I wasn't even sure myself if this perception was incorrect. But I pushed on anyway, filling the silence until Julio grew tired of listening to me and began to explain El Alto's relationship to Evo. After Evo's first year in office, he told me in careful deliberate Spanish, people in El Alto who had voted for him started to get frustrated; some even organized protests against his government. "Then in May 2006, Evo announced that he was nationalizing the natural gas, and that won back a lot of his support even though the nationalization law was mainly show; it didn't really take away the control of the foreign companies. In any case, it isn't just about the gas. People are upset because the neoliberal structure of the state is still largely intact."

I had, on more than one occasion, heard Bolivians say, "We elected Evo to do away with it and now he's governing it," so I understood what Julio meant. I took notes as he continued. "Sure, sometimes Evo's government offers powerful positions to leaders of our movements but then our leaders abandon their organizations, their roots, and become part of the same state bureaucracy we have fought against for so many years. All over Latin America we see the same problem. If social movements focus their energy on electoral outcomes we lose even when we win. How many leaders across the region have sold out, betrayed their base, or simply failed to change the direction of the massive state bureaucracy, oriented for the last two decades or more toward transferring power to the private sector? But if we ignore electoral outcomes, we severely limit our ability to influence state policy and thus we lose control over vital areas of our daily lives." Julio was right, I thought. Here was a contradiction at the heart of radical organizing, whether in Latin America, where strategies focused on electoral outcomes have had some success over the last decade, or in the United States, where it's difficult to imagine the radical left having any significant electoral impact at the national level.

I was particularly interested in whether El Alto residents favored an electoral strategy for social change or preferred militant street protests. But to Julio the dichotomy wasn't as clear-cut as it seemed to me. "Most Bolivians support democracy, the problem is that too often our elected leaders steal or do what Washington tells them, not what we elected them to do. Neoliberalism has undermined democracy by taking decision-making power away from national governments and transferring it to multinational institutions like the IMF. So, we have to take to the streets, keep the pressure on constantly. People in El Alto vote, and we vote for Evo," he told me. "But we also organize street protests because we understand the pressure our governments face from Washington, and the burdens they inherit."

Julio explained the rapid growth of El Alto into a city with, unofficially, more than a million people, most of whom are first- or second-generation arrivals from Bolivia's rural provinces. He told me that for at least two decades the city had provided support to protesters and movements coming into the capital from around the country. He argued that the rural roots, the close connections many families maintained with their communities in the provinces, and the widespread general poverty in El Alto, as in most of the interior of Bolivia, meant the recently arrived urban residents on the plateau above La Paz were natural allies to many of the groups from around the country that marched on the capital in protest. "The farmers, the *cocaleros,* the miners all have someone from their family or community here." I knew that in 2003, El Alto's residents led the way in overthrowing two successive presidents, Gonzalo Sánchez de Lozada, and then Carlos Mesa. But did the city's political significance go back further than that? I wondered. "Of course," Julio told me, looking steadily at me over the rim of his mug of coca mate. "Just ask the miners."

During my year in Chile back in 2002, I had visited Bolivia's mines for the first time. The University of Chile was on strike and I had taken the opportunity to travel more than forty hours by bus, across the Andes, through a high-altitude desert to the beautiful city of Potosí. Some eight hundred mines pockmark a fourteen-thousand-foot-tall mountain called Cerro Rico that looms above the colonial splendor of Potosí. The mountain has literally shrunk since the Spanish began mining its rich silver veins in the mid-1500s. Today, long after the silver deposits and the Spanish have disappeared, Bolivian miners remove five thousand tons of rock every day in search of tin, lead, and zinc.

While in a café in town eating a simple breakfast of eggs and toast, I met a local miner named Fecundo who invited me to see where he and his team worked. The next day, shortly after sunrise, I tied a red bandanna over my face, flipped on the headlamp strapped to my yellow helmet, and followed Fecundo into the bowels of the earth. The windswept entrance to the mine on Cerro Rico was through a crude, arched, beige stone tunnel that looked out onto warehouses, mineral processing sheds, and barrackslike dorms. Inside, the tunnel was black.

Barrel-chested, his left cheek bulging with coca leaves, Fecundo was one of ten thousand miners working on the mountain. I followed him deep into the dank shaft. All natural light disappeared and I had to crouch low to avoid banging my head on the ceiling. Fecundo steered me through a mazelike system of narrow tunnels, some of them dropping straight down and others heading off into the dark nothingness beyond the reach of my headlamp. In some places the ceiling seemed to be sweating beads of water; in others tiny stalactites hung from the roof. After a few minutes, I was panting for breath from the altitude and the dust-laden air and fighting acute claustrophobia, not generally a problem for me. I looked around anxiously to see if there was a place I could stand up straight and let my lungs expand. There wasn't.

Several hundred feet down into the shaft we came across a lone miner. He was coated with a thin layer of fine gray powder. He also had the trademark bulge of coca leaves in his cheek and the red-brown skin of Bolivia's indigenous people showing through the dust. Gloveless, he grasped a steel pick with his left hand and a mallet with his right. As he hammered into a piece of stone that, to me at least, was indistinguishable from the rest of the mine shaft, he slowly rotated the pick in between each mallet blow to adjust the angle. Fecundo yelled out to the miner in Quichua. Like most of Bolivia's miners and over half of the country's nine million inhabitants, Fecundo and his team spoke Spanish only as a second language. The man came over to greet us, smiling and extending a chalky hand. Fecundo offered him a pinch of his coca leaves, while I proffered one of the $3 bags of dynamite I had purchased, on Fecundo's advice, as presents for the miners from the shops selling mining supplies that lined the road to Cerro Rico. The small gray cylinders came in a clear plastic bag and felt almost weightless. It was hard to believe they had the power to bite into solid rock but that day I watched from a safe distance as the miners used carefully placed charges to turn a rock wall into rubble.

Farther down the shaft, we could hear a loud grating sound over a high-pitched hum. I could no longer see because the beam of my headlamp was reflected back into my eyes by the dense rock dust filling the air. Fecundo yelled toward where the noise was coming from. The two men working the machine heard him on the second try and cut the motor. They were both wearing goggles but no face masks, and a thick layer of rock dust coated them from helmet to boot. They showed me their huge power drill with its large bit for cutting into the rock. An adjacent nozzle sprayed water to reduce the dust—not at all effectively, judging by the air quality. They were drilling into the end of the shaft to test for mineral quality and extend the tunnel farther into the heart of Cerro Rico. Did they want a bag of explosives? Did I want to see them work?

They fired up the motor and the driller lifted the machine into place while his assistant took charge of the water and power lines. As soon as the drill made contact with the rock, the noise was overpowering and the dust began to fly. I tried to tough it out but my senses were overloaded: I couldn't breathe, I couldn't see, I couldn't hear myself think, and I couldn't figure out what I was actually supposed to be watching anyway. Reaching blindly for the wall I felt my way backward, stumbling and bumping my helmet but moving toward clearer air. I stopped, ripped off my bandanna now caked with rock dust, and crumpled to the muddy floor coughing. Fecundo was there in no time patting me on the back and chuckling warmly.

"*Vamos*," he said, "up a couple levels the breathing is better." In a few minutes we found ourselves in a spacious chamber with air that seemed deliciously clean and clear. There was a big winch with a cable going through a hole in the floor, and a few wheelbarrows lying around nearby. I was still trying to recover from the trauma of the power drill. I hadn't been able to tolerate the dust for even a few minutes and I had my trusty red bandanna to filter the air. The drillers, much closer to the source of the rock powder, had no filters or masks at all and, incredibly, appeared to be able to tolerate it all day, every day.

These miners, and how many thousands more like them, were working under conditions that couldn't have improved much since the Spanish colonial era. There were no bathrooms, no drinking water, no food. And at the shaft opening, where they dumped tons of mineral slag every day for sorting, I had seen plenty of young boys hard at work—age is difficult to estimate when in a different country but they were prepubescent, of that I was sure. My own physical discomfort began to seem paltry in comparison with their daily trauma. I was appalled. Sitting in the mine shaft that day I couldn't understand how anyone could subject themselves, much less their young sons, to this suicidal work. And for what? A starvation wage? The dream of finding a few ounces of silver the Spanish left behind? I began to regret going to the mines at all. Maybe my being there only added to the workers' humiliation. They had generously invited me into their hellish world, deep inside the earth. All I could offer them in exchange was a cheap present of a few sticks of dynamite.

But a small part of me also felt somehow redeemed: as a young backpacker and motorcyclist, Che Guevara had been profoundly affected by seeing the horrible conditions in mines in Bolivia. And my four parents had always decried the labor abuses perpetuated around the world to maintain a flow of raw materials for consumers in the United States. Here was proof of what they said, a justification of sorts for their political perspectives. And I was seeing it firsthand, not in Che's diary or in a film, not over dinner in Chicago. This was real.

Eduardo Galeano, a Uruguayan writer my parents encouraged me to read before I was even interested in Latin America, describes Potosí as a mine that "eats men." In *Genesis*, the first book in his Memory of Fire Trilogy, he writes of the "implacable rain of mine dust annihilating" the workers. "Their lungs turn to stone and their tracheas close. Even before the lungs forget to breathe, the nose forgets smells and the tongue forgets tastes, the legs become like lead. . . . When they emerge from the pit, the miners look for a party. While their short life lasts and their legs still move, they need to eat spicy stews and swallow strong drink." Remembering Galeano's words, I couldn't stop myself from asking how long men last under these conditions. "Silicosis. We all get silicosis," Fecundo answered. "The dust starts to destroy our lungs and when enough is gone, we die. Miners that are lucky enough to avoid dying on the job in a tunnel collapse or from the gas in the shafts generally end up suffocating and coughing up their lungs once the silicosis nears 100 percent. Drillers like those guys you saw are young and tough, maybe they will keep that job for three years, four max. The drillers get paid the most but they also get silicosis the fastest. If they're lucky they'll live to forty."

When I asked Fecundo how much he and the other miners earned, he was evasive and vague. In an unproductive month, he explained, they wouldn't make enough to cover the cost of their materials, but in a successful month, when they found a rich vein, they could afford to take the bus to and from work, buy meat for their families to eat, and maybe even school clothes for their children. Fecundo and the miners he had introduced me to were part of a cooperative and their shaft's profits were divided among the men according to their rank.

I later learned that in Bolivia most miners fall into two categories: those who work for the state-owned mining corporation (COMIBOL), who are unionized, salaried workers and who receive a steady paycheck and minimal benefits, and those who started or joined private ventures, called cooperatives, and who are paid based on the amount and quality of ore they mine in any given month and their position in the corporate hierarchy. This latter group often have a get-rich-quick, lottery-playing approach that leads a few to wealth and leaves most to "eat earth" for lack of food. Cooperative mining expanded rapidly in the 1990s and today around 80 percent of Bolivia's estimated 75,000 miners are in cooperatives. COMIBOL miners have no chance of getting rich but reap the benefits of stability and a long-term approach to reserve management and depletion. Almost without exception Bolivian miners, like two thirds of the country, live in poverty.

On October 5 and 6, 2006, in the mining town of Huanuni, dynamite blasts killed seventeen miners and injured more than a hundred others. These casualties were not accidents: a two-day conflict between COMIBOL miners and cooperative miners had started over access to the country's richest tin mines. The ensuing negotiations went on for months and led to the replacement of two mining ministers in the national government. The talks became more complicated still when tens of thousands of cooperativists marched on La Paz in February 2007 in protest of a proposed tax hike on the mining sector. Four months later, the COMIBOL miners union demanded that the government do away with the cooperativists all together. Both groups had supported Evo Morales's successful 2005 presidential bid and it was his government that was responsible for resolving the conflict.

cscscscs

The day after meeting Julio Mamani in El Alto, I tracked down José Montesinos, a friend of Julio's, in a seemingly endless line outside the government pension building in central La Paz. José was a miner who had retired to El Alto in 1987 after more than thirty years working in Potosí state—not far from where I first visited the mines with Fecundo back in 2002. Tall by Bolivian standards despite a slouch, perhaps left over from all those years in the short, narrow tunnels, he was sprightly for his age. His gray hair was thinning but neatly combed and his pencil-thin mustache was well trimmed. A thin glaze covered his eyes and I wondered if he had emerging cataracts. He asked someone to hold his place in line for an hour so we could have coca tea and cheese *empanadas* at a nearby café. I noticed that he was very thin and it occurred to me that perhaps his pension wasn't enough to make ends meet for him and his family. An old beige suit that was too big hung from his shoulders—I imagined it was the only one he owned and he wore it on special occasions, like collecting his monthly pension or meeting with a foreign journalist like me. When he talked, only one tooth was visible.

Once we were seated in the café I asked him to tell me about his life. He was born in 1936 in Tupiza, near Potosí, and began mining late, at age nineteen. He spent most of his career working in the mines and organizing in the miners union within COMIBOL. In the mid-1980s he was fired, and he decided to leave the mines and move to El Alto. I told him I was sorry he had been fired, but what I really wanted to learn about was his perspective on the mining industry, the role the mines and miners had played in national politics from the beginning. Though friendly, José's first responses were disappointing. He seemed cagy and unsure of what he wanted to say. As I sipped my green coca tea I began to think about making a speedy exit. But José's intelligence and insights would quickly prove my first impression wrong.

"You speak Spanish *muy bien*," he opined generously. "So you must have heard the expression '*vale un Potosí*,' right?" I had, and I knew it meant "worth a fortune," worth the mines at Potosí. The saying must have come into use back in the 1500s or 1600s when the Potosí silver mines were in their heyday. Now people use the expression all over Latin America without much thought as to where it came from. "Well the Spanish took more than sixty thousand tons of silver out of Potosí, so much silver that you could build a bridge across the Atlantic with it," he continued. "That silver, Bolivia's silver, funded the Spanish Armada in their battles with England, and, indirectly, fueled the European Renaissance as most of the wealth left Spain to pay off debts to northern European countries where the industrial revolution eventually began."

Talk about a debt. The IMF's worries about poor countries making their debt payments on time suddenly came into perspective. How much interest should Spain's debt to Bolivia have racked up over the last five hundred years? For José the tragedy wasn't the stolen wealth so much as the lost lives. The black slaves the Spanish brought over, accustomed to tropical conditions and freedom, lasted an average of just six months in the harsh conditions at high altitude (today Bolivia has one of the smallest communities of African descent of any country in Latin America). To address the labor shortage in the mines around the end of the 1500s, the Spanish systematized a forced labor system called the *mita*, inherited from the Incan empire. The *mita* obliged millions of indigenous men, more accustomed than Africans to the climate, to work long stints in the mines with little or no compensation. The Spanish encouraged the men to chew coca to cut their hunger and make it possible for them to work longer hours. Estimates suggest that several million indigenous people died working the mines for the Spanish.

Even after independence from Spain, Bolivia's mines continued to be lucrative for the owners and exploitive for the workers. "As late as the 1920s and 1930s," José explained, "just three families controlled the national mining sector. There were the Aramayos, the Hochschilds, and, most powerful of all, the Patiños." Between them they employed thirty thousand miners and owned 163 separate mines including the ones outside Huanuni where, in 2006, the cooperativists and COMIBOL miners threw dynamite at each other. It was under these barons, José told me, that miners began to organize in earnest for better labor conditions. In 1919 they won, at least on paper, the right to an eight-hour workday. And, a few decades later, the miners were one of the vanguard labor groups that made possible the 1952 revolution that nationalized the mines. José wished the owners hadn't been compensated—hadn't they already recouped their investment many times over?—but he still remembered the revolution and the nationalization as great moments in Bolivia's past. Che Guevara was in Bolivia during the revolution and described the miners busing in to support agrarian reform as "warriors from other worlds."

COMIBOL was founded to manage the newly nationalized mines and a few years later José started work. "It was a time of *mucha esperanza*," José reminisced, "there were high hopes in every sector of society for what the revolution would bring, but by 1954 the government had already sold out, become reformist rather than revolutionary, and rearmed the military." José went on to describe the tumultuous years that followed the 1952 revolution. He mentioned more military regimes and changes in government than I could keep track of, but it was clear that most of them offered very little for the miners. Still, José insisted, the mining unions represented the political vanguard in the country as late as the 1980s. "But then in 1985," his filmy eyes looked at me solemnly, "with mineral prices collapsing, and poverty and debt spiraling, the government embraced Washington's sociopolitical model."

I already knew this part of the story. Bolivia in 1985 was a classic example of the way that neoliberalism got shoved down Latin Americans' throats. Jeffrey Sachs, now a famed economist and onetime adviser to the IMF, the World Bank, and the United Nations, drew up a plan that would epitomize the term "shock therapy." Sachs's plan became Decree 21060, thanks largely to Planning Minister Gonzalo Sánchez de Lozada, who was later elected president twice only to have popular protests drive him from the country in the middle of his second term in 2003.* The stabilization plan prioritized Bolivia's

---

*Goni, as he is known in Bolivia, not only helped convert Sachs's plan into policy but he also benefited from the implementation. When the mining industry was privatized a few years later, he was buying. He developed a company called COMSUR, which owned the majority stake in five separate concessions and a foundry. The

debt payments to foreign and multilateral creditors like the IMF. It slashed tariffs and trade barriers, it froze public sector salaries, and it cleared the way for privatization of key industries, including mining.

"COMIBOL became nothing more than an administrative entity. They wanted to break our unions, and firing tens of thousands of miners was a good way to do it," José lamented. I had many more questions but our hour was up and he had to get back to his place in line to claim his monthly pension. I asked if I could see him again, and he told me where to meet him in El Alto the following evening.

Thus it was at 6 P.M. the next day I found myself back on a crowded minibus driving up to El Alto. As we climbed out of La Paz I could see the sun setting over the snowcapped peak of Illimani, one of the Andes's most beautiful mountains.

The minibus slowed at every traffic-jammed intersection and progress was further impeded by countless street vendors spilling out from crowded sidewalks into the road. Consequently I was a bit late when I arrived at the place José and I had agreed to meet, appropriately enough the Plaza del Minero, a large square dominated by the massive Statue of the Unknown Miner featuring a hardhat with a headlamp, and carrying a pick and dynamite. I spotted José waiting patiently on a nearby bench with a few other old men whom I presumed to also be retired miners. He jumped up to greet me and shook my hand with a warm smile before inviting me to his house, which, he told me, was just a few blocks away. I later learned that the neighborhood around the Plaza del Minero is largely populated by ex-miners. As we walked, I pondered his apparent excitement at seeing me: Had he expected me to stand him up? Did he think his meeting with a gringo would

---

1997 mining code was written during his first presidential administration and approved by him, despite an obvious conflict of interest. In 2004, shortly after being forced to step down from the presidency, he made millions when COMSUR was acquired by Glencore International AG, of Switzerland, for $220 million. The attorney general in Bolivia has brought charges against Goni stemming from a massacre that occurred while he was president.

impress his old mining buddies? Perhaps he was just pleased to have someone to talk to about his life. In any event, I was touched by the warmth of his greeting.

José lived in a comfortable but simple cement block house with broken glass bottles wedged into the top of the outer cement wall as a substitute for barbed wire—a security arrangement common throughout Latin America. Once inside, he invited me to sit in a poorly upholstered bright red chair while his wife went to get us each a glass of soda. A clock on the wall featured Jesus' face as the background, and a small television in the corner was playing music videos, including Coolio's *Gangsta's Paradise*. It was the last place I expected to see a 1990s rap video. I asked José to finish explaining what happened in 1985 when the government implemented its neoliberal economic plan.

"They wanted to destroy our unions," José picked up where he had left off the day before. "Miners were organized, our union members were mostly from radical left political parties, and we had a sense of solidarity with each other and with the country as a whole." In 1985, after the economic plan went into effect, COMIBOL shut down hundreds of mines, and for an opening salvo fired at least thirty thousand workers. According to José, more than seventy thousand *mineros* lost their jobs in mines and associated industries over the course of a few years following Decree 21060.

"That same year, in 1985, we organized a colossal *Marcha por la Vida* on La Paz," José continued, describing the March for Life while sipping his Coca-Cola. "But when we were just twenty miles outside of the capital the army attacked us brutally. Our blood flowed and we took refuge wherever we could. Although the city was much smaller back then, we received support from the people of El Alto and have looked to it as a center for solidarity ever since."

"So what did all of those unemployed miners do?" I asked, caught up in the dramatic narrative. I was wondering if Bolivia's abused labor population had responded to the changes that came with globalization as so many unions in the United States had—by focusing on narrow, short-term interests that ultimately precluded broader labor solidarity. "We have a saying," José answered. "*Sangre de minero, semilla de guerrillero.*" The rhyme is lost in translation but the meaning is the same: the miner's blood is the seed of the guerrilla.

I racked my brain for details of Bolivian history and guerrilla movements but I couldn't come up with anything apart from Che Guevara's fatal attempt to start an armed revolution there in 1967. Che had made numerous errors including learning Quichua, the highland indigenous language, and then basing his team in the lowlands where the indigenous people mainly speak Guaraní. His guerrillas lost communication with their contacts in Cuba, the Bolivian Communist Party refused to help, and the local community left them isolated and hungry. Without support on the ground or the mass uprising Che had anticipated, the Bolivian army, backed by the CIA, was able to hunt him down and summarily execute him. Che's 1967 guerrilla efforts notwithstanding, I thought of Bolivia as a peaceful country without guerrilla warfare in its past, despite widespread and perpetual political instability. "I don't get it," I said, feeling uncomfortable that perhaps I was taking José's saying too literally and connecting too readily with my own parents' years living underground. "Did some of you go on to form underground guerrilla organizations?"

José laughed a little, and told me gently that I was missing the point. He explained that after 1985 tens of thousands of Bolivian miners had no choice but to migrate away from the mines in search of a new life for themselves and their families. A few went to other countries in search of work, but more went to the campo and became farmers, especially of coca in the Chapare region, or moved into cities, especially the rapidly growing El Alto. What was crucial, José told me, was that even as "the new economic plan succeeded in destroying organized labor in the mining industry, it also spread the seeds of future political movements, including those that would carry Evo to the presidency."

I wanted examples and José had them. He told me about Filemón Escobar, who, after losing his mining job, became a coca farmer and union organizer and went on to become one of the founders of Evo's political party, MAS (Movement Toward Socialism), although he and

Evo had since fallen out. José himself was another example of a miner who had developed organizing skills and a radical political analysis during his decades in the mines only to lose his job in the aftermath of the 1985 economic plan. José moved to El Alto where he put his union experience to work in local movements and organizing efforts. When Evo was elected in 2005, it wasn't just the COMIBOL and cooperative miners supporting him, but also most of the 700,000 people represented by the neighborhood associations in El Alto, the estimated fifty thousand families of *cocaleros* in the Yungas and Chapare, and other groups around the country, many of which included ex-miners.

I sat back in the red chair attempting to make sense of what José was telling me. Jesus stared at me from between the minute and hour hands of the wall clock and several large-hipped, scantily clad women gyrated on the television screen. I tried to focus my attention. My mind filled with images of colonial slave drivers, coca-chewing labor organizers, a short-lived revolution, corrupt ministers, volatile global commodity markets, and a neoliberal economic program. Bolivia's history and that of the mines might be broadly summarized in a progression of just six words: colonization, independence, revolution, nationalization, privatization, and renationalization. Somewhere in the process the proverbial *sangre de minero* became a *semilla de guerrillero*, a seed whose germination gave way to broad national support for Evo in the 2005 presidential election. In Bolivia, the left was confronting similar challenges to those faced by progressive movements across the region, and in the United States too: how to win legitimate authority to make decisions and how, once you've done that, to deal effectively with the legacy of neoliberalism and its transfer of power from the state to the private sector, without stifling economic growth or civil liberties. How, in short, to ensure that young, charismatic leaders live up to the hopes of an idealistic electorate.

Returning home from José's house, I felt I had more questions than answers. I told Patricia I was heading to Potosí, to the mines for another visit. She offered to have her travel agent research the pos-

sible itineraries for me and invited me to a local German restaurant
for dinner. Between ordering bier and schnitzel she asked what I had
done during my days in La Paz. "Meeting friends of friends, mostly up
in El Alto," I answered, not sure what she would make of my spending time there.

"Really? Wow! What was it like?" she asked, apparently genuinely interested. "We talk about it a lot but we never go there except
on the way to the airport." El Alto was where poor people lived and
there wasn't much to attract someone with Patricia's privileged lifestyle. She was smart, politically astute, and socially conscious. People
in her family had even voted for Evo, believing his election would
save the country from a civil war; but none of that meant she had
access to a place like El Alto. As a gringo I could more easily transcend
the rigid divisions that separated the multiple worlds nestled in and
around Bolivia's capital city. I mulled over how to answer her question as I took a fork of sauerkraut. It seemed easier for me to cross
class boundaries in Latin America than for Latin Americans to do so
in their own countries or for me to do so in mine. Thinking about
it reminded me of my trips to El Salvador: the first time, as a naive
eighteen-year-old, I inadvertently stayed in a low-end brothel and
made friends with the women who worked there; the next time I was
there I stayed at the family home of a friend from college, a luxurious house with armed guards at the gate. Perhaps this ability to cross
from one side of the tracks to another stemmed from the simple fact
of being an outsider, removed from local class divisions. Or perhaps
it was something more my own, another dimension of growing up in
two worlds.

"Crowded," I answered Patricia's question, "and dirty. But the
politics are fascinating."

Back in Caracas

When I cleared customs in the Caracas airport, Jhonny was there waiting for me, his bald head shiny as ever, his stomach a bit larger since I had seen him seven months earlier after he'd driven the film crew and myself around the city on election day in December 2006. He gave me a big bear hug and asked, *"¿Cómo está mi gringuito querido?"*—How is my dear little gringo?—as we climbed into his Blazer. It felt good to be back but heading across a newly completed bridge toward Caracas, Jhonny warned me about a deteriorating economy and a more complex political situation in the country I had come to know best in Latin America.

It is, of course, a cliché for journalists to use their drivers as political barometers, but the ride from the airport to the city can sometimes be more revealing than the most detailed government briefing. Jhonny complained about Chávez's new United Socialist Party of Venezuela (PSUV), and the massive overhaul of the constitution that it was rushing through the National Assembly and toward a countrywide referendum. Both the new party and the constitutional reform had been announced in late 2006, before I left Venezuela the previous time. Lots of people in Chávez's coalition had been upset when he ordered them to scrap their existing political parties—which ran the gamut from the Venezuelan Communist Party (PCV), to the more centrist social-democratic Homeland for All Party (PPT)—but only a couple of parties had actually risked excommunication by openly opposing the merger. In theory, the move was intended to streamline the selection of local candidates and combat internal party corruption, bureaucracy, and hierarchy, thus distributing power to the grass roots. But in practice it appeared just as likely to concentrate power in Chávez's hands. The fact that the party developed a disciplinary tribunal before it even had statutes or an agreed structure was taken by some as an ominous sign.

The constitutional reform proposed numerous positive changes, including expanded social guarantees and creative mechanisms for empowering the grass roots like communal councils and a social safety net for the masses of self-employed. It also proposed abolishing presidential term limits and expanding presidential powers to declare potentially endless states of emergency. Jhonny had voted for Chávez on more than one occasion but didn't like the fact that he would have to vote on the reforms as a block—all or nothing. He also didn't want to do away with presidential term limits. "By the end of this term Chávez will have been in office thirteen years. If that isn't long enough to consolidate his revolution then nothing will be," he grumbled.

"Is there anyone else who might be able to step up and lead the political process besides Chávez?" I asked.

"That's the point," Jhonny insisted. "There isn't anyone else right now. But instead of spending energy training new leadership, he's pushing through a constitutional reform to allow himself to retain power indefinitely, or at least as long as he can win reelection every seven years. He still has five years in the current term, isn't that enough to train a new leadership to replace him? And why not at least try? If it doesn't work out, he can ask the people to reform the constitution at the end of the term."

Jhonny's logic made sense. It was hard to overlook Chávez's efforts to entrench his own hold on power. I still believed Chávez's primary motivation was a desire to help the poor majority of his citizens. But it would be dangerous to conflate the interests of the poor majority with his own power simply because he was the only politician capable of leading the coalition government at the moment. Lots of policies that the opposition criticized as centralizing power, undermining opposition groups, or weakening the independence of the other branches of government had valid alternative explanations, but it was troubling to a gringo in the Bush era that so often an apparent side effect of their implementation was more power to the executive. And it didn't seem right to make expanding constitutional guarantees for social security contingent on doing away with presidential term limits: why couldn't people vote for each individual amendment?

As I paid Jhonny and hauled my bags up to a friend's apartment where I would be staying for the next couple of months, I reflected on the challenges of state power itself, not just in Venezuela but across the region. Even where radical movements had won electoral victories, they faced myriad obstacles to achieving the change their electorates had waited so long for. I had seen the disillusionment of my friends in the Landless Movement in Brazil with Lula's presidency, the struggle between government and private miners in Bolivia, the tension between Correa's government and the national indigenous movement in Ecuador. Perhaps the realities of governing, of state power, made disillusionment and disappointment likely outcomes when these leaders took office. Certainly the left has more experience criticizing from the outside than running from the inside, a weakness sorely felt after a successful electoral campaign.

After unpacking, one of the first friends I met up with was Miguel Sánchez Navarro, who had been a classmate of mine at the Universidad de Chile. I had kept in touch with him over the years and had recommended him for a job in Venezuela at the same think tank where Marta and Michael now worked. He had been there a few months, and had managed to get both of us invited to give a joint lecture on regional experiences with progressive governments and twenty-first-century socialism at a university in Barinas state. Over a dinner of rotisserie chicken and fried plantains, we planned our presentation and caught up on the years since he had visited me at graduate school in England. Apparently, lots of our classmates in Santiago were still hanging around the university; a couple had yet to finish their undergraduate degrees. Miguel, on the other hand, had spent a few years in Paris where he earned his master's from the Sorbonne. He had then made a down payment on his own apartment in Chile before deciding he needed a change of pace and a more radical political environment.

He had walked away from his comfortable, successful intellectual life in Chile for a short-term job in revolutionary Caracas. His salary in Caracas was in bolivars, but he wanted to be able to make monthly payments on his apartment in Chile. The problem was that the currency control meant there was no way for him to send his money abroad; he either had to spend it all in Venezuela or use the black market to buy a convertible currency. The black market, he explained, was not only illegal, it was worth only a third of the official rate.

The extent of the economic difficulties facing Venezuela was underscored repeatedly during the first days of my visit. Miguel Sánchez Navarro was just one of at least a dozen people who wanted to know if I was selling dollars, and most of them were Venezuelan. More troubling, when I went to the grocery store I couldn't find milk or sugar. Far from the endogenous development that Chávez advocated, and the vision in the "Walking on Two Legs" working paper of Michael Lebowitz's that I had translated on my first days in the country back in November 2004, Venezuela now imported more than ever, including roughly 70 percent of its food. Policies to promote domestic food production were failing because of a range of factors: higher rates of profit in the oil, finance, or import sectors decreased investment in agriculture; government price caps to guarantee affordable food to the poor decreased production; and currency controls encouraged producers to sell in Brazil or Colombia for a convertible currency. Many policies that had been put in place for justifiable reasons had ended up contradicting other key policy goals.

Most of my Venezuelan friends expressed concerns about Chávez's new political party. One, who was heavily involved in neighborhood politics in Caracas, told me she had been told who to vote for in the party nomination process, not as a suggestion but as an order from above. It sounded more like old-school Chicago machine politics than revolutionary participatory democracy. Likewise, people had reservations about the constitutional reform, but no one said they expected it to fail. When I asked people if they planned on voting against it, or criticizing it in policy circles or the media, I was dismayed at the answers I got because of the deep-rooted problems with the political process they indicated. My old roommate Humberto's response was typical: "I have always voted, whenever I have the chance. But I can't vote for a reform that would do away with due process—that is the kind of thing the Bush administration in your country would do. And I can't vote against it either because then I would be voting against the communal councils, the worker protections, and social security clauses. Worse still, I would be voting with the opposition. The government has effectively curtailed critical debate from within, so I think I'm going to abstain."

On the night of the referendum, Miguel, my other Chilean friend Pablo, and I all headed out to the Miraflores palace to wait for the results. The atmosphere couldn't have been more of a contrast to that of a year earlier when the streets had been filled with thousands celebrating Chávez's victory in the 2006 presidential election. A band was playing on a big stage and a few hundred red-shirt-wearing chavistas were chanting noisily, but the atmosphere was tense rather than celebratory because the result had yet to be announced and everyone knew it was too close to call. As usual at such times, I was receiving a steady flow of text messages—from friends inside the palace, at home in front of the television, in the opposition campaign headquarters, and in the rural interior of the country. Rumors were flying: the reform had been approved 52–48 and the opposition was claiming fraud; the reform had been defeated and there would be protests; the results wouldn't be announced until overseas ballots were counted; we should go home immediately because there was an opposition destabilization plan in effect and violence was sure to ensue.

Pablo wanted to make contingency plans for what we would do if violence broke out. Miguel thought we should stay put near the presidential guard and, if necessary, seek safety in the palace itself. I suggested we might flee into La Pastora, the barrio where Humberto still lived, and take refuge in his apartment. By midnight the results still hadn't been announced and the streets had fallen eerily quiet. The band had played its last set and was now packing up hastily. Miguel thought it was time to go home. Pablo agreed: there was nothing left to see and the chances of us finding a cab would only get worse as it got later. Finally, around 12:30 A.M., we decided to call it a night—at that point no matter what the results turned out to be it wasn't safe in the streets. A few minutes later we were squeezed into the back of an ancient taxi with the exhaust pumping directly into the car and the upholstery long gone from the seats. Luckily, the radio still worked and the driver had the news on at full volume.

Just as we pulled up to the building where Miguel lived, the head of the National Electoral Council came on the air live to announce the results: the reform had been voted down by a margin of less than 2 percent. The opposition had maintained almost exactly the same number of votes Rosales had won a year earlier in the presidential election. Widespread abstention among chavistas—three million people who voted for him in 2006 this time stayed home—had handed the opposition a narrow victory. We raced up the stairs and turned on the television in time to watch Chávez responding to the defeat. He looked somewhat stunned but graciously accepted the result. There was to be no delaying, stalling for time, or trying to fiddle with the outcome. Chávez was taking the high road and proving that his commitment to the democratic process extended to defeats as well as victories. He promised to continue the struggle, announcing that the defeat was just "for now," as he said after his failed 1992 coup attempt in a televised interview on his way to prison, instantly making him a national hero. He called on all Venezuelans to peacefully accept the outcome. The opposition had already printed up thousands of shirts with "FRAUD!" across the front and would now have no use for them.

The opposition's track record left little room for doubt that had the outcome been the other way around—an approval of the reform by a narrow margin—they would have refused to recognize the result and would have taken to the streets in violent protest. The international media would have sided with the protesters and the country would have been thrown into chaos. Instead, after what could only be regarded as the narrowest of victories, right-wing commentators on talk shows began to announce that the referendum had not really been about the constitution but about Chávez's presidency in its entirety and that the majority of the country no longer supported him. The assertion was so out of touch with reality that it could only undermine those sectors of the opposition that wanted to play by the rules of the democratic process. Meanwhile on the other side the government and its supporters accepted the defeat and continued with their regular work—no doubt there were plenty of chavistas who were relieved at the outcome.

Despite a variety of contradictions and causes for concern, Venezuela's political experiment is still a democratic and courageous effort to invent an alternative model, based on the insistence that another way, another world is possible. The majority of Venezuelans have refused to accept that the only way to do things is the Washington way. The political changes in Venezuela are by, for, and about the most excluded, impoverished, and downtrodden citizens. The Bolivarian Revolution has helped to create political space for countries throughout the region to embark on their own democratic, political experiments. Sometimes cynicism and pessimism descend and I resign myself to the idea that these Latin American political experiments are doomed to failure. But I hope I'm wrong. Certainly never, not once, have I thought they shouldn't be tried. Humanity can benefit from political diversity the way that it does from linguistic, cultural, racial, or religious diversity. The political status quo is antiquated and in need of urgent, radical change. Democratic political experiments like those in Venezuela, regardless of their long-term viability, inspire hope and political creativity across the globe.

Shortly after the referendum, Miguel and I set off for Barinas state. After a comfortable overnight trip in an air-conditioned bus replete with plush recliner chairs, we arrived at the university that was hosting our talk. I was nervous about weighing in on any of the tense domestic political issues in front of a Venezuelan audience, especially in Chávez's home state where his father was governor. Miguel and

I agreed to focus our comments on non-Venezuelan developments. About forty people had gathered to hear us in a sweltering auditorium. Miguel kicked off with a twenty-minute historical and theoretical analysis of the socialist experiments in Cuba and Chile. The audience listened attentively with only the occasional cell phone interruption.

When it came to my turn, I explained my connection to Latin America and then, drawing on my experiences traveling through the region, described the shift I had witnessed over the previous nine years from neoliberal dominance to progressive democratic uprisings. I told stories of Guatemalan sweatshops and border crossings, Chilean coups and free trade deals, Argentine economic crisis and rebound, Brazilian riverboats, landless movements, and a working-class president, Colombian displaced communities and neoliberal development projects, Ecuadoran Indians and oil, and Bolivian hearts and mines.

I explained that what had started out as a way to pass time before college, to learn a new language and seek adventure, had become a dominant theme in my young life. But language, Spanish and Portuguese, was only the beginning, a prerequisite key to peoples, cultures, and politics. The more I spoke and comprehended, the more I was able to understand what was happening in the region around me, to build friendships through my wanderings.

Though my initial interest in traveling south had been primarily to learn a language, I soon acquired profound affection for the landscapes I traveled through and the people I met along the way. The food was pretty good too. I found I thrived on a life on the road where buses and planes served as portals to new worlds. As I came of age, changing in myself, I found a region that was also in the midst of the most profound transformation. I came to see Latin America as a prism through which I could better understand my own roots in the radical left in the United States, and the role my country plays in global society. It was easier to be self-aware, self-critical, to clarify what I valued in life beyond the comfort and familiarity of home.

Since before I could remember, my learning and life in the United States had been rooted in multiple, almost mutually exclusive, worlds, which happened to overlap intimately in me. I combined two lives: one immersed in the stability of privilege, and the other in the challenges of deprivation. When I set off on my first international adventures I knew no other way to live or to learn, and so, in my travels, I sought out the extremes of different worlds wherever I went.

I've lived in rough Caracas barrios, hitchhiked through the Andes, slept on cargo boats on the Amazon, and spent weeks in towns without running water. Throughout my travel life I've saved pesos by sleeping in bus stations or on buses rather than in hotels. Ever the frugal traveler, I economized and thus extended my trips. But I also benefited from global networks of friends and the gringo wild card by staying in luxurious mansions, gated communities, penthouse suites, and by interacting with political and economic elites throughout the region. I became familiar with multiple worlds wherever I went in Latin America.

All my experiences, the various worlds of class, race, culture, geography, and politics that I've visited, have shaped my understanding of Latin America and beyond. Yet, in my storytelling, I dedicate little space to the elites for a number of reasons. Having the most in common with the United States they have the least to teach my compatriots; possessing resources as they do, their voices are regularly transmitted across the globe via mass media; speaking multiple languages and traveling extensively, most of them can and do speak for themselves. James Boswell put it well in his *Life of Johnson*: "Gentlemen of education," he observed, "were pretty much the same in all countries; the condition of the lower orders, the poor especially, was the true mark of national discrimination." The majority of Latin Americans inhabit a parallel reality to that known throughout much of the United States and to their own national privileged classes. It is, primarily, the lessons I've learned from the poor, the excluded, the voiceless, that I seek to recount when speaking and writing about Latin America.

I talked for too long, as usual, at the university in Barinas. But the audience seemed to pay close attention throughout and had lots of comments and questions for us both afterward. An old man with a white shirt and a blue hat resting on big ears insisted on the need for continental unity, like the European Union, but with a more socialist orientation. A young man, probably a student, with his hair gelled into waves, asked what *estadounidenses* thought of Chávez's efforts to negotiate the release of hostages, including United States citizens, being held by the Colombian guerrillas. A round woman in a pink dress suit talked about the risk of U.S. intervention and argued that the only way to resist was to unite with other Latin American countries. A man in the front row wearing a Che Guevara T-shirt energetically denounced United States government plans to invade Venezuela—*los gringos son capaces de lo que sea,* the gringos are capable of doing anything—and reminded the audience that the Bush administration had totally ignored the United Nations in the invasion of Iraq. A young woman with long dark hair and glasses asked about the burgeoning Latino population in the United States, its impact on national politics and the upcoming presidential election.

As I answered questions and listened to comments, I realized that the specter of United States intervention, well founded in Latin American history, if exaggerated at times in Chávez's Venezuela, could easily become a distraction from the immediate challenges the region was facing. Revolutionaries in Venezuela needed to focus on overcoming bureaucracy, corruption, nepotism, incompetence, a rentier state mentality, an economic dependence on oil, and the challenges of innovating a new policy model. United States support for the 2002 coup, and continued funneling of resources to opposition groups, fueled the paranoia of a possible military intervention. Maybe if we *estadounidenses* did a better job of making sure our tax dollars didn't go toward undermining democratic experiments or overthrowing or destabilizing governments unwilling to adhere to U.S. policy imperatives, people in countries like Venezuela could do a better job resolving their own internal problems.

I wasn't in a position to tell the Venezuelans how to do things, and they probably didn't want to hear it from me anyway. At times I had fretted that my years in Latin America, perhaps especially my political engagement there, might be little more than an expression of a liberal escapism that seeks to do good abroad where the problems and the politics are expected to be more straightforward, less fraught than those close to home. But the longer I stayed in any country, or the region as a whole, the clearer it became that the political struggles there, including in highly polarized places like Venezuela, were no easier to decode than those in my own communities.

Over the years I traveled south, Latinos became the largest minority group in the United States, and the fastest growing. The Latino presence in the United States is everywhere from the highest echelons of business and government to the poorest ranks of undocumented busboys and maids, although still concentrated in the latter. The Hispanic vote will play an ever more substantial role in local, state, and national elections. I went to nursery school with children of Central American refugees, I waited tables in a restaurant where the kitchen was staffed exclusively by Mexican cooks, I befriended Salvadorans in college, and I visited prisons where more than 25 percent of the inmates were Latino. On reflection, it sometimes seems strange that I went so far to find the people and the region that were coming, quite literally, to a town near me. Yet the United States has always been a country of immigrants and no one is an immigrant for long here. There may well be more Puerto Ricans and Dominicans in New York than in San Juan and Santo Domingo combined. But the Colombians who live in Queens, the Brazilians in Providence, the Mexicans in Boise, the Venezuelans in Miami, the Chileans in San Francisco, and the Guatemalans in Atlanta are part of their host country. Their lives straddle multiple worlds, as does mine. It is impossible to understand Latin America simply by spending time with immigrant communities in the United States, just as it is impossible to understand those immigrant communities without spending time in their countries of origin.

In 2008, I tried to settle into a less nomadic life in New York City. A comfortable bed, a shower, a closet, and a well-stocked refrigerator were luxuries I readily accepted. Living in the same neighborhood, not to mention time zone, as friends and family was a welcome change. But the daily routines offended my sense of freedom, and I experience the inward-oriented consumer lifestyle as a kind of reverse culture shock.

I followed from afar as Chávez introduced a new currency, removed price controls on milk, and successfully brokered the release of hostages held for years in Colombia. Then, the FARC-EP began to disintegrate with one of its leaders dying, another getting killed, and all of its high-value hostages being rescued. Ecuador and Colombia had a border spat and Chávez got involved. Paraguay elected a former bishop with progressive tendencies named Fernando Lugo to the presidency. And Venezuelan aid to Latin America reached more than five times that given by the United States. Bolivia and Venezuela kicked out the U.S. ambassadors as Bolivia's secession movement turned violent. Friends from a dozen Latin American countries popped up regularly in my e-mail but seemed, were, a world away. Though New York has millions of Spanish speakers, I often felt it was inappropriate to speak to them in their own language. In New York, I was just one of millions, no longer occupying the distinctive position of being a gringo. That part of my identity was inevitably lost and as it blurred, other parts of my life—particularly family—were brought into sharper focus.

My mom, Kathy, was released under parole supervision in 2003 after serving twenty-two years of her twenty-year minimum sentence. The pure joy of her freedom, of her reentry into family and community, was more powerful than words can express. And yet it made the reality of my father's situation that much starker. My dad, David, has served barely a third of his minimum seventy-five-year sentence for exactly the same crime for which my mom was given a twenty-year minimum. I now live just hours from his prison: it's easier to visit and communicate regularly. Yet I have also found the proximity suffocating: how can I be in the United States, in New York, and not throw myself into an all-out fight for my father's freedom, or at least better treatment within the prison system? What essential element of humanity do I have to suppress to go about my daily life as though everything were normal when one of the people who made me, and helped raise me, is gratuitously deprived of his most basic liberties? With an impossibly long minimum sentence, there isn't much hope of winning his freedom, no matter how perfect his prison record, how little risk he poses to society, how remorseful he may feel, or how desperately I want him out. As an unarmed first offender who never intended for anyone to get hurt, he has served his time. My gringo wild card is wasted on the Department of Corrections just as my father's humanity and commitment to those worse off than him is viewed as a threat. Perhaps my traveling and living a full life can extend my freedom, and his too. Most parents live, at least to some extent, vicariously through their children. Even the restrictions on bringing maps into his prison can't entirely prevent me from sharing my adventures with him. One thing is clear: whether at home in the United States, or abroad on the road, I will have to keep living in at least two worlds.

Afterword

The journeys that this book is based on took place over nine years. Inevitably, I lost touch with some people along the way; others have kept in touch but from afar as our lives roll by. Here, I provide a brief update on some of those who shaped my experience in Latin America.

The last time I visited San Andrés, Guatemala, was in 2003, to drop my brother Malik off for his own language immersion experience. The prospect of reconnecting with Flor, my girlfriend when I had lived in the town back in 1999, had me dreaming about possibilities the entire bus ride up to the Petén. When I arrived, I learned she had a second baby and was living with her partner. I found her at the store where she worked, but, she told me, now that she lived with her babies' father, she couldn't have people in town seeing us together— *pueblo pequeño, infierno grande*. Juan, my best friend who worked at the language school, was much the same as I remembered him, more of an alcoholic to be sure, and perhaps with a face that had become a bit droopier with the passing years. When I invited him for a Gallo beer he talked almost obsessively about getting to the United States, about the various contacts he had through the language school in random places like Winnetka, Illinois, and Lancaster, Pennsylvania. But he still had to save up enough money for the long, dangerous trip to *El Norte*. His mom was sick, which left him to take care of his little siblings and made it impossible to put money aside. Did I want another beer? My host family, Doña Eugenia, Delia, and Jesús, were all doing well, living in the same house, and no longer dependent on hosting language students for their income after Jesús's recent promotion.

In Chile, Auntie Helen still lived off her pension, though now her son had grown up and moved out to study law in Santiago. She still e-mails regularly to ask about my family and encourage me to visit Chile soon; she has yet to miss one of my birthdays. Miguel Sánchez Navarro, my friend from the University of Chile who came to work in Venezuela, now lives with his Canadian girlfriend in Ottawa. Professor Luis Vitale still teaches classes in the same run-down building where he told his harrowing stories on September 12, 2001.

In Brazil, as of 2008, Lara was in a custody battle with her ex-husband over their three kids. She had moved back to Pará, near her father, to be able to claim residency in the area where her kids were in school. I receive regular updates from her younger sisters and nieces in Manaus, who frequent the so-called LAN houses, or Internet cafés, where they spend hours chatting on instant messenger.

Elizabeth, who had made possible my time in Ecuador, is back in the United States, studying at Fordham Law School. Her friends in Ecuador—Ana, Inéz, and the rest of the crew—are still working in indigenous communities, prisons, youth centers, and keeping busy with their political organizing.

Sister Carolina, in Colombia, wrote me with an update on the communities we visited on our pilgrimage through the Chocó. A flood had wiped out the Wounaan village Join Poboor, near where she and my mom were lost in the jungle. The good news from the Chocó was that the paramilitaries and their banana export operation were finally cleared off the community land at La Balsa. Our presence, the legal campaign, and, most significantly, ongoing community pressure had finally succeeded despite the odds. Del Monte was being sued in the United States courts for its ties, through its subsidiaries, to paramilitary violence in Guatemala and a jailed paramilitary leader testified to taking payments from Del Monte in Colombia. The communities were worried, however, about Venezuela's plans to build an oil pipeline to Colombia's pacific ports to facilitate oil sales to China. The challenges facing them continued.

Marta Harnecker and Michael Lebowitz are still living in Caracas and working as intellectuals and organizers in support of the Chávez administration. Humberto installed a water tank with a pump so his apartment has running water seven days a week. He also got married and has a daughter. Jhonny upgraded his taxi from a 1996 Blazer to a 2008 Explorer.

My grandfather's old Cuban friend from the airplane fiasco in New York, Luis Martínez, had himself spent a few years living in Venezuela. His time there coincided with a previous oil boom and the rule of a president, Carlos Andrés Pérez, who, like Chávez today, had dramatically improved relations with Cuba. When, at the end of 2007, he learned that I had been living in Caracas, he told me about his years there, and how much he liked Venezuelans. "They look you in the eye, like a *cubano*," he said. "Despite the problems and contradictions," he continued, "Venezuela is playing a crucial, necessary role in Latin America's ongoing political transformation." He thought it was a great place for me to spend time. "The corruption and rotten elements teach you to make principled decisions in life's gray areas." Though he seemed to give me the benefit of the doubt, I couldn't help but wonder how well I had held up or would face the temptations and hard decisions ahead.

Acknowledgments

There are so many people, in so many countries, who made this book possible that there is no obvious starting point. The people I encountered all across Latin America welcomed me, opened new worlds to me, and generously shared their passion, time, and perspectives. They are why I fell in love with the region and how I had material for this project. I hope I have fairly and accurately represented them and their voices.

My editor at Scribner, Colin Robinson, helped me develop this project from the beginning, and gave me the confidence and support to make it a reality. Without him, it's safe to say, not only would it be a less polished book, but there would be no book at all. His patience, attention to detail, insightful comments, politics, and, most of all, his friendship are as rare as they are cherished qualities in an editor. I can't say enough about what a pleasure it was to work with him. Thanks also to Kate Bittman, Tyler LeBleu, Alexis Gargagliano, and Karen Thompson at Scribner.

My agent, Jill Grinberg, helped keep my vision for the project on track and gave valuable feedback at key points in the writing and editing process. She also worked hard on the details so I could focus my energy on traveling, writing, and editing. Thank you.

For funding that allowed me to keep traveling and studying over the past nine years, thanks go to my publisher, the Rhodes Trust, and Rotary International.

Dozens of friends and colleagues provided me with support, feedback, inspiration, encouragement, and places to stay as I bounced around the world writing and researching. It would be impossible to list everyone but here are some of the people I owe a debt of gratitude: Maggie Alarcon, Darius Anderson, Daniela Arriagada, Sonia Assad and family, Luis Bonilla and family, Matthew and Michelle Carpenter-Arevalo, Nancy Carrion, Betanha and Adriana Carvalho, Mariana Cook, Francine Damasceno, Ben Dangl, Elena Escapini, Liza Figueroa-Clark, Nancy Gear, Marta Harnecker, Stalin and Luis Hererra, Helena Kennedy and family, Anna, Eleanora, and Michael Kennedy, Mona and Rashid Khalidi, Dorothy Kronick, Coty Krsul, Jean Lathrop, Sara Latorre, Michael Lebowitz, Phillip Lopate and the Skidmore College Summer Writers Institute, Alex Main, Michelle Martin, David Moskowitz, Fernando Muñoz, Mwaniki Mwangi, Pablo Navarrete, Francisca Nuñez, Tanya Olsen and family, David Palmer, Carolina Pardo, Elena Pereira, Carlos Pizarro, Gideon Rafel-Frankel, Thomas Rigo, Jeremy Robbins, Miguel Sánchez Navarro, Alejandra Santillana, Daniel Schulson, Kevin Simmons, Gui Stampur, Malcolm and Sue Terence and the whole Butler crew, Dayana Valecillos and family, Peter Van Agtmael, and the prodigious Juan "Velocidad." Thank you. You know who you are and how much you mean to me.

John Coatsworth read a late draft and provided expert feedback on the analytical content of the book. Elizabeth Joynes and Sam Kass, lifelong friends of mine, both traveled with me at various points on my wanderings in Latin America and also provided me with valuable input on this project. Thai Stein-Jones gave helpful suggestions and support on an early draft of the first half of the manuscript. Cyrus Habib and Michael Ellsberg generously brought their considerable editing experience to bear on both the book proposal and the drafted manuscript. Sarah Stillman held my hand all the way through the writing process; without her encouragement, insight, patience, and generosity I can't imagine how I would have done it.

Finally, I owe an eternal debt of gratitude to my family for their lifetime of support, love, and guidance in ways too numerous to mention. My siblings, Malik Dohrn and Zayd Dohrn and Rachel Dewoskin; my fathers, Bill Ayers and David Gilbert; my mothers, Kathy Boudin and Bernardine Dohrn, are my world, no matter which continent, country, or city I happen to be in. My nieces Dalin and Light are the future.

About the Author

Chesa Boudin, a Rhodes scholar, completed a second master's degree in public policy in Latin America at Oxford University in 2006. Chesa translated into English *Understanding the Bolivarian Revolution: Hugo Chávez Speaks with Marta Harnecker,* co-edited *Letters from Young Activists: Today's Young Rebels Speak Out,* and coauthored *The Venezuelan Revolution: 100 Questions—100 Answers.* He is currently a student at the Yale Law School.